TRAVERSING LIFE

TRAVERSING LIFE

THE GUILDED PEN ANTHOLOGY

TWELFTH EDITION, 2023

SAN DIEGO WRITERS AND EDITORS GUILD

The Guilded Pen, Traversing Life, Twelfth Edition 2023

is a publication of the San Diego Writers and Editors Guild

2307 Fenton Parkway, Ste. 107-266

San Diego, CA 92108

www.sdweg.org

©San Diego Writers and Editors Guild

All rights reserved.

Published by: SDWEG

2307 Fenton Parkway, Ste. 107-266

San Diego, CA 92108

ISBN: 979-8-9895976-0-4

Managing Editor: Tamara Merrill

Copy Editors: Al Converse, Bob Boze, Cornelia Feye, Janice Coy, JR Strayve JR, Ken Yaros, Margaret Harmon, Rick Peterson, Sandra Yeaman, Shujen Walker, Steve Corkery, Suzanne Shepard

Proof Editor: Sandra Yeaman

Book Design and Formatting: Konstellation Press

Cover Design: Teresa Espaniola

SAN DIEGO WRITERS AND EDITORS GUILD

To Promote, Support, and Encourage the Writing Art for Adults and Youth.

SDWEG is a nonprofit group of writers and editors and those interested in writing and editing. The Guild has been a collaborative partner in the larger San Diego writing community since 1979 and takes part in author showcase events and fundraising for literacy and skill-building projects.

We continue to develop and grow as a Guild, recognizing the substantial changes in communication and publishing over the past forty years. Every innovation is driven by the passion and commitment of our members.

Visit the Guild website at www.sdweg.org to learn more about what we do, who we are, and the benefits of membership.

Guild membership is open to all, and guests are welcome to the meetings for a small donation. We hope you will join us and be a part of all the new and exciting projects.

A WORD FROM THE PRESIDENT

The members of the San Diego Writers and Editors Guild write memoirs, romances, westerns, science fiction, young adult stories, thrillers, health books, poetry, and on and on. The annual anthology provides an opportunity to stretch our imaginations and perhaps try our hand at something new and different.

A theme often is chosen which presents certain parameters to the scope of our submissions. It provides an opportunity to publish something for the first time for newer and aspiring authors. For them, it also provides an introduction on how to submit a written document for publication within well-defined parameters.

A team of volunteers goes over each submission several times to ensure it meets publication requirements.

This anthology, *Traversing Life*, is the Guild's twelfth edition. Its new managing editor, Tamara Merrill, a well-known author with many accolades, has been a Guild member since 2018.

Since 2017, I have submitted something to each of our anthologies and often more than one submission.

How a simple theme could create such diverse views makes

for a fun read. I hope you enjoy this edition of our latest anthology.

Mardie Schroeder
President

"If it sounds like writing, I rewrite it. Or, if proper usage gets in the way, it may have to go. I can't allow what we learned in English composition to disrupt the sound and rhythm of the narrative."
Elmore Leonard

ACKNOWLEDGMENTS

The Guilded Pen Anthologies owe their existence to the San Diego Writers and Editors Guild Board of Directors. In 2010, their dedication to the mission of the Guild and their foresight resulted in the establishment of the annual anthology. *The Guilded Pen, Traversing Life, Twelfth Edition 2023* is the result of their continuing dedication to the writing arts.

Board of Directors 2023
Mardie Schroeder, President
Bob Riffenburgh, Vice President
Audrey Walz, Secretary
Marcia Buompensiero, Treasurer
Sandra Yeaman, Financial Administrator
Patricia Bossano, Newsletter Editor
Penny Paugh, Event Coordinator
ShuJen Walker, Manuscript Review
Reina Menasche, Director at Large

When, in March 2023, I was asked to assume the Managing Editor role for the Twelfth Edition of the San Diego Writers and Editors Guild, *The Guilded Pen* Anthology, I approached the task with trepidation. These were some "big shoes to fill." The Guild under the directorship of longtime members, Marcia Buompensiero and Rivkah Sleeth, has produced eleven excellent anthologies over the past eleven years and I did not want to f ail.

Our 2023 theme, Traversing Life, combines two words: Life —what we call the condition of living, growing, and reproducing, and Traversing—which means to move or travel through. The theme was chosen to give the members an opportunity to create a short story, an essay, a memoir, or a poem about the activities we do and the continual changes we experience as we participate with the human race in this thing called "living our lives."

For some, it is all about happiness, building a family, or leading life as it comes. For others it is about writing, travel, accumulating wealth, and for still others, it is all about love and relationships.

The forty-five pieces, by thirty-nine writers, accepted for the 2023 Anthology explore, explain, and have fun with those ever evolving, constantly changing trips we take or watch others take as we all traverse life.

The daunting task of putting together the 2023 *Twelfth Edition of The Guilded Pen Anthology – Traversing Life,* could not have been accomplished alone. Al Converse, Bob Boze, Cornelia Feye, Janice Coy, JR Strayve JR, Ken Yaros, Margaret Harmon, Rick Peterson, Sandra Yeaman, Shujen Walker, Steve Corkery, and Suzanne Shepard contributed their time and energy to review, critique, edit, and support the writers and the process. This talented group of volunteers were invaluable. I sincerely thank each and every one of them for their time, skill, and support, and wish them the very best in their writing careers.

It is our hope that you, the reader, will find enjoyment, meaning, and emotion in the content presented and that you will take the time to contact any or all of the writers with your thoughts. (Contact information has been provided in the About the Authors section.) As always, a great way to support the writers and the Guild is to leave a review.

Thank you,
Tamara Merrill, Managing Editor 2023

CONTENTS

SECTION ONE - SHORT STORIES

1

HERE'S WHERE THIS STORY ENDS
ANNA HALLETT

Here's where this story ends. Ted is in the green lounge chair on his back patio. On the ground next to him is a plastic tumbler of warm iced tea.

On his feet are his favorite loafers. He bought them because they look like the brown boat shoes that all the cool, rich kids wore in sixth grade. He couldn't afford them then, so why shouldn't he have a pair now? That's what he'd thought as he clicked 'buy'. Even as an old man, Ted is still trying to be one of the cool kids. But in a more self-aware, ironic way, of course.

He's dressed in Bermuda shorts and the golf shirt he won in a golf tournament in Las Vegas a few years ago. He was pleasantly surprised to find that not all of his trophies were in the past. It was just a little office competition at the annual conference, but still....

On his right ring finger is his class ring, a wide gold band with a green glass stone for St. Patrick College of Engineering. Good times. Dating pretty girls and making bad decisions with his buddies. Nothing catastrophic: too much beer the night before parents' weekend; up all night to make out with Kim instead of studying for the physics test; skinny dipping with friends and losing his glasses in the mud at the bottom of the lake. Childish choices made by a boy who thought he was a man.

Whenever Ted noticed the ring, maybe when it tapped on the mouse as he typed at his computer or when it clinked against a glass of cold water, he wondered what happened to those college buddies. He never did stay in touch. Not even on social media when, years after graduation, it became a thing. There was so much of the world to conquer—first school, then jobs, travel, family. Letting go of old friends just happened.

On his left hand, his wedding ring. A plain gold band, scratched and nicked on the outside and smooth around his finger. It used to be a little loose. He'd had to be careful when he washed his hands that it didn't slip off. When he felt anxious, he would spin it around his finger. Over time it became tight. Sometimes uncomfortably so. But it's been there for fifty-two years and he feels naked without it.

When he was twenty-eight, Lois slipped the ring on his finger at the altar in front of family and friends. She'd looked so beautiful. When Ted sees the wedding photo hanging in the hall, he marvels at how young they both were. He knows this sounds cliché, but it's true.

Noah, his friend at Berman Engineering, set him up. Noah's girlfriend, Marie, brought her friend Lois for a double date. A blind date. It wasn't love at first sight, but he and Lois had an easy rapport from the start. Two years later he couldn't imagine life without her so he'd proposed. Nothing elaborate. He was too self-conscious to be showy. Besides, what if she said no? Dinner at his apartment and a simple, single stone diamond ring.

Covering his mostly bald head is the floppy hat Billy gave him for Father's Day. Billy's a good boy. Not always an easy kid, but good.

Ted and Lois thought they might have two or three children. They both had good jobs and big hearts. But life's a kicker sometimes. With a total of five pregnancies, Billy was the only one to make it to birth. Ted doesn't remember ever seeing his own father cry, but he remembered crying after all four miscarriages. He cried for Bridget, Maya, Philip, and Sarah. He also cried when Billy was born. Big, wet tears that dripped down his face and pooled in the corners of his smile.

As a child, Billy was smart, kind, and mostly well-behaved. Ted and Lois were blessed. But, as a teenager and young man, he became anxious and depressed. In college, his first girlfriend broke up with him. To be fair, she didn't dump him. She just knew he wasn't the one and moved on. She ended it just before winter break, but kindly after midterms. He came home and barely left his childhood room. He slept or watched TV.

Ted and Lois fretted but didn't know how to help him. They worried about what would happen when he went back to school in January; when they wouldn't be able to keep an eye on him. Lois found a psychologist near the school and set up a recurring appointment. Ted took the day off from work and drove the hour and half to Billy's school so he could drive him to his first appointment. He hadn't wanted the kid to have to go alone and that way he knew Billy was really going. Lois took him to the next appointment and Ted to the one after that. With time and medication, Billy learned to live with his depression.

This morning, Ted woke just before sunrise, as the sky was brightening from black to gray to red and finally blue. He fixed himself an egg, over easy, and a cup of tea with milk and stevia. He completed the online jumble puzzle while he ate. After breakfast, he checked his email. Billy sent him a photo of his daughter-in-law Sue and his grandchildren, Zach and Fiona, at the beach. He read the news online, but it was all bad, so he gave up.

Before the day got too hot, Ted filled a glass with iced tea from the fridge and relaxed on the green lounge chair on his back patio.

From here he gazed out at the Borrego Springs desert. In the distance was the dark silhouette of the Santa Rosa Mountain range. Across the road were the palm trees and cottonwoods of the golf course, and just beyond the patio, the catclaw shrubs and creosote bushes.

Next to him is the other empty green lounge chair where Lois used to sit. Living in the desert had been Lois's dream. She hated being cold. Said the cold felt like pain.

When she received the diagnosis, they'd decided to buy this second home in the desert. On the good days, when she didn't need to be in or near the hospital, they lived here in Borrego and enjoyed the warmth. In the beginning, they tried all the local restaurants, played golf, hiked Palm Canyon, and watched the local theater company performances. Lois joined a writing group at the library and Ted played cards at the Senior Center. Billy and his family would visit most holidays, sleeping in the spare room and the den. Ted played pickleball with the grandkids on cooler winter days.

They did their best to make each other happy.

A few years ago, Lois finally succumbed to death and Ted was alone.

The warm breeze blew across the landscape and the ebb and flow, reminiscent of the waves of the ancient sea that once covered the land here, lulled him to sleep. He felt Lois's hand take his. He didn't question it. He didn't want to question it. He accepted it: welcomed her.

Ted did not do great things. He did not do anything terrible. No one will ever find his name in a history book. He lived a simple life and that's a beautiful thing. He is a patch in the breathtaking multi-colored quilt of life that stretches back and forward in time.

He is still now, his breath silent, not even his heart beats. A family of quail pass in front of his chair, bobbing and pecking, and a butterfly pauses to rest on his shoulder.

2

THE UNPLUGGING

BOB RIFFENBURGH

Where am I? It's all so dark. I'm not hurting. I don't feel a thing. How strange …. What time is it? I have no clue. I listen. All is silent. I try to move, but can't seem to. I drift off again.

I hear a voice ask, "Dr. Hansen?" It begins to bring me to consciousness. It's Lola's voice. My wife. My love. It wraps me in warmth. I hadn't noticed how cold I am. I realize I'm hearing voices for the first time in a while.

∾

"Mrs. Rodriguez? Yes, I'm Dr. Hansen. I asked you to meet me. I'm afraid I have some rather serious issues to discuss with you."

"You make it sound alarming, Doctor."

∾

Lola's speaking again. Is that fear in her voice? Her words seemed to waver over the "doctor."

Lola's voice wavering? It carries me back to the time I first really noticed her. She'd been in my introductory psychology class, but what's one more classmate on the other side of the room? This day, she had come in late. The professor was something of a mean shit, badgering students at every opportunity. This day he made sarcastic comments about students who were so disrespectful as to be late. But he made general comments, not addressing her directly, so she couldn't reply or explain. I felt outraged. After class, I caught up with Lola.

"Hey, Lola, I want you to know that Professor Burns was totally unfair. What happened?"

She turned and looked at me with those big brown eyes. Her full, soft lips were quivering. Her voice wavered. "My ... my bus was in an accident. We had to wait for the transit company to bring another around."

Her loveliness and her vulnerability drew me in like a bee to pollen. I knew right then that she would be special to me.

"I suppose you could say it is ominous, Mrs. Rodriguez. Maybe you should sit down."

The legs of the flimsy plastic chair screeched on the tile floor as she sat.

Dr. Hansen paused. Then he continued, speaking a bit too quickly.

"He's been in this coma for six months now. He's a number three on the Glasgow Coma Scale."

"What's that mean, Doctor?"

"It means he's never opened his eyes, never made a sound, and never made any movement."

"Does that mean he's ... brain dead?"

"Not quite. There's still a trace of electrical activity in the brain. His pupils still contract with light. He's not completely dead, but we have to look at the probability of his never becoming conscious."

"Then he's still alive," came a new voice, redolent with fear. "We have to keep trying."

~

It's my daughter's voice. Gabriela. Dear little Gabi, now a mother herself. I remember the first time I heard that anguish in her voice years ago. She was fourteen, dumped from her first crush on a boy. He didn't bother to tell her. She found out when she saw him with his arm around Rosie Reynolds. When she confronted him, he said, "Who do you think you are, Gabi? Keep your ass away from us."

Gabi cuddled up to me on the sofa. "Daddy, I'm all broken. I'll never get over this. I'll never be right again. I wish I were dead."

I held her tightly. I told her, "It's the emotional equivalent of a broken bone. It will mend, but slowly. And then you'll find another beau and forget all about this boy." Of course, she didn't believe me. All I could do was hold her so she'd know there was a place where she was still loved and wanted. I needed to reassure her for a few months until she healed.

~

"Well, Gabi," Dr. Hansen said, "we've been trying for half a year already. We've run out of options. There's nothing more we can do."

"Except keep trying." Lola again. "As Gabi said, we can keep trying."

"Mrs. Rodriguez, you have to look at the reality. He's taking up a hospital bed we need for other patients. Patients we know we can help. And then, there's the cost. At six months, the extended health insurance is capped. It's run out. From now on, you will have to cover the cost. You know how expensive a hospital stay is. It's running, with physician's care, $3,000 to $4,000 per day. In a week, you'll go through your retirement savings and Chikki's college fund. The next week, you'll lose your house."

"I don't care," Gabi sobbed. "I can't lose him. And Chikki can't lose her grandfather."

"Gabi," Dr. Hansen said, "I think you have already lost him. In my 25 years of practice, I've encountered quite a few comas. Not one has ever recovered from a GCS of 3 lasting over six months."

∾

I HEAR *Gabi making little noises—half sobbing, half choking sounds. She spoke again.*

∾

"YOU WOULDN'T BE SAYING this if we weren't Hispanic. You'd keep trying if he were a white guy."

Dr. Hansen's voice was harsh. "Absolutely not. No way. It has nothing to do with that, nothing at all. It's just that it's time to unplug. It's time."

∾

TIME TO UNPLUG. *Where have I heard that before? Oh, yes. The vet. A couple of years ago, our beloved Goldie was hit. Lola, a pregnant Gabi, and I were sitting on the front porch on a sweltering summer Saturday, making small talk and trying to cool off with iced tea. A delivery truck ran slowly by on the street, its driver looking at street numbers. Goldie made a streak for it, barking fiercely to drive off the threatening monster. I saw her pass the front wheel and then move in front of it. She got too close. The wheel caught her and rolled over* her. She gave one great howl and then lay still on the edge of the street.

The vet said some of her internal organs had been injured. He couldn't tell which or how badly. She was alive but unconscious. He put her on life support with tubes and monitors and stuff. We all took shifts sitting with her. We talked to her, sang to her, stroked her, held her. She didn't respond.

After two days, the vet gave us the ultimate news: there was no hope. It was time to unplug. In tears, we let him unplug her. We cried for days.

$\sim$

"No," Lola moaned. "No. We can't unplug him."

Dr. Hansen sounded even more irritable, his harshness a defense to keep his feelings away from reality. "Yes," he said. "I'm afraid so. We'll have to do it sooner or later. Later would just prolong your misery. It wouldn't change anything. Do I have your permission?"

Gabi's sobbed softly. There was no other sound. Lola didn't give permission.

$\sim$

MY FOG IS CLEARING A LITTLE. *Did I hear "unplug?" That meant the end of life support. I would join Goldie. Was that such a bad thing? I still miss her. But then I would lose Lola and Gabi and Chikki. Three generations of women I loved. They represent my journey through life. They are my reasons for living. I must not abandon them. I must not.*

A thought occurs to me. Why not just tell them you've awakened? Because you can't talk, moron. Can you raise your hand? Can't seem to do that, either. Finger? Oh, shit. Nothing. I haven't moved in six months if I'm to believe Hansen.

So what am I going to do about this? Just lie here and let him pull the plug? I'll put all my focus on moving my right index finger. Try. Try ... It won't move.

～

DR. HANSEN SPOKE AGAIN. "Do I have your permission?"

Lola answered, choking over her words. "I guess so. If there's nothing else we can do."

～

I WATCH Dr. Hansen look over at the nurse standing by the wall. She nods, signifying that she had witnessed the permission.

Wait! I watch? I'm seeing? My eyes must be open. I'm waking up just as they decide to let me die? I struggle to speak, to move, to make some sign.

Dr. Hansen obscures my vision bending over me to reach the tubes. I feel one tube slip out through my throat and exit my nostril. I swallow. I SWALLOW! But that's a reflex, not a conscious act. It must have been a feeding tube he pulled. I feel another slipping out, exiting the other nostril. I feel like I'm smothering. I have to breathe. I begin to see black spots. At last, my lungs suck in a breath of air. It feels so good.

～

"OH!" Gabi shouted. "Doctor. His chest is moving. He's breathing!"

Dr. Hansen pulled back and straightened up. He stared down.

"My God! It looks like he is!" he said. He grabbed the stethoscope draped around his neck, inserted the earbuds, and placed the diaphragm on the chest. "Sure enough! He's truly breathing," he said after a moment. His eyes were big and staring as he shook his head. "It's possible that the removal of the tubes shocked his system into functioning."

"You mean," Gabi said, "that if you had pulled them six months ago, he'd have waked up?"

"No. I don't mean that," Dr. Hansen rejoined sharply.

"Gabi," Lola said, through tears, "let's not look our gift horse in the mouth."

"Eduardo," Dr. Hansen said, "can you hear me?"

I STRUGGLE TO SAY YES, but can't make it. I try to nod. Finally, I manage. I hear him ask, "Do you know where you are?" I manage to nod again. He asks, "Can you blink?" I blink. He reaches down and pinches the skin on my forefinger. Ow! This time I manage to pull it away.

"HALLELUJAH!" Dr. Hansen said, almost shouting. "Spontaneous eye control, knowing appropriate words, and withdrawal from a painful stimulus. That's a 12 on the Glasgow Scale. We've got a conscious, cognitive man here!"

SUDDENLY LOLA and Gabi are on me, hugging, crying, laughing. I feel like I'm smothering all over again. But, oh my, I will take that sort of smothering any day.

3

LIZZIE'S RUN

LAWRENCE CARLETON

I took my place on the launch platform in Transporter B. I, Medic Lizzie Ryan, had been ordered to Substation Draco, where an ensign had caught his hand in a blender. They needed a medical specialist in limb regeneration, so there I was, waiting to be teleported. Ensign Arthur Dent, the on-duty operator of the transporter, verified that the beam path was sufficiently clear, told me to be still, and energized the device.

I stood there, pretending not to be terrified. This would be my first teleportation experience. Transporters are cutting edge technology, and space station Waterloo and its substation satellites are the first to deploy them for regular use.

"Ready, in five, four, three..." counted Ensign Dent.

I braced myself. There was the initial whir and things momentarily went blank. I closed my eyes. When I opened them, I expected to find myself on Draco, but the room was the same room I supposedly left. Ensign Dent was behind the control panel muttering to himself.

"Something is wrong with the system," Dent said. He rechecked all the controls and monitors. "Well, I've heard that this happens sometimes. Maybe some impurity in the beam path has caused an auto-abort. I'll check with Uncle Ben to see whether I should just try again."

"Uncle Ben" is Dr. Benjamin Forager, the supervisor of transportation for our station. He was one of the chief engi-neers on the team which developed the technology.

After Ensign Dent left the transporter bay, I decided I should go in search of a bathroom—quaint that we still call them that. It took me longer than expected to locate one. I hurried back, worried that I was causing a delay. As I approached the transporter doorway, I saw Ensign Dent and Uncle Ben standing at the control panel discussing the incident. "It's the oddest thing," Ensign Dent said. "Nothing happened while I was here for several minutes, but now Substation Draco reports they did get our specialist."

Relieved, Uncle Ben assured him, "These things happen, Arthur. It's always wise to be careful. No harm done. I'll have an engineer investigate the delay." I slid away from the doorway as Uncle Ben left to return to his office.

What to do? The transporter was supposed to disassemble your body into a code which is beamed to a distant spot separated from your current location mostly by space, then at the distant spot render the code back into the original you. People who have been transported report that they have full memory functionality and the same awareness of body parts, movement, and posture. They have every reason to believe that they are the same person who stood in the transporter a few seconds, or at most, minutes earlier.

My mind was racing. "What has happened? Can there really be another me out there? Would she try to take over my life? What will the authorities do if they find out there are two Lizzies? I need a place to hide and think." I sensed that it would be unwise to go back to my quarters. In fact, it would be hard not to be seen going there, and I decided I didn't want to be seen. Medics' quarters are some distance from the transporter bays, but engineers' quarters are scattered throughout. Aha! I thought, "I know an engineer."

Engineer Nelson Prince's place wasn't far. Prince had invited me there on previous occasions, though not for discussions of technology. I decided it was time to pay him a visit. His door was ajar, and he was in night clothes at his desk. I spied the little bookshelf he once described so fondly to me, with its three books: 1) *Fahrenheit 451* by Ray Bradbury. Prince liked to remark that we don't burn books anymore. We don't even publish them in paper. He's the only person I know who still chooses paper over electronic when he can. 2) *Things Fall Apart* by Chinua Achebe, his distant relative. 3) *No Easy Walk to Freedom* by Nelson Mandela, a copy so beaten up that it would fall apart if anyone tried to read it. Prince had told me he just felt good knowing it was there.

His choice of books was totally unexpected, given the way we first met—at the Halloween costume party in the gravity simulator. He was there in his Wakanda outfit, which for him wasn't much more than a loincloth, gloves, and a scary necklace. He was totally into the role, his enthusiasm growing into danger of getting out of hand. (I, by the way, went as Wonder Woman, and wasn't wearing much more than he.) That was the occasion of my first declining his invitation to visit his quarters. Now, after more no-thank-yous, I will be visiting for the first time.

Prince didn't seem to notice me as I approached. He muttered to himself, "What am I missing? What? What am I missing?" as he looked back and forth between two piles of documents which on my closer peek turned out to be about our space station's transporters. He suddenly looked up as I leaned in to get a better view. He said softly, almost whispering, "Am I dreaming, or have you at last taken up my offer?"

I looked into his brown eyes and said, "I need you awake so you can help me." His smile nearly melted me. I continued, "I had an incident with one of our transporters."

"I've been reviewing the logs. So, you're the one. Trouble-maker," he chided, but I could see he was smiling. "I don't understand how you can be in two places at once. Somehow, they lost track of you and think it was just a delayed delivery. They don't know you're still here on our Battlestar Galactica, do they?"

I told him in detail what had happened.

He confirmed, "Well, you're right not to want to be seen. They can't afford this kind of thing to be known. Stay here. Please stay here."

I wasn't sure whether this was simply for my protection or there were ulterior motives in play.

Prince continued. "Do you remember Todd Friendly? It might have been before you got here. The same thing happened to him and he reported it to Uncle Ben, who made him keep it a secret. He didn't mention to Uncle Ben that he'd already told his fellow engineers, including Vince, Kwame, and me. Within 24 hours Todd was gone. 'Reassigned.' When we asked him, Dr. Benjamin Forager replied that he will never say where and there's no record of it. You're here for now, kiddo, at least for the night. I've got spare jammies." He grabbed a pair from a drawer and tossed them at me. After I stood there assessing the situation for a few seconds, he smiled and assured me his motives were pure—this time.

When I came out of his changing room he was standing by his bed. The sheets were drawn to one side, and a bedroll had been spread on the floor. "Your choice," he indicated.

I didn't have to think. I knew what I wanted. I strode up to him, pulled off this outfit top, ran my fingertips over his perfectly muscled chest, looked deeply into his eyes, and kissed him softly. "I've made my choice," I murmured. He kissed me hard.

I felt safe in his hands. He transported me in a way I'd never experienced, safe and free in my own land of dreams.

Early next morning, in the fashion we have such things as

mornings in a space station, I heard voices outside the door. Vince and Kwame were there with Prince. Kwame congratulated Prince, "You nailed Lizzie Ryan? The Queen of Tease bites the dust! We all thought no one could have her—especially you."

Vince added, "You're the champ, Prince—oh that's right you are the Prince! Remember, though, she is too good for you."

Kwame wanted to know, "What's she like?"

I was angry and could almost feel Prince cringe. He cleared his throat and paused for a few seconds, then said, "I have been favored by a goddess. But we've got a situation, and how we handle it is crucial both for Lizzie's safety and that of anyone who teleports from this home-away-from-home of ours. Come in. We've got to think."

I pulled the sheet around me as they entered and said their hellos. I swallowed my anger, but I could feel myself blush.

At first, our main thinking gravitated toward getting me back to earth and away from the authorities who'd "disappeared" Todd. Vince thought it would have to be by shuttle, given our experience with transporters. Kwame thought we'd probably have to invent, or steal, an identity to get me on some shuttle, and we'd have to line up someone we could trust on the other end to handle my case.

Soon I realized that I didn't want to leave. I didn't want some clone taking over my life here, especially not Prince, and I wanted to help the guys expose the problem with the transporter. The guys agreed reluctantly when I argued, "It's my life. What I know of biology should be helpful in understanding what various parts of the transporter system are meant to address."

I hid in unoccupied supply bays sometimes, sometimes at engineers' quarters. The three amigos were pretty clever moving me around and providing me with necessities. The need for anonymity among people who knew me made it hard for me to contribute to our secret cause, but with my specialized help we did get the feeling we were getting close to an answer.

Meanwhile after some weeks' delay, "Lizzie Ryan" returned by shuttle from her visit to Substation Draco and upon going back to "her" quarters, reported some of "her" things missing. Prince warned me to stay away from my quarters, but I couldn't help myself. After all, that clone was taking over my life. I lurked down the passageway, waiting to follow her, thinking she would head to sick bay. Instead, she started walking toward me. I quickly returned to Prince's quarters, thinking she hadn't seen me. Wow, was I wrong! Soon Station Commander Joan Valjean issued a bulletin warning of a possible thief and security breach.

Then about six weeks after my transporter mishap, I found myself spending most of the day in Prince's bathroom, suffering from nausea. What was that we drank to celebrate Vince's birthday the night before? I had assumed it wasn't alcoholic. Now I wished I had some of my mother's menudo. I heard the outer door open and called, "I'm in here, Prince."

The bathroom door opened and two security officers entered. One of them said, "You are an unauthorized person on Space Station Waterloo. We have orders to apprehend you and escort you to the commander's office."

As we entered Commander Valjean's office, I saw the commander and my clone seated at a table. The commander stared at me in astonishment. My clone said, "I knew I'd seen the imposter entering that cabin."

The commander addressed me, "Sit down and explain yourself."

I responded angrily, "I'm Lizzie Ryan, and she's my clone!"

Before I could continue, Prince entered, accompanied by two more security officers. The commander listened as he explained what had happened in the transporter bay. She announced, "I want complete medical tests run on both of these women, and keep them in sick bay until the results are back."

Commander Valjean called a formal hearing and held it in her boardroom. Advocates called witnesses to testify to the identity of both Lizzies. The physical exams and DNA analyses had shown that we were identical. We were grilled on our verifiable personal memories, on the customary assumption that continuous memory establishes identity, even though we all know that everyone has noticeable gaps in their remembrance of personal history. Still, our memories matched except for the understandable differences covering the most recent weeks. The commander pronounced her conclusion that the transported Lizzie was a duplicate of the original Lizzie. She explained, "Since obviously the two of you exist at the same time, it's clear that the transported one was made by copying, not by decomposing, beaming, and recomposing the original." That raised the question of what normally happens to the originals after they are copied. Prince, Vince, and Kwame were assigned to research this.

After the hearing Commander Valjean took Prince and me aside. She said, "Lizzie, the preliminary medical tests you underwent revealed a little hitchhiker growing inside you."

Dumbfounded, Prince and I looked at each other.

This piece of luck afforded Commander Valjean an opening for a face-saving solution. We are now officially conducting a study of human reproduction in space, with Betsy—she hated being called "Twin Lizzie"—as a control and me as the variable. This, and not the transporter, is getting all the publicity.

Quietly in the background, Prince, Vince, and Kwame found and removed the code which had resulted in the destruction and disposal of the original person during normal teleporting. The break came from examining old paper documentation of the devices. The electronic documentation had been altered to hide the fact that there was a cleanup step, but it hadn't occurred to anyone that someone might have been making a paper trail. Uncle Ben and a few coconspirators are now serving time back on earth. The commander has ordered that all transporters be disabled.

My life is heading toward a new normal. I tolerate the Betsy clone but still feel uncomfortable around her. I have moved in with Prince. At first, we could not imagine ourselves as parents but now we are excited. Today we are relaxing in our quarters after a long day at work. Prince looks at me and jokes, "Looks like we're stuck together for some time."

I reply, "Do you think we'll last?"

He says, "No way to tell. I guess we'll have to." He smiles and continues, "After all, the first American to be conceived in space is on her way!"

4

ROBBY AND ANNE EAT TOGETHER

CAROLINE MCCULLAGH

We threw ourselves
Into the future together seizing the day ...
from "Carpe Diem" by Jim Harrison

Sunday, September 29, 1968

I dried my hands on the dishtowel and picked up the receiver. "Hello," I said.

"Hello. Anne Bennett?"

"Yes."

"This is Robby O'Malley. We met a couple of weeks ago."

I couldn't place the name, but the voice was familiar. "Robby? ... I'm sorry. Where did we meet?"

"At the conference. In Sacramento."

I thought for a moment. "Again, I'm sorry. I don't recall ... Oh! Wait! Do you mean Professor O'Malley?"

"Yes. I didn't want to say 'professor.' It seems a little pompous."

"Not at all, Professor. What can I do for you?"

He'd been the keynote speaker. Who was I? Nobody. A novice teacher who had been dragooned into representing our school by her fellow teachers. They all had families and didn't want to waste a weekend. I didn't either, but I couldn't get out of it.

There was a pause.

"I hope I'm not interrupting anything."

"Well, yes, you are." I chuckled. "I'm washing breakfast dishes."

He laughed.

"I could call back."

"No. That's okay. I have a couple of minutes to talk before the water gets cold."

"In that case ... I going to be in San Diego on business next week. I enjoyed our conversation on art in elementary education. You brought up some really interesting ideas."

"But I argued with you."

"That was the fun part. Most people don't care enough to argue for their ideas ... In any case, I thought since I'll be there, maybe you and I could get together for lunch on Saturday and talk a little more about it."

"Oh, that would be nice. I don't have anything I have to do next weekend except grade papers, and you know first grade papers don't really take a lot of time."

"Shall I pick you up on Saturday then?"

"Do you know San Diego?"

"I'll get a map."

"Why don't I come to you? It would be easier. Where will you be staying?"

"I'll be at the Surf 'n' Sand Hotel in Pacific Beach."

"Ah, that's about a half hour from here depending on traffic. What time?"

"Noon?"

"Okay, I'll see you then."

I hung up and walked back to the kitchen, my mind going

in a dozen different directions. Then I walked back to the phone and called Jay. Trying to sound sad, I broke my date to go to a beach party with him Saturday afternoon. And just in case, I cancelled my Sunday brunch date with Steve too.

At the conference, Professor O'Malley had been the Friday dinner speaker. He moved around the dais and gestured as he spoke. He was graceful and rhythmic. It was almost like watching a dancer.

For an older man, he was really handsome too: tall, slender, blond, a face with purpose, beautiful hands with long slender fingers.

I found out later he had hazel eyes.

On Saturday, I decided to go to his seminar. I didn't really know who he was, but I had been impressed with the ideas in his talk. There were fourteen of us. He led a lively discussion. He had a talent for drawing people out. We talked for a long time. He invited all of us to join him for lunch, and we talked some more. Finally, in ones and twos, the other teachers left. I was the last one there with him.

"Miss Bennett," he said. "Let's walk a little. It seems we have more to talk about."

We had dinner together and then lunch the next day before he left to catch a plane to New York. He didn't wear a wedding ring, and he didn't mention a family, so when he asked for my phone number, I gave it to him.

I never thought he'd call.

ON SATURDAY, we walked to a good Mexican restaurant near his hotel. After lunch, we took a long walk through Pacific Beach. He'd told me in Sacramento that two of his favorite things were walking and bicycling in new cities, so I'd worn good walking shoes just in case. In the late afternoon, we sat in the hotel coffee shop, still talking about everything under the sun.

"I don't even know where you live," I said.

"Mostly in hotels. I travel all the time. But I get my mail and vote in Minneapolis, so I guess that's home."

"You have a house there?"

"An apartment. It's hard to maintain a house when you're never there."

Still no mention of family. I glanced at my watch. "Oh, it's late! It's been a lovely day, but I'd better get home."

"Do you really have to go, Miss Bennett? It's almost dinnertime. I could take you to dinner."

"Don't you get tired of restaurants?"

He shook his head. "The food all tastes the same after a while."

"I could cook for you."

His face brightened. "I'd love that."

"I'm not gourmet."

"I don't care."

So I showed him on his map where I lived. "Do you think you can find it?"

"I spend most of my life with maps in strange cities. I'll find you."

I DIDN'T HAVE a dining room in my little house, so we ate our spaghetti alla carbonara at the kitchen table. The air was redolent of garlic and pancetta. After he helped me with the dishes, he asked, "Are you busy tomorrow?"

"Not really." I gave fleeting thought to the brunch I wasn't having with Steve.

"The Symphony is playing a concert featuring pianist Claudio Arrau. Do you like that kind of music. Would you like to go?"

"I love classical music, Professor O'Malley. Unfortunately, a symphony ticket really isn't in my budget."

"Well, it is in mine, Miss Bennett. Please let me treat you. It's so much more fun when you have a companion to share with."

So I agreed.

AFTER THE CONCERT, I offered to cook for him again to thank him, but he said, "Oh, no. You look so beautiful in your red dress. You should be out in public where people can see you." He took me to an early dinner at Mr. A's, an upscale restaurant near the concert hall. Then he drove me back to his hotel so I could pick up my car.

As he opened the car door, he said, "I doubt you want to walk far in those high heels, but let's go look at the water for a few minutes before you go."

We followed the paved path through the heavy tropical landscaping to the edge of the bay. It was dark now. The evening was cool, the moon up, almost full. Lights sparkled in the distance on the other shore. A few groups lingered at the concrete fire rings. We could hear one of the groups singing with a guitar accompaniment.

We were quiet as we strolled, savoring the beauty of the scene.

He seemed tense though, the first time I'd seen him that way. For a moment, I thought he was going to say something, but he shook his head and was quiet.

"I should go, Professor O'Malley. I'm sure you have things you have to do to get ready for your meetings tomorrow. Thank you for such a special day."

He turned to face me.

"Miss Bennett ... Anne ... I'm not married. I've never been married. I have no children that I know of. I'm not seeing anyone right now. If I were to kiss you, do you think you could call me Robby?"

"Yes, I think I could do that."

I usually wear my shoulder-length brown hair down, but I'd pinned it up for the concert. He reached up and took the pins out to allow it to fall free. He brushed it gently into place with his fingers. Then he took me in his arms and kissed me as I'd never been kissed before.

When he finished, I said softly in his ear, "Oh, Robby, do you think you could do that again?"

And he obliged.

It was strange. There was no awkwardness between us. It was as if we'd always known each other and were just renewing our friendship. He put his arm around my waist, and we walked back to his hotel suite.

HE SAT ON THE BED.

"I don't know what you expect," I said. "I know I'm young—I'm twenty-four—but I'm not a virgin, so if you were hoping for—"

He shook his head. "I'm not either."

He laughed joyfully and patted the space next to him. "Come here."

I sat and he kissed me. Then he turned me so that my back was to him.

"I'm forty-six."

He unzipped my dress, kissing down my back as he did.

"Have you ever had an older lover?"

"Is that what you're going to be?" I asked. "This isn't just for tonight?"

He slid my dress off my shoulders and kissed the nape of my neck. "Oh, my god, you smell so good." He rested his cheek on my shoulder. "No. It isn't just for tonight ... Now, there are some advantages to an older lover. I can give you what you want. The only question is, do you want to tell me what that is, or should I find out for myself?"

I turned to him again. "I'd like to let you find out for yourself."

"Ah." He nodded. "Stand up then."

I did.

He pushed my dress down over my hips to the floor ... and then proceeded to find out.

And when we finished, all I could say was, "Oh, Robby."

THE NEXT MORNING, as I was getting ready to leave for school, there was a knock on my front door. When I opened it, a woman stood there holding a large bouquet. I could smell the fragrance of the amethyst-colored roses from where she stood.

"Anne Bennett?"

"Yes."

"These are for you." She handed them to me.

"Me?"

"Uh-ha. Boy, you sure impressed someone! It took him forever to choose the right flowers, and then he paid extra to make sure they were delivered before you left for work."

"The right flowers?"

"You don't know the language of flowers?"

"No."

"The white liatrises are for happiness, joy, bliss ... and desire. The purple roses are for love at first sight."

"Oh, my gosh!"

"Yeah." She smiled. "Enjoy them. There's a card in there."

She left.

The card simply read "Robby."

I called him.

He answered on the second ring.

"Oh, my gosh! Those flowers! They're gorgeous."

"Bet you didn't know there are 24-hour florists."

"I had no idea."

"You're going to be late for work."

"Yes."

"Shall I come to you this afternoon when you get home?"

"You don't have a dinner meeting?"

"No. I'll tell you about it later. Five o'clock?"

"Yes."

MY STUDENTS DIDN'T HAVE my full attention that day. It seemed like I spent most of the time counting minutes.

When he came to the door, I said, "Bed first, then conversation and dinner, or conversation and dinner, then bed?"

He laid his jacket on the back of the sofa and took me in his arms. "I think bed first. Then we'll see what happens after dinner."

"You don't think I'll wear you out?"

"Well, if memory serves," he said, "you were the one lying there last night trying to catch your breath. You didn't ask for mercy, but ..." He shook his head and smiled.

"Okay, bed it is."

In the bedroom, he kicked off his shoes. Then, without undressing, he lay down on the bed and rolled over on his back. "Anne, I need to tell you something first. I sort of ... Well, no 'sort of.' I lied to you."

Was he married after all?

"About what?"

"I didn't come to San Diego on business. There are no meetings. I came to see you."

"Why?"

"Because I already knew that I love you. What we're doing here is figuring out whether you could feel that way about me."

"Oh ... Do you tend to fall in love easily?"

He rolled over and sat up.

"I've never felt this way before. It's overwhelming. I haven't been able to think about anything since the conference but you. Still, if you don't think you can feel that way about me, just tell me. I won't bother you again.

I sat next to him. "As long as we're admitting our lies, I lied too."

"What about."

"I told you I didn't have anything planned for the weekend, but I broke dates for a beach party Saturday and for brunch yesterday."

"Why did you do that?"

"Because I already loved you, and I wanted to be ready in case you wanted anything from me."

He lay down again, pulled me down on top of him, and kissed me.

"You might want to think about checking out of your hotel and staying here."

"The bed's bigger there."

"Yes, but I can cook for you here. You should know whether I can cook before you make any kind of commitment. You know, spaghetti doesn't really count. What if it turns out I'm a bad cook?"

"There is that," he said, smiling. "Let me think about it."

"Yes, you lie there and think about cooking, while I do this."

I unbuckled his belt and unzipped his trousers ...

He groaned with pleasure.

"Yes, cooking," he said softly.

HE REALLY MEANT it when he said he lived in hotels. He was booked two years in advance for speeches, seminars, and conferences, including in Europe and Asia. But we talked on the phone several times a day, every day, no matter where he was. And he sent flowers.

Oh, the flowers! I learned Robby's language of love through those flowers.

A month later, he came for a weekend, and then later for a week when we went house hunting, and finally, four months after I met him, I carried red roses on the day I became his wife, and we started our new life together.

5

ROBBY'S DEATH

CAROLINE MCCULLAGH

Doors are opened that never before were opened,
New ways stand open, but quietly one door
Closes, the door to the future; there it is written,
"Thus far and no farther"—there, as at Eden's gate,
The angel with the fiery sword.
from "Dear Men and Women" by John Hall Wheelock

January 15, 2003

I adjusted the covers.

Robby was in our bed at home.

When the doctor had said it was time for hospice, he'd made me promise that I wouldn't put him in the hospital. He thought it would just prolong his dying. Neither of us wanted that, so he was home.

He didn't move much, but it was enough to disarrange the covers a little. There wasn't much else I could do. The hospice nurses were in charge of the pain medication, and he wasn't eating or drinking now, so I couldn't help him with that. He'd always been a bit of a dandy, so I kept his hair, white now, combed as neatly as I could. And I read to him when he was a more awake, poetry mostly. I chose short poems that I knew he liked. I could usually read a whole poem before he drifted off into a deeper sleep.

We'd both assumed this time would come. He was twenty-two years older than I was. We never talked about it before we married ... There were so many things we didn't talk about, but still, we managed to make a good marriage.

Ultimately, he said we had to make plans. I didn't want to think about it, but he said, "Sweetheart, all marriages end in tragedy, either in divorce or death. We need to do this."

HE WAS forty-six when I married him. I'd never thought much about death. I knew lots of men died in their sixties, so I thought maybe I'd get twenty years with him. When he reached his seventieth birthday, it surprised me how much of a relief that was. But then there was the next significant milestone. His grandfather, who was the longest-lived male of his family—we'd done a lot of genealogy, so we knew—died at seventy-five. That birthday loomed large for Robby. He was sure he wouldn't outlast his grandfather, but he did.

Now here we were.

"Are you ready, Mrs. O'Malley?" The day nurse, Amy, asked.

"I'll get Carola."

I walked into the kitchen where she was putting together a lunch for us.

"Time," I said.

"Okay, I'll get Ernesto."

Carola and Ernesto had been our employees since the early days of our marriage and our best friends.

The three of us helped Amy shift Robby so that he wouldn't develop bedsores.

At first, I was uncomfortable with the nurses around. We'd lived sort of an insular life. We had friends, but nobody close except Carola and Ernesto. I soon realized that since this was all the time we were going to have together, I couldn't fritter it away worrying about what the nurses thought. So when I wanted to, I laid down with him, and some nights I slept with him. But most nights I was too restless, so I'd move to the cot I'd put next to the bed.

He knew who I was. His body was failing, but his mind was as sharp as it had ever been. He couldn't carry on a conversation anymore, but he could communicate when he was awake enough, especially when we adjusted his position.

One of those times, he reached up to touch my breast and said, "Touch me." The nurse heard, and when we had him settled again, she excused herself to go make a cup of tea, so that we could have some privacy, and I could show him how much I loved him still.

Another time, he was in obvious discomfort. The morphine pump had four possible settings. Amy increased the dosage from level two to three, but the next time we moved him, he said, "Too much."

"Too much what?" I asked.

He pointed to the IV.

"Too much pain medication?"

"Yes."

Amy reset the pump to two, and he drifted off to sleep again.

I'd adjusted to this new and different reality of our marriage, and I halfway thought it would just go on like this. Still, I waited every day for the call from the doctor's office saying that they'd just come up with a miracle cure, a shot, a pill, some kind of treatment, but that call never came.

What did come was the day I hadn't allowed myself to think about.

It didn't seem different from any of the other days. The four of us had shifted Robby in the bed. I washed his face with a warm washcloth and combed his hair. Then I sat next to the bed and held his hand. He squeezed my hand, and then his eyes closed as he drifted off. He took a deep breath in ... and then breathed out, and he just didn't breathe in again.

After a few moments, Amy said. "Mrs. O'Malley, it's over. He's at peace now. He's not in pain anymore."

She quietly went about the business of turning off the pump and removing the IV tube from his arm. Then she left the room.

Carola and Ernesto, tears in their eyes, hugged me and followed her out, leaving me to say goodbye.

I had no tears. I'd shed them in private long ago.

I sat a while holding his hand. Then I adjusted the blanket one last time, kissed him, and followed them out of the room.

6

GO BABY WHALE

BOB BOZE

After lying awake most of the night, rehashing the fight with my ex-wife, I decided I needed a walk on the beach to clear my head. Halfway across the beach, I heard a scream.

What is going on? Then I heard another scream.

Two steps later, I rounded the base of the cliff and looked down the beach. A hundred yards away, a woman was standing next to a giant gray rock, screaming at the top of her lungs. "Help! Someone, please help!"

My first thought was that the rock had rolled off the cliff and injured someone. *This is San Diego, cliff collapses and boulders rolling down onto the beach happens all the time.* Then I remembered last night's news; the videos and warnings about the recent rains and high tides causing daily collapses. *How stupid can someone be to walk on the beach below the cliff and not pay attention? They had to have heard a rock that size coming, tumbling, and crashing its way down the cliff.*

Suddenly the rock moved. "Holy crap! Is that a rock?" I mumbled to myself as I started to run toward the woman and whatever the gray thing was.

The woman looked up and saw me. "Oh God! Please help! The baby is trapped and I can't get her out!"

Baby? What baby? My mind was racing a thousand miles an hour. *The rock crushed a baby? But the rock moved. How could a baby move a rock that big?*

That's when I heard a strange, low grunting sound. A sound that instantly took me back to the delivery room and the only sound I would ever hear from my son. The sound that took me years to forget was back and I immediately knew it would change my life, again.

I felt the woman staring at me like I was some kind of imbecile. "God damn it! Don't just stand there! Help me get the baby loose! I need a knife or something."

Things began to come into focus. The gray thing wasn't a rock. It was a whale. A giant whale. The whale was wrapped up in a fishing net and under the front of the whale was a baby whale. The fishing net was wrapped around both of them and holding the baby tightly against mom's belly.

"Are you stupid or something?" the woman screamed, pulling me out of the trance I was in as I stood there trying to analyze what was going on. "We need to cut them loose. They're both dying and mom is crushing the baby."

Suddenly I remembered my pocketknife. Oh crap, *It was on my dresser this morning. Did I grab it before I left*? I reached into my pocket, felt the pocketknife and, without thinking, said "Ta da," as I pulled it out.

"You have to be dumber than dirt and heartless," she said, as she snatched the knife out of my hand.

It only took trying a few cuts for us to realize we needed to work together. I sat next to her, held the net tight, away from the baby, while she cut the net. Then she passed the knife to me, we scooted over to the other side, and she held while I cut. When the baby was almost free, the lifeguards showed up, with a Sea World Animal Rescue crew right behind them.

We gladly let them take over while we scooted out of their way and collapsed on the beach.

"Thank you," she said. "I'm sorry for calling you names. I was in panic mode and scared to death. I really didn't mean whatever I said." After a short pause she added, "I don't know what I would have done if you hadn't come along."

"No problem. I completely understand," I told her. "I think they'll be fine... thanks to you."

We turned our attention to the rescue group and a few surfers who had joined them. They had finished cutting the fish netting from around mom and were pouring seawater over both whales while a woman with a stethoscope checked out mom and the baby.

Abruptly, we both looked around, realizing how quiet it was. No one was talking and the only sounds were from the water being poured over the whales and the surf breaking on the beach. We looked up to find a woman in a Sea World Animal Rescue uniform standing in front of us. She pasted on a smile, then sat down next to us. "I'm afraid mom didn't make it."

Without thinking, I let out a moan and whispered, "Please, I can't take losing another baby."

The Sea World woman's smile broadened and she put her arm around my shoulder. "Thanks to both of you, I think the baby will be okay. We're going to take her back to Sea World for a more thorough examination but I'm pretty sure she'll be okay." She looked at the woman next to me. "I'm Doctor Alicia Reed, a veterinarian with Sea World." Turning back to me she said, "Are you okay? You're awfully pale... but I suspect that's to be expected, given the trauma of trying to cut mom and her calf loose."

"I'll be fine," I said, not wanting to discuss my private life with two strangers.

The woman next to me somehow sensed my discomfort and quickly changed the subject. "I'm Fae, by the way." After shaking hands with first the doctor and then me, she added, "And you are?"

"Oh, sorry, I'm Kevin." I just nodded at each of them, not wanting them to see how badly my hands were shaking.

THE NEXT HOUR was organized chaos. All of us gathered around a large tarp and helped roll the baby whale onto it. Then, about twelve of us took an edge and loaded her into a Sea World pickup truck with a padded bed liner. Once the baby whale was on its way to Sea World, a large crane and dump truck took care of loading mom so they could dispose of her giant body.

The only thing I remembered afterward was the constant grunts the baby whale made as she tried to locate her mom. Each grunt became more desperate, and heart wrenching, and they only trailed off when the pickup got far enough away that we couldn't hear her anymore.

Once the pickup was out of sight, Fae and I found ourselves staring at each other. Uncontrolled tears rolled out of our eyes as we grabbed each other and sobbed.

After a good healthy cry, I jumped up and ran over to the fishing net that was still laying on the beach. Frantically, I searched every square inch of the net.

"What are you doing?" Fae asked.

"I want to find out who owns the net. Who left if where the whales swim... who is responsible for trapping mom and her baby."

"Even if you do find the boat that the net came from, ultimately it's global warming that killed mom... along with thousands of other animals," Fae said, as she watched confusion wash over my face. "Kevin, if anyone is protective of the whales and other sea life it's the fishermen. But global warming has forced the whales, and the sea life they eat, out of their normal habitat. The whales are just following their food and the fishermen are just following their fish. Thanks to global warming though, their territories have collided."

"That's just a bunch of crap," I told her. "The world has just decided to blame everything on global warming. Frankly, I'm not even convinced there is such a thing as global warming. The earth has been temperature cycling since it began and every time the temperatures peak or dip, everyone screams 'Global Warming.'"

"Oh wow!" Fae said, looking totally stunned.

"Let me guess; you're a tree hugger and global warming sign carrier," I came back with. I wasn't sure where that came from. Then, I decided to make a bigger fool of myself. "Oh, I get it. You were out here roaming the beach just looking for something to rescue. If it hadn't been the whale and her baby it would have been a clam someone dug up and was going to take home and bake."

"You... you have to be the biggest jackass I've ever met."

"Why? Because I don't buy your global warming argument?" By now, I'd convinced myself that my anger from yesterday's argument with my ex-wife was boiling over to today, and I was taking it out on Fae. "Look, I'm sorry. Today is not my best day and I'm afraid I'm just arguing with you so I can prove I'm right about something."

"Sounds like you've been arguing with a woman," Fae said, adding a chuckle.

"Yeah. My ex-wife. Over something that happened more than two years ago."

"My guess is you still need to blow off some steam." She looked at her watch then added, "I've just missed the last express bus, and it'll be two hours till the next 'stops at every corner' one gets here. So how about if I buy you a beer while you pour your heart out and tell me what a bitch your ex-wife is."

"Two reasons why that's not a good idea. First, my dad told me 'never talk to a woman about a problem with another woman, because no matter what, you lose'. Second, you'll likely try and turn me into a climate change hippie protestor and have me sleeping with you in a palm tree so the city can't cut it down."

Fae's stare was boring a hole in me. "Let's start with my sleeping with you. While you may be cute, you're so enamored with yourself that your head would never fit in a palm tree. Second, I don't sleep around... well... at least not in palm trees. That's because I'm afraid of heights and who knows what might be living up there. Finally, my main reason for inviting you for a beer is because I've two hours to kill, I'm a good listener and I need to get the baby whale out of my head."

"I'm sorry, this is going like the arguments with my ex-wife and that's my fault. Grabbing a beer is a great idea," I told her, then deliberately reached down and took her hand, trying to change the mood. "Is the pub across the street okay for that beer?" She looked down at our hands, made no attempt to pull hers away, and nodded.

As we crossed the street I said, "Just to be clear. My ex-wife is not a bitch in any sense of the word. In fact, she's a wonderful, intelligent, kind person who is just having an awful time adjusting to something."

"The loss of your child?" Fae asked.

All I could do was nod. "Please don't take this wrong because losing my son broke my heart. But I guess, having been in the service and seeing people killed means you deal with death differently. You quickly learn to separate yourself from it and convince yourself there's nothing you could have done differently. Unfortunately my wife blamed herself the second the doctor told us he had died during birth. 'If only I had', 'I should have done this or that', 'a decent mother would have known'. And on and on.

"Therapy has helped, but once she quit blaming herself, she shifted the blame to me. I know it's natural to have to place the blame somewhere, but after a year of the accusations cutting deeper and deeper, I gave up defending myself and called it quits."

By this time, we were in the pub, where we settled down at a high-top table off in a corner so no one could overhear our conversation.

"First round's on me," Fae said as she headed for the bar. A few minutes later she was back with two beers and a basket of pretzels. We bumped beer glasses and she picked up where our conversation had left off.

"I'm sorry," Fae said. "Death does funny things to people, and everyone reacts differently. The death of my mother tore my family apart. None of us realized she was the only thing holding us together. Then one day she was gone and what little glue she had used to hold us together dried up and we fell apart. That's rubbed off on every relationship I've had. Each time I expect my mom's ghost to tap me on the shoulder to let me know, 'He's the one.'"

"And?"

She squeezed my hand to tell me, *It's time for a subject change.*

"If you're going to convince me to hike up into a palm tree with you, you'd better start persuading me that climate change is real and eating Brussels sprouts for the rest of my days will save the world."

Her face scrunched up. "Yuk! If eating Brussels sprouts is the only way to save the world, they can kiss it goodbye."

"Ah ha. Not a fan of Brussels!" I teased. Just then, as if on cue, the TV next to us launched into a two-hour special on climate change. "You planned this, didn't you?"

"Nope," she said. "The man upstairs must have known you were going to be a hard sell and that I'd need help."

～

THE NEXT TWO hours were spent glued to the television special. The coverage started with who was being impacted the most by climate change: Animals. How almost every species was losing its habitat at an alarming rate. The glaciers were melting, drought was killing off vegetation, water sources were drying up, rising water tables were wiping out habitat and animal migration trails. Adding to that was the loss of habitat caused by human expansion, as mankind tried to adjust to these same issues.

I sat there stunned as the program moved on to the effects climate change was directly having on mankind. Crops and farm land no longer able to produce because of drastic, long term changes in weather patterns. Islands, coastal property and tide lands now submerged by the rising tide waters. Sealife and their habitats being wiped out by oft recurring El Nino and La Nina and other weather phenomenon. This portion of the program went on to delve directly into the plight of fishmen as the habitat of their normal catch kept moving or was wiped out entirely.

Finally, the program closed with horrific scenes of houses, businesses, and entire towns along the shoreline that were devastated during the most recent storms. Pictures of houses that had been there for years, floating away as their stunned residents helplessly looked on. Businesses turned to rubble. Family farms and ranches now submerged. On and on it went.

As we sat in silence and watched, I kept looking over at Fae, waiting for her to say, "See. I told you." But she never did. Finally, I turned it off, unable to watch any more, and realizing that I owed Fae a big apology.

We ended the night with me taking her home so she didn't have to ride the 'stops on every corner bus', and I could apologize; which I did on her doorstep. That was quickly followed by my invitation to take someone, that I now tremendously admired, out to dinner the next night.

W<small>ELL</small>, one dinner turned into two, then a bunch of breakfasts and lunches and finally, six months after our whale rescue episode, Fae moved in with me.

D<small>ID</small> the whale episode and my meeting Fae change my life? You bet, and all for the better. By the end of our bar visit and the TV specials, I was convinced that what happened to the whales was driven by climate change, not by the fishermen being greedy and careless.

I also adored the fact that my tree-hugging, sign-carrying, anti-Brussels sprout, now partner, never once lectured me or gave me the raspberry. She has given me raspberries but never over climate change and only occasionally in public.

So, what are our lives like now?

Both of us fight climate change in every way we can, big or small. We patrol the beaches every year during beach clean-up day. We volunteer at Sea World, the San Diego Zoo, and the California Wolf Center, as part of their on call Animal Rescue teams. We also do presentations, anywhere we can on the massive impact climate change has on the animal and human world.

Oh, and if you pass a bunch of flowers down on the beach at the base of the cliff... that's us. A memorial to mom whale, from us and her calf, who is out there somewhere, hopefully avoiding mankind and their fishing nets.

Go Baby Whale!

LOST AND FOUND

JEFF MASON

The wooden clapboards needed painting and the front yard was covered with wet fallen leaves. *Twenty years, a long time or no time at all,* Jason thought as he climbed the four steps to the front porch of the large nondescript two-story house on Clark Avenue in Ames, Iowa. He hadn't intended to be here. He hadn't weighed the consequences, yet here he was.

He rang the bell, once, twice, and a third time before he heard anything from the other side. When the door opened a crack he asked, "Is Catherine here?"

An older woman peered out and said, "Who? Who are you after?"

"Catherine Masters. She used to live here."

"Cat hasn't lived here for twenty years, since 2000."

Jason handed her a business card. It read Jason Clay, Esq. and gave a Des Moines street address, an e-mail address, and phone number. "Do you remember me, Mrs. Masters? I haven't seen you in years. I think Catherine might want to talk to me."

She stared at the card and said, "I'll let my daughter know you stopped by. Care to tell me why?"

"It's between Cat and me. Just let her know I was here."

The thirty-mile drive back to Des Moines from Ames gave Jason a chance to reflect on his impulsive visit. At least he'd found out Cat was still alive, not much to go on but a start.

A weak November sun radiating little warmth was low in the west when Jason returned to his law office. His partner had left for the day. They could only afford a part-time receptionist so at four p.m. on a Thursday the office was locked, dark, and vacant. Jason didn't bother to turn on the lights in the waiting room but switched on his desk lamp. He sat alone in his somber office.

He picked up the letter still atop his in-basket of his desk. It had arrived in yesterday's mail and was handwritten on plain stationery. The hand-lettered envelope had been postmarked from New Orleans three days earlier. The writing was neat and precise.

I have reason to believe that you are my biological father. I was able to acquire a copy of my Story County birth certificate listing Jason Marcus Clay as my father and Catherine Ann Masters as my mother. I was adopted as an infant and raised in Nashville. I'm a junior at Tulane in New Orleans. I haven't been able to locate my mother, but you are the only Jason Marcus Clay I could locate in Iowa. I would like to meet you. Please contact me.

Your Hopeful Daughter,
Jean Marie Duncan

AN E-MAIL ADDRESS and phone number were written below the signature. Jason re-read the Tulane University return address on the envelope.

Jason reviewed his memories of Cat. When he'd known her she was a senior at Iowa State University still living at home with her mother. He had been a sophomore who lived with his fraternity brothers but worked busing tables in the student union to help pay for his tuition. That's where they met. She'd thought he was funny. He'd thought she was beautiful but remote. They'd gone out a few times and gotten drunk more than a couple of times, usually at fraternity parties. They'd made love whenever they could, but always with protection. He tried to remember if he had been in love with Cat, but he only remembered the physical attraction.

He'd met her mother a couple of times when picking up Cat. He didn't think he ever had a conversation with her. She had always been cool if not cold toward him. He had no memory of Cat talking about her mom but thought she was divorced. Cat never mentioned her father.

They'd broken up after Christmas. He'd gone home to Des Moines and when he returned after New Year's Cat had ended it. She didn't say why, just that she needed a break. He hadn't pursued her. Now he wondered why he hadn't.

Jason put the letter and a couple of depositions he needed to review into his worn leather briefcase. As he drove home he remembered Cat as aloof, almost regal in her bearing. She was tall, at least five foot ten. Her dark hair and dark eyes lent her a mysterious air. He pictured a younger woman with Cat's features but also somehow with his rounder face and darker complexion.

He stepped through the kitchen door and the usual pandemonium enveloped him. The twins, three-year-old boys, were yelling for their mother, and the baby was crying loudly. Jason found Michelle trying to burp the fussy baby, a soiled blanket covering her shoulder. He kissed her on the cheek, took off his sport coat, took the baby from his wife, and began walking to and fro in the living room while murmuring baby talk.

After fifteen minutes of pacing the baby calmed and Jason placed her in her crib. She kicked her legs a few times, tried but failed to suck her thumb, and fell asleep.

A loud timer went off and Michelle called out, telling him to take the things out of the oven. Jason removed a bubbling pre-packaged lasagna and a baking pan with almost browned French fries. He made a green salad and poured two glasses of Chardonnay from yesterday's half-empty bottle. He prepared two child plates putting French fries in one compartment, apple sauce in a second, and cottage cheese in the third.

He sat the twins in their highchairs, fastened their bibs, and placed their plates in front of them. They'd learned to use child utensils and could get a considerable portion of their food into their mouths if they wanted to. They liked cottage cheese and apple sauce and recently had discovered French fries, so they were actually eating when Michelle came into the kitchen. She'd changed her blouse and run a brush through her hair.

Jason served lasagna and salad to Michelle and himself. As soon as he began to eat, the twins demanded attention. Determining that they had eaten as much as they were going to Michelle undid their seatbelts, pulled them from their highchairs and sat them in front of the TV. She started the DVR which played an inexhaustible supply of Thomas and Friends train videos.

When she sat down again Jason told her he wanted to discuss something important after they'd put the children to bed.

"Why can't you tell me now," she said. "Is something wrong?"

"No. That's not it. I want to wait unit the kids are down."

At nine the dishes were in the dishwasher, the twins bathed, read to, and tucked into their beds. Jason and Michelle settled in the living room to talk.

Stuttering slightly Jason said, "I, I don't know how to tell you this. I found out I might have a twenty-year-old daughter."

Michelle gave him a dour look, "You're kidding? Right? How in the hell did you just find this out."

Jason took Jean's letter out of his briefcase and handed it to Michelle. She read the brief letter once, then read it again.

"Let me explain," Jason said. He told Michelle about his brief relationship with Cat while they had both been students. "I reached out to Catherine after Christmas vacation, but she firmly told me she needed to end our relationship. She never said why, and I never saw her or talked to her again. I should have followed up, but I had no idea."

"Why do you think Cat chose not to tell you?"

"I don't know. I didn't think we had a committed relationship. I might have mentioned that I planned to see my old high school girlfriend when I was home at Christmas."

Michelle considered that. "That was in 2000 and abortion was legal. Why didn't Cat get an abortion?"

"She as very Catholic. I don't think that would have been an option for her."

"And you never even saw her again?"

"She did a semester abroad that spring. She was two years ahead of me so she should have graduated in May. No. I never did see or hear from her again."

Michelle stood and walked around the living room. Then looking directly into Jason's eyes she said, "If Jean is your daughter, then she is part of our family. We have to meet her."

THE NEXT MORNING Jason sat at his desk trying to decide how to respond to his daughter. He started a few e-mails but deleted all of them without sending any. He reached for his desk phone and dialed the number from her letter. The phone rang several times before a message said, "This is Jean, if you want me, tell me how and when, and leave a number." A beep followed. Jason hesitated before he blurted, "This is Jason Clay. I received your letter, and we need to talk. Call me back at this number."

After he hung up, Jason realized he had forgotten to leave his number. A few minutes later when a phone rang outside his office, and he heard the part-time receptionist say that she would check and see if Mr. Clay was available. The intercom buzzed, and the receptionist told him, "You have a call from a Jean Marie Duncan."

Very tentatively Jason picked up the receiver and said, "Hello."

"This is your daughter and I'm so happy I found you and that you called me."

" Are you sure? I had no idea I had a daughter."

"I'm sure everything fits if you're the Jason Clay who went to Iowa State in 2000."

"We, my wife, and I, would like to meet you. Is there any chance you could come to Des Moines?"

"I have a four-week winter break. Maybe I could visit after Christmas? Do you know anything about my birth mom?"

"Sorry, no."

They talked for a few more minutes and promised to talk soon and arrange her visit. He offered to pay for a round-trip flight from Nashville, but she said she would rather drive, and that it was only ten hours from Nashville to Des Moines.

"I'm so happy I found you," she said. "And I can't wait to meet you in person."

ON MONDAY MORNING, Jason's receptionist notified him that he had a call from Mrs. Masters.

"Hello, Mrs. Masters," he said as he picked up the phone.

"Mr. Clay, I talked to Cat yesterday and told her you were looking for her. She told me to call you and tell you she didn't have anything to say to you."

"It's important that I talk to Cat. Do you know where she is? Do you have an address or an e-mail for her?"

"I don't think Cat wants me to give those to you."

"Do you have any grandchildren, Mrs. Masters?"

There was a long pause before she answered. "Cat is my only child. I don't think she wants to have children, so no."

ON THE DAY AFTER CHRISTMAS, it was already dark and threatening snow at six p.m. when an older Honda Civic pulled to a stop in front of Jason and Michelle's single-story tract home in suburban Des Moines. The young woman who emerged from the driver's side of the car wore a parka, faded blue jeans, and a knit wool cap which still allowed her curly raven-colored hair to cascade over her shoulders. She pulled an overnight case from the trunk and walked to the front door.

Jason and Michelle, who had seen her pull up, flung open the front door and greeted her before she had a chance to ring the bell.

"Jean?" Jason said.

"Dad?" Jean said.

Neither Jason nor Michelle said another word. They each opened their arms and hugged her then stepped back. "We're so glad you're here," said Michelle. "Come out of the cold and we'll get you settled."

Twenty minutes later the whole family including the twins and Michelle holding the baby assembled in the living room. The twins stared at Jean but were too shy to talk.

"Are you old enough to have a drink?" Jason asked.

"Of course," Jean said. "I turned twenty-one in September,"

Jason poured eggnog laced with bourbon for himself, Michelle, and Jean. He put a couple of ounces of unaltered eggnog in sippy cups for the twins.

"Tell us about yourself," said Michelle. "Where were you raised?"

"I grew up in Nashville. It's really the only place I've ever known. My parents, Jack and Yvonne gave me as normal a childhood as possible. I fit right in, with aunts, uncles, and grandparents. I guess my parents couldn't have children, so they got me. I'm an only child. They always said I look just like the daughter they thought they could have."

"How did you find us?" Jason asked.

"I didn't know I was adopted until I was in high school. That's when my parents told me. I wanted to meet my birth parents right away, but my parents thought I should wait, and that you might not want to meet me. I didn't try to find you until this year when I transferred to Tulane. I contacted my adoption agency and found out I was born in Ames. The agency refused to give me information about you or my birth mother."

"How did you find out I was your father?" Jason asked.

"I called the Story County clerk who was kind enough to help me get a copy of my birth certificate. I knew I was named Jean Marie and that my birth date is September 29, 2000, so it didn't take her long to locate my birth certificate. It listed Jason Marcus Clay as my father and Catherine Ann Masters as my mother. I used the Internet to find you. You're the only one in Iowa, but I struck out looking for my birth mother.

"Did you know Catherine's mother lives in Ames?" Jason said.

"Really, when can I meet her?" Jean blurted. "Don't you think we should call her to tell her we're coming?"

"I suppose, but I haven't told her you exist."

"I was born in Ames. Don't you think she already knows I exist?"

"She'll probably tell us not to come."

"Why?"

"I don't know, but I think she and your mother don't want to have anything to do with you or me."

ON TUESDAY JASON cleared his calendar and they drove, in silence, north to Ames past corn stubble under a gray sky. Patches of white snow gave the only relief to the otherwise somber day. In Ames, Jason navigated the streets bringing the car to a stop in front of a modest two-story clapboard with an enclosed front porch. Large bare limbed trees stood in front of the house. Dead blackened leaves still covered the walk and the part of the front yard where the snow had melted.

Jean trembled as they walked to the front door. Jason rang the bell twice while they waited.

The front door opened and Mrs. Masters looked at them through a closed glass patio door. Why are you here?"

"I brought your granddaughter, Jean, to meet you," Jason said.

"You must be mistaken. I don't have a granddaughter."

Jean fished in her purse, pulled out a stamped copy of her birth certificate, and pressed it to the glass of the porch door.

Mrs. Masters studied it through the glass before slowly reaching down and unlocking the door. She stepped back, and Jason opened the door. He and Jean followed Mrs. Masters through the house to the kitchen in the back. Without a word, Mrs. Masters gestured for them to sit at the kitchen table, lit a burner on the gas stove, and put a large tea kettle over the flame.

Jean and Jason each took a chair at the table.

"I knew about you," Mrs. Masters said. "Even saw you when you was born. A brown baby to my blonde daughter. When you was adopted right away by that mixed couple from Tennessee we figured that was the last we'd hear from you. What do you want coming here now?"

"I want to know who I am and who my birth parents are," Jean said.

"Jean wants to meet her mother," Jason said.

"I don't think you should," Mrs. Masters said. "She has a life for herself now and she don't need reminding of her past mistakes."

"Have you even told Cat that I've been looking for her?" Jason asked.

"You ruined her life once. Now you're trying to do it again."

The tea kettle whistled but Mrs. Masters ignored it until the whistle grew too loud. Then she turned off the gas.

"I'm going to help Jean find Cat," Jason said. "I think it would be better if you told her, but one way or the other, we'll find her."

Mrs. Masters looked at Jean. "She has a husband and family, and they don't know anything about you."

"Well you can tell Cat we want to meet. Or we can show up on her doorstep. It's really that simple."

Mrs. Masters folded her arms in front of her chest but didn't say a word.

Jason and Jean stood and left never having been offered tea.

On the drive back to Des Moines Jason said, "As Cat's daughter you can get a copy of her marriage license just by asking for it from the Iowa Department of Public Health in Des Moines, assuming she was married in Iowa."

"Is a marriage license a public record?"

"Yes, but only specific people are allowed to request it without a court order. Children are one of the categories allowed to get copies. Once we know Cat's married name we shouldn't have too much trouble finding her."

AT TWO THE next afternoon Jean sat in Jason's waiting room. The receptionist ushered her into Jason's office as soon as his last client for the afternoon left. Jean smiled broadly as she opened her purse and removed the envelope containing a copy of Cat's marriage license and handed it to Jason.

The license read Catherine Ann Masters was married to Martin Dale Altshuler of Des Moines, Iowa on June 20, 2010.

"There are only five Altshulers listed in the Des Moines directory," Jean said. "Only one is Martin."

Jason looked up the phone number online and dialed. When a woman answered he asked for Cat.

"I go by Kate now."

"Cat, I mean Kate, this is Jason Clay."

"I don't know any Jason Clays and I have to go."

"Cat it's me and I have a young woman with me who would like very much to meet you."

"I, I don't know."

Jason handed the phone to Jean. "Mother? I'm so happy I found you."

AT NINE THURSDAY morning Jason and Jean sat at a table at the Waveland Cafe, a breakfast place Jason loved and that was only a mile from his office. Jean was so antsy she couldn't sit still, folding and unfolding a paper napkin until Jason took it away from her.

"What if she doesn't show?" Jean said.

"Then we'll have the best hashbrowns in Des Moines, and I'll have a couple of hours to show you around town."

A tall woman in an overcoat, gloves, and woolen cap came through the front door and scanned the restaurant. She spotted them and headed for their table. Jason and Jean scooted out of the booth and stood to greet her.

"Kate," Jason said. "You'll be glad you came."

"Mother?" Jean said and extended her hand.

Kate took Jean's hand. Her mouth moved but no words came out.

"Let's sit down and order breakfast," Jason said.

Kate removed her coat and cap and set them on the seat beside her.

For a moment no one said anything, then Jean's words flowed out in a torrent. "Mother. Is it okay if I call you that? I've been searching for you, and now I've found you. I've wanted to meet you to find out where I came from. Jason's been helping me. Now that I've found you, I have so many questions."

Jason held up his hand and said, "Jean, take a breath. Give Kate a chance."

Kate spoke slowly. "It was so hard to give you up. I was sure I couldn't endure seeing you again. I'd put you out of my mind. I didn't exactly forget you, but kept you in a place where I didn't need to think about you, and I really haven't. Not for years."

"So your mother never told you that I was looking for you?" Jason said.

"I don't talk to my mother anymore. She made me give my baby up. I tried, but I never could forgive her."

Kate turned to Jean and said, "Do you hate me?"

"Why would I hate you?" Jean asked. "I only want to know where I came from. Loving parents raised me, but you know—I still wonder."

Tears brimmed in Kate's eyes and slid silently down her cheeks.

Jason reached out and took Jean's hand. "It's a joy for me to find someone I didn't know I'd lost."

8

CONTINENTAL DIVIDES

SANDRA YEAMAN

One smiling face caught Becca's attention when she took her seat behind the thick pane of ballistic class separating the visa section from the waiting room. Serious, even dejected faces topped the rest of the chairs. Not one empty seat in sight. And the line waiting for seats led out the door and down the sidewalk to the street. Becca couldn't see how far down the block it reached.

What's he doing here again? It wasn't surprising that an Iranian turned up in Stuttgart to apply for a visa, but she had refused him yesterday. Becca mused on the coincidence that led to her first assignment as a Foreign Service Officer in Stuttgart being because of her prior experience teaching in Iran. Frankfurt was the westernmost point Iran Air flew. Iranians with enough money and dreams of traveling to the US often turned up in the waiting rooms of US consulates in Germany.

She had turned her back on all things Iranian when she left that country four years earlier, except for her thoughts of Zac. But the departure of the shah and then Ayatollah Khomeini's return changed everything. Zac's letters stopped then. Becca yearned to know why and whether her connection to him endangered him.

She turned her attention to the row of documents on the counter and grabbed the closest one. A young woman wanted to travel to spend her gap year in the US before beginning her university studies. Like so many other young German women, it appeared she planned to spend the year as an au pair in the home of a friend of the family, unaware that a special visa was required to do so.

Becca didn't find anything in the passport, on the application, or in the many letters and documents the applicant had submitted to suggest a different explanation for the requested long stay in the US. She also didn't find the au pair special paperwork. Confident she had enough information to complete the interview quickly, she pressed the button for the microphone that broadcast into the room and called out the number on the "now-serving" paper tag clipped to the cover of the passport.

Three minutes per interview. That was the goal. If Becca took longer than three minutes for each interview, people would still be in chairs at noon, and she and her staff could not leave for lunch. After confirming her initial suspicion, she explained the reason for her refusal to the young woman and watched her walk away, her shoulders slumped forward.

Becca knew without opening the next package which applicant was next. It was thick—one passport with two previously refused applications. *It's* his *application.* The Iranian man who sat smiling in the front row. At the end of the previous day's interview, she had told him what she told all Iranian applicants —she recommended he wait at least six months before reapplying since it was unlikely his circumstances would change sufficiently in less time. But here he was again today.

She unfolded the previous application. She recalled he had two children, both of them living in Los Angeles, having left

Iran seven years earlier, before the revolution. They hadn't ever traveled back to see their father.

Among the documents filed with the previous refusals Becca found a letter she remembered reading when it first arrived several weeks ago, but she hadn't seen it the day before. As she began reading it again, she realized it was about this applicant. A rabbi in Los Angeles wrote to the consulate to explain he would be applying for a visa to attend his son's wedding. In the letter, the rabbi explained that the young man had been raised Christian in Iran and that he would be marrying a Jewish woman, also from Iran. The father, in contrast, was Muslim. The rabbi closed with his wish the consulate staff would view the father's application favorably since he had not seen his children in many years.

Why didn't he say anything about his son's wedding yesterday? She pressed the waiting room mic button and read off the number clipped to the passport cover.

The man approached the booth, still smiling.

"Good morning, Mr. Javadi," Becca said. "Do you have translator today?"

"No. I can speak English enough."

"OK. My first question is why did you come back again today? I told you yesterday that you should wait at least six months before reapplying."

"I want to explain to you for myself. I think my translator, my friend, not explain enough. But I think you understand."

"Why didn't you tell me yesterday that you wanted to travel to attend your son's wedding? I would have understood that explanation. We received a letter from a rabbi in Los Angeles."

"I want to see my children. I not see them for many years. First they go England. Then, after revolution, they go America. If I arrive too late for my son's wedding, I don't care. I just want see my son."

"Why isn't your wife traveling with you?"

"My wife not my children's mother. Their mother and I, we divorced. My wife now stay at home."

"I'm also confused about one other thing. In his letter, the rabbi said your son was raised Christian."

"Yes, my first wife Armenian. Christian. The children also Christian."

"But you are Muslim."

"Yes."

"There is one other problem with your application I must understand. You marked the question about whether you had ever been arrested with *yes*."

"Yes. That is true."

"Please tell me about it so I can understand why I should believe you will return to Iran after your visit. If you were arrested in Iran, why would you want to go back?"

"I say you truth. I was arrested and in prison. But I do nothing wrong. I have friend who tell me he leaving Iran. He tell me but he not say when or how. So when police look for him, they come to my house and they ask me. They ask me where he is. And I say truth. I say I not know. The day before I knew. The next day, I might know. But that day, I not know. So they arrest me."

"How long were you in prison?"

"Four, five months. I not sure. My hair turned white in prison."

"What do you mean?"

"In prison one guard, he like me. And he know I friends with other man in my cell. He try take care of me and him. One night, in middle of night, he came my cell and took me to different cell. When guards take people from cell at sunrise, we know they execute them. When guards take people from cell at sunset, they release them. But he take me from cell at midnight. Put me in different cell all night. Next day, he come back and he say my hair is white. I ask him why he take me from cell. He say he not want me see they take the other guy away at sunrise. He know I unhappy if I see. So he take me to another place so I not see. When he come back, he say my hair is all white."

"Okay. Let me ask you the most important question. Why should I believe you will return to Iran at the end of your visit."

"I must return. My wife in Iran. My job in Iran. My house in Iran. In Iran is everything but my children. In United States is only my children."

"Thank you, Mr. Javadi. Your answers are very different from the answers many Iranians tell me."

"I say you the truth."

"And I believe you." Becca paused and considered whether she should continue. She knew she would be crossing the line between interviewing an applicant, a requirement of her job, and asking for information for herself. Her curiosity won the battle. "I have another question for you. It isn't for your visa application. It is for me. Okay?"

"Okay."

"Since you are going for your son's wedding and your son will marry an Iranian woman who is Jewish. I would like to know if you can find an Iranian Jewish family in Tehran. When you go back to Tehran, will you see if you can find that family?" Becca wrote Zac's name on a blank piece of paper, adding Pars Garden Hotel on Takhte Jamshid Avenue under his name, and her own name under that, and handed it to Mr. Javadi.

"I ask my Jewish friends in Munich. The man who he came with me yesterday to translate. He is Iranian Jewish. Maybe they know this family. Maybe they know if the family in Iran or someplace else."

"Thank you, Mr. Javadi. If you find out anything, you can send me a letter at the Consulate to let me know. My name is at the bottom of the paper. Come back this afternoon after 2 p.m. to pick up your passport and visa." Becca noticed her heart pounding as she folded all the papers into the passport and placed the packet onto the shelf behind her for the consular

staff to stamp the visa into the passport and prepare the application for filing.

"Tank you." Mr. Javadi continued to smile while he
backed away from the interview window and headed for the
door.

TWO WEEKS LATER, Becca received a call from an Iranian
woman, the wife of Mr. Javadi's friend in Munich. She told
Becca Mr. Javadi had found the family and would return to
Germany to explain what he learned.

When Mr. Javadi finally called to say he was again in Stuttgart, Becca arranged to meet with him at a café at the Stuttgart
train station.

"I pleased to see you," he said when Becca arrived and
joined him at one of the outdoor tables.

"And I am pleased to see you," Becca said. "How was your
son's wedding?"

"I arrived one day before. Very nice. He marry very nice
woman."

"I received a phone call from your friends in Munich. You
found the family?"

"Yes, I found them. They in Los Angeles. Here is phone
number." He handed Becca a small paper with only a number
beginning with a Los Angeles area code. He then looked down
and remained silent for several seconds. When he looked up,
he said, "I sorry I also have some bad news."

Becca thought she saw a tear in the corner of one of his
eyes. "What is the bad news?"

"I found your friend's family. But your friend not with
them."

"Do you know where he is?"

"Yes, I know."

Becca watched as he took a deep breath.

"I knew when you said his name. I knew that name, but I not able to say I knew him then. I afraid."

Becca felt her head jerk slightly backwards. "Why would you be afraid to tell me?"

"Because, your friend is the man in my cell in prison, the one the guard take from cell after he move me to a different cell. Your friend is my friend. I not sure when you say his name, but I afraid you change your mind about my visa if I say I know man with that name."

Becca felt her body grow limp and grabbed the edge of the table to steady herself. "Do you mean my friend was the man who was executed?" Becca recognized her voice rising in pitch as she spoke.

"Yes. The same. I not sure then. But now I know. Now I can tell you more about him. About why he was in prison. You want me say?"

Becca leaned forward with her elbows on the table, her hands in front of her mouth, and her eyes closed. "Yes. Yes, I want to know more."

"Your friend, he and family own a hotel, right?"

Becca nodded, her eyes still closed.

After Mr. Javadi described what he had learned about Zac and his family during his trip to Los Angeles, Becca sat up straight and looked directly at him. "When was this? How long ago was this?"

"In summer."

"Last year? In 1980?"

"Yes. After that, your friend's whole family leave Tehran. They all now in Los Angeles. The number I give you," he said, pointing to the paper with the LA phone number on it, "is number for your friend's relative. He have the same name as your friend. He waiting to hear from you."

Becca and Mr. Javadi talked for another half hour, arranging how they could remain in contact once he returned to Iran. Becca knew she couldn't tell any of her colleagues about her meeting with Mr. Javadi, that it would remain her secret. But she knew she had to tell her boss about what happened to Zac. She knew it would affect her work when interviewing other Iranian applicants. She needed a break.

THAT EVENING BECCA worked out the difference in the time between Stuttgart and Los Angeles before she picked up the phone to dial the number on the paper Mr. Javadi had given her. She felt her heart beating faster than normal and a lump rose in her throat while she waited for the ringing to stop. *Why am I sure Mr. Javadi talked with the family? Maybe he just talked to someone about the family and then tried to pass on what he heard as personal experience? I have no evidence to believe what he said? Maybe Zac is still alive. Maybe the Isaac Hamadani Mr. Javadi heard about was a different man. Maybe . . .*

When an unfamiliar male voice answered, Becca said, "I'd like to speak with Isaac Hamadani."

"I am Isaac," said the voice on the other end.

"I'm Becca Lysne. I stayed at your hotel a few years ago. Do you remember me?"

"Yes. I remember you. I've been waiting for you to call. We are all safe in California. And we are happy to hear from you."

"A man I met in Germany told me he saw you in Los Angeles recently. Is that true?"

"Yes."

"Did he tell you he had been in prison—with Zac?"

"Yes, but not at first. I heard he was looking for Zac. I was suspicious. I didn't know why anyone would be looking for Zac. Anyone from Iran, that is. The government announced his execution on the radio, so I thought everyone in Iran would know Zac had been murdered by the Iranian government. When we learned that a guy from Iran was trying to find Zac, I asked my father for advice. He told me I had to pretend to be

Zac so I could tell you myself what happened. We didn't want you to hear from a stranger. When I met Mr. Javadi and learned he knew Zac, I explained that Zac was my uncle."

"He told me Zac was arrested because the government wanted the hotel."

"Yes. They took the hotel away from my family. And I knew we had to leave. You know I helped the Americans at the embassy? Back in February right after Khomeini returned."

"I didn't know that."

"I did. Because our hotel is close to the embassy, when I heard armed thugs had entered the embassy the first time, on Valentine's Day, I sent my driver to the back gate of the embassy with food for the employees. Thank God that attack ended. I knew then that I had to get my family out of Iran. Then the Pasdaran took the hotel."

"Why didn't Zac leave at the same time?"

"We tried to convince him to leave. But he was certain my grandfather, his father, could prove the family owned the hotel and the land, and he wouldn't leave his father alone to do that. He was the only one without a wife or children. He said he had to stay to help his father. He agreed the rest of us should leave, but he was always the optimist, never the realist."

"So Zac and your grandfather stayed in Iran after you left. Did your parents stay, too?"

"They stayed until Zac was murdered. Did you know they made the family pay for the bullets that killed him before they would release his body? And that they defaced his body by writing horrible things all over it? They wanted to make sure we couldn't bury him and thought their blasphemies would prevent it."

"Isaac, I am so sorry to hear that."

"Will you send me a photo of you? I remember you, but I don't remember your face."

"I'll send you the photos I have of Zac as well."

"And I'll send you photos of my family so you can see that

we are doing well in the United States. When you come back to California, you must come to see us. The family would like to meet Zac's friend again. And we need to be sure you find a nice American husband. Or have you found one already?"

"I'm still not looking for a husband. I'm very happy with my career and am not sure a husband fits in with that future."

"We'll see," Isaac said. "Let's talk later. Give me your telephone number, and I'll call you in a few days, after you've had time to think about what I've told you."

Becca gave Isaac her phone number and address, and they arranged to speak at the end of the week.

AFTER THAT PHONE CALL, Isaac called Becca several times to talk about Zac and the takeover of the family hotel by the Iranian Revolutionary Guards. He expanded on what Mr. Javadi had told her and explained more about how he helped a small group of American embassy employees in February 1979.

In November that year Iranian students again overran the US Embassy in Tehran, this time taking hostages—American staff members and two other Americans who happened to be at the embassy that day. The students claimed the embassy was a nest of spies. They pointed to shredded documents they pulled from the embassy—evidence, they insisted, of the spying.

After the embassy takeover, Isaac said Zac worried the students might find evidence of the help Isaac provided back in February. They were both relieved Isaac had already left Iran. Zac stayed with his father, and together the two took steps to get the hotel business back.

In the spring of 1980, Zac's father was summoned to Qasr Prison for another discussion about his case. The caller also demanded that Zac accompany him. The caller implied that everything was now settled for the family to once again regain possession of the hotel. Instead, once they reached the prison, they arrested them.

On July 30, 1980, guards led Zac out of his cell and into the prison's courtyard in front of a squad of armed men who shot him. They released Zac's father to return home without seeing his son.

The authorities later admitted a case of mistaken identity led to Zac's execution. Becca wasn't convinced. It's too easy to excuse an action as a mistake or a misunderstanding.

9

EASY PICKUP

MARDIE SCHROEDER

Thursday around 10am I was picked up at the Mission Hills library by a tall slender man in logoed attire who carried me to his shiny red sports car parked across the street. Oh boy, I thought, I'm in for a wild ride. Didn't happen. He just sat there staring at my cover. Well, that's nice. Some people don't even do that. Some just throw me on the back seat and zoom off. I remember one time I was left in the car overnight . . . how sad is that? Nothing to keep me amused.

We turned the corner onto Washington Street going east. And let me just say here that it was not the wild ride I had anticipated. Too much traffic for one. Anyway, on a crowded city street what would one expect?

Soon we stopped at a coffee shop. I'm always nervous going into a coffee shop—spills you know. Jelly donuts are the worst. But I stayed in the car. It's always a crap shoot not knowing who you go home with. The worst are people who eat and read. Toast is the absolute worst. Crumbs end up between my pages. It's really very uncomfortable.

I've met some very interesting characters on my travels. One elderly lady lived alone in a huge three-story mansion and had piles of books in her bedroom waiting to be read. She'd read me in the afternoon downstairs in the living room and carry me up to the bedroom late at night. She would doze off in the middle of a sentence. I don't think she was bored because as soon as she jerked awake she was back at it exactly where she left off. I just waited patiently for her to continue reading.

I had a very scary experience once when a woman got so mad at her husband because he kept reading me when she wanted him to talk to her. She grabbed me out of his hands and threw me to the floor yelling that a lousy book was more important to him than she was. I don't think that marriage lasted very long.

I really like it when groups of people get together after reading me. It's quite fascinating how interested they are in discussing minute details about the story and the author.

One lady who picked me up had two cats who competed to curl up on her lap as she read. Purring is such a pleasant thing and cats do seem to like books. Dogs certainly have their place but they seem to be less book friendly. They tend to chew the edges when they think no one is looking.

Some people turn down the corners of the pages. It would be nice if bookmarks were furnished so that doesn't happen. In the past, some books had a ribbon attached which made for an elegant presentation. Sometimes even the edges of the pages were gilded in gold.

As you know, I'm many copies in various places. I just love bookstores. Everything is brand new and shining. The aroma of fresh paper permeates throughout the store adding a certain serenity to the space somehow. We're on display seeking admiring glances from people walking in. At the first crack of being opened you want to shout, "pick me pick me."

You can see I get around a lot. Sometimes copies of me make their way around the world. One time I was left in the airport bathroom. I almost got tossed in the trash by the loo lady (I was in London) but she ended up taking me home.

On my first ride on a double decker bus, a soft drizzle fogged up the windows. The loo lady tucked me inside of her coat to keep me dry when we walked from the bus stop to her apartment. She walked us up four flights and entered a tiny room. She put a kettle on a two-burner electric plate and had tea and biscuits. Turning on a very small lamp next to a tiny table, she started to read. I was very grateful she managed to avoid any crumbs falling on my pages.

Anyway, when she finished reading me, she dropped me into the lending library at the airport. Who knows where I'll go next.

Oh here comes my person. Off again.

My my, I had not expected such a cozy bachelor pad. A true sanctuary if I ever saw one. Very neat and tidy. I could stay here quite a long time. I hope he's not a fast reader.

All too soon he finished reading me but he didn't take me back to the Mission Hills library. Instead, he took me to the Mission Valley one.

More adventures await me. Until next time.

10

THE PATH
MICHAEL O. GIBBS

Drama, a day in the cultural training of a Native American boy
*A child born to the people of the plains soon learns that every
decision he or she makes touches, in some way, all the others. This
oneness in the struggle to survive is our triumph.*
Crow On The Ridge, *Holy Man*

urtle, a youngster of five winters, watched as the village elder pushed his way free of the reeds and shuffled toward him. Pony Man, the elder, was returning from somewhere beyond the pond.

Upon coming to where Turtle squatted at the path's edge, the old man abruptly plopped himself on the ground and pulled his moccasin off. Grimacing, he twisted the exposed foot around and examined its pink bottom.

"Turtle," he said, lifting his yellowed eyes momentarily. "I would tell you a story of the Stone Nation."

Turtle squirmed—sure he knew the cause of the elder's

discomfort. He let the obsidian point he had been working on slide from his fingers to the ground behind him.

Pony Man squinted at his foot, rubbing a calloused finger over its soft surface while Turtle looked on.

"Ahuhh," Pony Man said, bending closer. A small drop of blood formed on the foot. He brushed the blood aside and plucked a tiny black flake from the wound beneath.

Sun glinting from its smooth black surface unhappily confirmed Turtle's fear. It was an obsidian shard—one carelessly dropped on the path by Turtle moments before.

"As you know, Turtle, each of Mother Earth's nations must move in their own sacred circle of life. And so it is with the Stone Nation, for they are among the Beings who live here with us."

"Yes, Grandfather." By custom, Turtle addressed all village males older than his father as Grandfather. This grandfather, he knew, made fine arrow points for many of the village's warriors, but more important to Turtle, he was their band's Storyteller.

Turtle loved sitting beside the campfire at night, gazing into the depths of its flickering flames, listening to Pony Man's tales of long-ago times and exciting battles.

"And did you know that the Beings of the Stone Nation journey in the earth's waters to reach the ends of their sacred circles, Turtle?"

"No, Grandfather." Turtle's worry gave way to captivation. He was going to hear a story.

"It is so," Grandfather explained, "for the Beings of the Stone Nation have no legs or wings to carry themselves. And for these reasons, they must find their way to the waters of this living world so that they might tumble to the Great Maker's lodge in the Spirit World on the other side of this one. This is how they close their sacred circles, Turtle, just as the Beings of each nation must."

Turtle pulled his knees close to his chest. *Legs? Wings?*

While Grandfather slipped his moccasin back on, Turtle glanced over his shoulder long enough to assure himself that the point he dropped in the dirt had neither legs nor wings.

"The Food Stone Beings," Grandfather continued, "give us their strong backs upon which we grind our gathered herbs and nuts. And the Sweat Lodge Stone Beings share with us the power of their magic when we breathe in the sacred steam they release to cleanse our spirits. Just as the Hunting Stone Beings give us fine points, like this one you have been making, Turtle." He jutted his chin out. "And each must make its way to the Spirit World that it might be swallowed up before the Great Maker spits it back out as a fine mountain."

Turtle flushed—his eyes downcast—sure now that he had done something wrong.

"Each Stone rubs itself upon the floor of the stream during its journey so that it might be bright and shiny in the eyes of the Great Maker when it reaches the Spirit World. Yet the Great Maker does not swallow up each Stone, Turtle. And do you know why this is so?"

"No, Grandfather . . ."

"This is so because each grain of sand cannot become a mountain. The earth would soon collapse under such weight and fall in upon itself. The Great Maker honors only those who respect the Beings of all his Nations. The rest are cast away—no one knows where—but it is a sad thing when other beings that live here with us cannot close their circles."

The old man sat still for a moment, gazing westward at the distant mountains. At length, he shifted himself, grunting as he straightened his legs.

"But the Stone Beings still have no legs, Turtle. So how are they to get to the stream that they might tumble to the Spirit World and become fine mountains to protect our people from fierce winter storms?" He lifted his eyes once again to the faraway horizon.

Turtle, still looking down, hunched his narrow shoulders. He had never seen a stone tumbling over the ground, except, of course, those tossed by him and his friends.

Grandfather's eyes dropped to his callused hand, looking at the tiny shard, the one taken from his foot.

When he did not continue, Turtle prompted him to do so. "How, Grandfather? How do they get to the stream?"

"We carry them, Turtle," the old man replied, his eyes searching the earth between his spread legs for additional shards. "It is how our people honor the Stone Beings for the gifts they bring us. We take them to the stream so they can begin their journey. And the Great Maker, knowing this, honors them for their respect to his other nations."

Pony Man fell silent while pinching several additional black flakes from the dirt path. "And so it is that all the Beings of Mother Earth are bound together, and we must help one another when it is in our power to do so."

Unsure if the story was over, Turtle waited.

After a moment, Grandfather reached over and tousled Turtle's hair, and when the boy looked up, he winked, smiling so that the many wrinkles in his face multiplied.

"So, Turtle," he concluded, "the young brave who throws his stone shards into the stream brings much pride to his people, for in doing this kindness, he protects his people from injury. And at the same time, he honors those of the Stone Nation for their service to our people. And, the spirits from beyond our world look upon such young braves with great favor. It is a thing to think about." Grunting, the old man climbed to his feet and held out the fist containing the shards he had collected.

Turtle stood, sticking out his tiny hand to receive the rock chips—vowing in silence to never again disrespect those of the Stone Nation.

Pony Man folded the black shards into Turtle's outstretched hand, and laid his hand on the boy's shoulder, leaving it there, waiting for the boy to raise his eyes again.

When their eyes met, Pony Man shifted his gaze to the litter of shards still remaining on the dirt path, smiled, and once again winked. "Make your people and the Great Maker proud," he said, then turned and limped away.

11

LUCKY LADY, LIVING IS A GAMBLE

CHAVAH SIEGEL

Elana jumped as a roadrunner darted past her and disappeared underneath a fancy sports car parked near the entrance to the Vegas Cactus Apartments. "How," she muttered, "do those birds have so much energy in this heat?" She glanced at a combination clock and thermometer above the front door. It displayed a temperature of eighty degrees at ten o'clock in the morning.

Stepping into an igloo-cool lobby, she wheeled a small suitcase down the hall to the manager's first floor office. She slid keys under the locked door, along with a note giving her forwarding address in Chicago. On her way to the exit, a delicate rose scent surrounded her. She noticed a man with shimmering blond hair perched on the arm of a love seat in the lobby.

He smiled and tipped his fedora. "Shalom. How are you this heavenly August morning?"

His words reverberated in her ears like delicate harp notes. She studied his flawless complexion before nodding to him. "I'm okay. And you?"

"Wonderful as always. Elana, could I give you a ride downtown?"

She paused, assessing his pinstripe suit, crisp white shirt, and gold cufflinks. "Absolutely not," she murmured. Shaking her head, she hurried to the front door and stepped outside. She gasped, almost colliding with him. "How did you sneak out here so fast? Please tell me you have a twin."

"I have many earthly duplicates of myself. By the way, your bus just left. It's going to be 110 degrees by early afternoon."

She pictured herself frying like an egg while waiting almost an hour for another bus. Checking her watch, she noticed it had stopped. "Darn." She squinted at him. "Have we met before? Your face seems familiar, but I don't know your name."

"Raphael." He pulled out an antique pocket watch from his suit jacket. "I'll keep track of the hours." He pointed to a sports car the color of a ripe tomato. "We have plenty of time. Since your doctor got a late start today, your appointment has been pushed back. And your hotel room isn't ready yet for check-in." He picked up her suitcase. "I'm your escort for today."

She frowned. "How did you know my itinerary? I have to admit you have an honest face, so I suppose I'll just have to trust you." Following him to the car, another roadrunner sprinted past her. "I can't believe how quickly those birds move. Scary."

"The Hopi Indians, among other Pueblo tribes, believed roadrunners held medicinal powers."

"That's interesting. Maybe I should have been viewing them in a different light all this time." She shielded her eyes against a relentless blue sky. "I hate this infernal sunshine and can't wait to leave this hot desert town. One more night and by tomorrow afternoon I'll be back in the Midwest." She hesitated. "Okay. I'd appreciate it if you could please drop me off at the corner of Fremont Street and Las Vegas Boulevard."

"Excellent." He snapped his fingers, and the engine turned on. After stashing her suitcase in the trunk, he helped her get in, buckling the seatbelt for her. "I'll take good care of you. Sammy Davis, Jr., often sat in your seat. And I drove Howard Hughes all around Summerlin."

"Really? You can't be that old. I'm thirty-two, but I've already noticed spider web lines around my eyes. Your complexion is flawless—I'm sure due to a good plastic surgeon."

"I'm ageless."

"Good for you." She pulled a silk scarf out of her purse and wrapped it around her neck, covering a prominent scar.

"That's a lovely Hermes scarf," he said, touching her wrist, "but you don't have to hide your surgical scar. It will heal in time."

His hand feels like a fluffy cloud, she thought. "Complete strangers insinuate I've tried to slash my own throat. It's a thyroidectomy incision. Not a sign of a suicide attempt."

He grinned. "You can always tell people you were a Jewish pirate during the Spanish Inquisition, and that you got into a sword fight. But good news. You won."

"Thanks for trying to cheer me up. I doubt, though, I'll live to see a new year."

"Even in 2010, miracles still exist." He pulled out of the parking lot and headed toward Highway 95, driving with one finger on the steering wheel. "You aren't dying."

"How would you know? I won't get the biopsy results until this afternoon. However, I'm sure the cancer has spread to my lymph nodes." She sank further into the plush bucket seat. "I like your car. What kind is it?"

"I'm the original owner of this 1953 Alpha Romeo Spider." He waved his hand over the control panel. Icy air filled the car.

"I'm guessing you're one of those amateur magicians populating Vegas."

"There's nothing magical about what I do. You require healing. And I'm your man."

"So, Raphael, did your parents name you after the Renaissance painter?" His name tasted like honey on her lips.

"That's a good guess. But wrong again."

"Any other tricks you can show me?" *Mr. Houdini wannabe,* she thought.

"Abracadabra," he said, tapping on the steering wheel three times. "You'll need these."

A pair of pink rhinestone sunglasses appeared in her hand. Her jaw dropped. "Impressive. Anything else?"

He placed a hand on her forehead.

Elana opened her eyes. She stood next to Raphael in front of a Fremont Street Experience souvenir shop. "What happened? How did we get here so fast? I don't remember a thing."

"You fell into a restful sleep."

"Who are you anyway?" She stared into Raphael's deep sapphire eyes.

"You already have the answer." He pointed to a display in the shop window.

Studying a T-shirt with a grinning image of Bugsy Siegel, a halo above his head, and holding a machine gun, she laughed at the caption. Trust Me. I've Been a Perfect Angel in Vegas. "I've got it now." She glanced at his black-and-white wing tip shoes. "You're an actor rehearsing for a mafia movie." She looked around. "Where are the cameras?"

He took her arm and guided her toward the Golden Nugget. "I have another client."

"I don't understand." She followed him past the hotel's front desk and into a packed casino. Walking past multiple slot machines, she said, "I should tell you—I don't gamble."

He led her to a poker table occupied by cigar-smoking men and pulled out a chair for her. "Stay here. Don't leave no matter what." He snapped his fingers, and a four-by-six postcard appeared in his hand. Giving it to her, he said, "If you get into any trouble while I'm gone, just concentrate on this." Raphael disappeared into the cloud of cigarette smoke coming from a nearby roulette table.

"Excuse me," she said to the card table dealer. "Do you have the time?"

The dealer, a man with angel wing tattoos on each side of his neck, winked at Elana. "Casinos never have clocks. But you don't need one to know you're in good hands."

A cocktail waitress with an angel pin on her collar came to the table and placed a cold drink in front of Elana. "Your favorite. Lavender lemonade."

The man sitting next to Elana adjusted his angel cuff links and pushed a pile of chips toward her. "Enjoy your good fortune," he said. "You'll have a long and happy life."

Elana stood. "I'm sorry. I need to leave." She hurried out of the casino and toward the hotel entrance, a blast of frigid air surrounding her. In the lobby, she approached a woman in a blue suit standing next to the front desk. "Could you please tell me—"

The woman, wearing an angel ring, handed her a brochure. "Welcome to the First International Convention of Female Elvis Impersonators. Show starting soon."

"No thank you," Elana said, waving away the brochure. "I'll just wait in the lobby until my room is ready." She saw a vacant couch and gravitated toward it. Sitting on the plush cushion, she examined the ivory-colored card Raphael had given her. His name, R. Malak, was embossed between a pair of wings. *That name means angel in Hebrew,* she thought. Turning the card over, she stared at an image of the biblical Jacob wrestling with an angel. Tears flooded her eyes. *I don't have any faith,* she thought, *And I have zero control over my future.* She opened her purse and stashed the card inside.

Four Japanese women wearing blue velvet pantsuits strolled by, their faces covered in heavy pancake makeup and bright red lipstick. As they stopped in front of her, their glittering diamond angel necklaces mesmerized her. They separated into two groups.

Raphael emerged in a cloud of gray smoke, wearing a blue

suit, the shade reminiscent of a Chicago summer skyline. "Come," he said, reaching out his hand to Elana. "I have to escort you back to the casino."

"Why?" she asked, straggling behind him.

"Your only job is to trust." He led her to a vacant slot machine before floating over to the poker table.

Elana sighed. Plunking down in the seat, she heard a jingle coming from the machine next to her, followed by a robotic game-show voice announcing a big win. She glanced at the player, a woman wearing a sequin-studded cape and a gold belt with Elvis imprinted on the buckle. "Lucky lady," Elana said, motioning to a steady flow of coins pouring into a bucket.

The woman glared at her. "I saw you come in with that archangel Raphael."

"Everyone seems to know him," Elana said. She stared at the woman's black Pompadour hairstyle. "I just met him this morning."

The woman laughed. "Raphael and I go back an eternity. He believes himself to be superior because he's a healer. The reality is he's jealous because I get more business, especially in decadent places like Vegas. It's a jackpot all the time for me in this town."

"What are you talking about?" Elana asked. An odor reminiscent of decaying flowers drifted past her.

"You can't be that much in denial. I'll never understand you humans. Just when you're busy traversing through life, I come along and put the kibosh on all your cherished plans." She deposited a gold coin in the slot and pulled the lever on her machine. Diamonds, emeralds, and rubies began to fill a second bucket. "Yeah, Baby, that's more like it. I have to change things up once in a while. It gets so boring around here while I wait for my next assignment." As she turned to Elana, her eyes glowed red and seemed to become volcanoes overflowing with lava.

Elana looked around the casino. *When,* she thought, *is Raphael coming back?* "You're not making any sense."

"What's not to understand? I'm an angel, too. By the way, Raphael and I receive our orders from the same Higher Source. But, unlike him, I don't represent the living. Haven't you guessed my identity by now?" She tapped her name tag.

Standing, Elana tiptoed closer to the woman and read the words. "Hello. My Name is the Angel of Death." She took a step back, her heart pounding. "I don't believe you."

"No? Watch this. I can change into anything, or anyone, I desire." She snapped her fingers and morphed into Marilyn Monroe before becoming Al Capone and then turning back into her original Elvis impersonator incarnation. "Most humans never see me coming. They delude themselves into thinking tragedy only happens to other people. Then I arrive on the scene."

"I'm not ready to die," Elana said. "I'm young, and I haven't achieved my goals. I doubt I've even come close to finding my purpose in life."

"What do you know about living? You've wasted so much of your days on ridiculous pursuits." She pointed a skeletal finger toward a poker player. "There's one of those vulnerable humans I had my sights on right before you walked in. Let's see if Raphael comes to his rescue."

Elana watched as the man clutched his chest, fell forward, and hit his head on the table before collapsing on the floor. A few seconds later, she heard the siren of an approaching ambulance. "Will he survive?"

The Angel of Death shrugged and pointed upward. "There's always someone watching from above. Security reacts like lightning to any hint of trouble, including a medical crisis. It looks like Raphael won this round. At least for now."

"Lucky for that guy. He'll recover."

"There's always another human to take his place," the Angel of Death said. "You'll do."

Elana gulped and pulled out Raphael's card from her purse. She felt it vibrate in her hand. "Raphael gave me this for protection."

"So what? Here's my business card."

Examining the purple ink, Elana read from the Twenty-third Psalm. "Though I walk through the valley of the shadow of death . . ." She shook her head and glared at the Angel of Death. "I told you I'm not ready to die. I'm going to fight you. I have too much to live for."

"Good luck. You're going to need plenty of it. I'm stronger than you. You won't win. Not without significant help."

As the Angel of Death changed into a dark menacing form, Elana heard a rustle behind her. She turned around, catching a brief glimpse of a pair of wings. Raphael hovered over her.

Thunder rumbled throughout the casino. A plume of black smoke surrounded the Angel of Death, followed by a cloud of pure white.

Seeing a flash of lightning, Elana crumpled in a heap onto the carpet. She awoke to a pure white cloud and the sound of harp music. Rubbing her forehead, she detected a pleasant rose scent enveloping her. Looking around the vacant casino, she saw Raphael standing in front of her, his wings fluttering. "Is this the afterlife?"

"Of course not." He held out his hand and helped her stand next to him. "We won."

"The Angel of Death is gone?"

"For now. You won't have to worry again for decades to come."

"I guess I'll trust you." She clutched his hand, walking with him out of the casino and onto the Fremont Street Experience. "Everything looks so normal." She looked at groups of tourists wandering past hotels and shops. "Isn't that the mayor of Las Vegas?" She smiled at the familiar man in front of the Four Queens Casino, flanked by two showgirls sporting life-size angel wings. "Everyone looks so happy." *Did I dream it all?* she thought, noticing Raphael's wings had disappeared.

"We're here," he said as they crossed Main Street at the end of the shopping district and stopped in front of the entrance to a medical office building.

"Will I ever see you again?"

"If and when you need me." He waved and disappeared, blending into a group of doctors leaving the building.

Taking the elevator to the seventh floor, Elana stopped at the reception desk and signed in. "I like your angel pin," she said to the receptionist. "Lots of people seem to believe in those supernatural beings."

"They're real to me." She reached into a drawer and brought out a ceramic angel pin, offering it to Elana. "I make these for anyone in need of spiritual assistance. This one is for you."

Elana examined the angel's face surrounded by porcelain roses. "It even looks like me. Thank you." She pinned the piece of jewelry to her collar.

A nurse appeared in a doorway next to the reception desk and beckoned to her. "We're ready for you." She led Elana into an exam room. "Doctor will be in shortly. He's finishing up with another patient."

Elana chose a random magazine from a rack before taking a seat. Closing her eyes, an image appeared of her walking in the sand along Lake Michigan, a cool glass of lavender lemonade in her hand. *If only,* she thought. She sighed and fanned through the magazine before dropping the open magazine onto her lap.

"Do you believe in angels?" her doctor asked, entering the room and standing beside her. He pointed to the magazine. "I see you're reading an article about them. After reviewing your biopsy results, I'm inclined to believe in them myself."

"Excuse me? Just tell me the bad news. You had warned me that my presurgical biopsies didn't look good. All this time, I've been expecting the worst. That my cancer has spread. Tell me right now how much time I have left. I need to get my affairs in order."

He smiled. "Your angels must have been working overtime because your postsurgical biopsy came back completely clear. No sign of cancer at all. I'm astounded myself." He shook her hand. "I love giving patients good news. Just follow up with your doctor when you get back to Chicago. And don't forget to thank your angels. You're a lucky lady."

"Are you sure you didn't mix up my results with someone else? If I heard you correctly, you're saying I'm to going to live." She paused. "Yes. As a matter of fact, I do have an angel to thank." Glancing at her watch, she noticed the minute hand moving again. She smiled at her doctor. "Everything's in good working order."

The scent of roses followed her as she walked out the door and into the waiting room, a warm breeze seeming to push her toward the elevator. Getting in alone, she looked upward. "I shouldn't ask, but could I please get one more sign? Something to remind me that you're still here with me. Always." She closed her eyes and took a deep breath.

A single blue feather floated slowly through the air, landing on her head.

12

FAMILY MATTERS

STEVE CORKERY

ike Hagerty wore a haggard look as he hurried down the polished linoleum corridor of the Woodland Convalescent Home. A group of relatives and his three small children trailed behind him like ripples. Henry and Kate, the older children, were valiantly trying to keep pace with the longer strides of their aunts and uncles. Claire, the fledgling three-year-old, had slipped out of an uncle's grasp, choosing to prance rather than march. The family slowed, and kept a respectful distance as Mike approached and stopped at a doorway.

Brightened by the cloudless sky of an August afternoon, the sun-washed room had a faint scent of fragrant flower arrangements that failed to overwhelm the bleached hospice odors. A doctor in wrinkled scrubs and two uniformed nurses stood at the foot of a bed. The doctor glanced up and motioned Mike to enter. Rubbing his tired red-rimmed eyes, and releasing an extended breath, Mike crossed the threshold of the room where his wife, Amelia, lay dying.

The children wriggled free from their relatives and joined their father at the head of the bed where their paralyzed mother lay. Only her dark eyes indicated signs of life as she looked at Kate, and then to Henry, finally resting on Claire's face. Claire squirmed her way in front of her siblings to touch her mother's hair that lay in soft, black waves on the starched white pillow.

The doctor took Mike aside. "I came straight from the hospital." he said. "We did all we could. The embolism was acute, more advanced than expected, and the clot moved quickly. Her body is shutting down fast. She'll pass soon. I'm sorry, Mike." He looked at the three huddled children, and then at the relatives who had entered the room, lined up against the wall as though posing for a portrait. He put his hand on Mike's shoulder as he left the room. "Thank goodness for family."

The children watched closely with wide eyes as the nurses detached the futile drip tubes and IVs from their mother. Only six-year-old Kate grasped the finality of her mother's condition, and she started to cry. A nurse loosened Amelia's stiffened fingers and removed a handkerchief. She gave it to Mike, pressed it into his hand and said, "Use this. It will help; it has her smell."

Mike wiped Kate's tears and turned to face his relatives. Several were shaking their heads, eyes downcast. Some clutched frayed leather prayer books, and others moved their fingers around a chain of rosary beads. Mike coughed, cleared his throat, and struggled to find words. "Please pray for Amelia. Say goodbye and send her with your love."

He ushered his children out of the room into the hallway where he knelt and brought them close to him. Henry and Claire sniffled, and Kate sobbed as she leaned into her father's arms. He struggled to remember the words he had tried to rehearse. "It's time to...Claire honey, Henry, Kate. . ." His strained voice broke under the weight of the terrified look in his children's eyes. "We must do something that is hard to do, very hard. We have to say goodbye to Mom."

"Where is she going?" Henry whimpered. "Is Mommy going

back to the hospital? I don't like it there; I don't want to go there."

Claire chimed in, "Can we go with her too, Daddy? I want to be with Mommy!"

Sniffling, Kate blurted out, "Mom is going to die and go to see God. Right, Daddy?" Her sister and brother looked at her with wide, puzzled eyes and open mouths. Tears trickled down their cheeks and they moved in closer to their anguished father, waiting for his answer.

"Hush." Mike brought his steepled fingertips together and studied the children. "She is not going to the hospital. Not this time. She is dying." His prayer steeple collapsed.

The relatives began filing out of Amelia's room, holding one another for support. They stopped to embrace Mike and bent down to kiss the children. Virginia, Mike's youngest sister, gently lifted her brother by the arm, steadied him, and spoke in a soft undertone.

"Mike, we'll be at the house. Amelia's sisters are making dinner. Everyone needs to get back home, so they'll be leaving after church tomorrow. I think it's a good time to talk and make decisions tonight while we're all here." She paused, "After the children are in bed."

A storm of voices whirled through his mind as he watched the somber shadows of his relatives fade toward the end of the hallway. No decisions had been made—the unexpected whims of a heartbeat had precluded steady decision-making. Recent talk had been a loud, verbal tug-of-war; plaintive arguments, rancorous debate. It was a cruel crossword puzzle they were trying to solve. He had penciled in, and then erased, the slow answers to quick questions about what lay ahead for him–and more pointedly–for his children.

A nurse appeared at the door and beckoned Mike and the children to enter. "Please hurry, she has little time left." Mike nudged Henry, and Kate took Claire by the hand. There was a faint rise and fall of the blanket covering Amelia. Her eyes were closed, and Mike spoke in a sobbing staccato.

"Amelia. Sweetheart. I can't...don't know how, I don't want to say goodbye. I love you. You will always be the love of my life. The children are here with me. They are so beautiful, like you. They want to tell you how much they love you. Amelia, I'm scared, but I promise to do the best for them. Goodbye my love." Tears ran down his face and his breath escaped in soft bursts. He looked at the thin green line on the beeping monitor. "Come, girls. Henry. Talk to Mom, touch her, say goodbye. Tell her you love her."

Kate sniffled. "Mom, I'll be kind, like you taught me. I'll help Daddy and Henry and Claire. Goodbye, Mom. I love you." She kissed her mother and moved aside for her brother.

Henry sidled in next to the bed and tenderly touched his mother's closed eyes and her face. He wept, "Mommy, I don't want you to die. I love you too much for you to die. I'll be nice to my sisters and I'll do my chores for Daddy. Goodbye, Mommy. I love you."

Claire climbed on her mother's bed. "Is it my turn? Can I tell Mommy I love her and that I'll be good and that I hope she has fun with God and the angels in heaven? Is it time for me to say goodbye, Daddy?" He nodded. Claire wrapped her arms around Amelia and tears ran down her face. "Goodbye, Mommy. I love you to the moon and back."

Amelia's chest rose, fell, and with a final heartbeat, the folds of the blanket froze. The monitor stopped beeping as the green lifeline flattened. The nurses led the grieving family out of Woodland Convalescent Home into a fractured afternoon of listless air falling like a veil.

The route home was short and well-traveled. Mike, distant and pensive, followed his children. Henry ran ahead, stopping to turn around at the corner of each block to reassure himself that his father and sisters were still in sight. Kate walked with Claire, and as she neared a park, she waved to a group of friends. She slowed to wait for her father, who had stopped to observe mothers laughing with their children on a brightly painted merry-go-round.

"We're almost home!" Henry hurried up a hill, stopped in front of the small, well-kept house, and waited for his family. The children jumped up the porch steps, pausing to wake up an uncle who had fallen asleep in a chair.

The house smelled like Amelia's cooking: olive oil and garlic, fragrant basil, and ripe tomatoes mingled with the familiar aromas of warm bread and fried peppers. Every chair in the house had been pulled up to the dining room table. Folding chairs were hauled from the basement and squeezed around a card table. Amelia's sisters were busy filling plates. They fed the children, and then served the men, who attacked the meal set down in front of them.

Mike noticed Amelia's vacant chair at the table. He wondered where her soul was now, and realized he was crossing from devout faith to doubt, from Amelia's trust in him to crumbling uncertainty. He sat down beside her empty chair. The men at the table tried to engage him in talk about corn prices, weather, machinery. Their efforts went unheard.

Mike was distracted by the echo of other voices from recent conversations with his fellow workers at the tractor factory. They had been there for him after Amelia's stroke, lending their support, taking his place on the welding line at the plant, and helping him with the children. They were like brothers, their advice and encouragement both sympathetic and direct.

One had told him, "You mourn and move on. A friend of mine lost his wife to pneumonia in May. He has kids, moved in with his mother. They're doing ok. You come from good stock, Mike. You'll be alright. The kids will be alright."

Another had counseled, "Mike, that younger cousin of yours. His wife, she died a year ago. Tuberculosis. Three children, sent one to your sister and the other two to a sister-in-law. You said he cried like a five-year-old for months. But he moved on. Trust me, you don't want to spend tomorrow unable to make amends for what you should have done today."

The house was soon filled with supper and noise. Amelia's oldest sister leaned against a counter and ate while she watched Henry show Claire how to twirl spaghetti on a fork like his mother had shown him. Several women washed dishes and re-cleaned what had been cleaned the day before. Finally satisfied with the godliness of cleanliness, they poured coffee and took their places at the tables, preparing themselves to assist in making deferred, looming decisions.

One brother lifted himself from a folding chair and set his glass of wine on a counter, ready to say something. Another began rearranging chairs around the dining room table. Mike, and Amelia's empty chair, were suddenly at the end of a family peninsula, surrounded by waves of well-intentioned relatives.

Mike's youngest brother, a freshman at a nearby community college, found the middle cushion on the davenport. With Henry on the floor at his feet, and the girls on either side of him like bookends, he finished reading a chapter from a book about a family who crossed the prairie in a covered wagon from Nebraska to California. He chuckled, "Okay, that's it. Next time I'll tell you a funny story about a guy named Einstein." He looked at Mike. "And his theory of relatives. Goodnight, you knuckleheads. Give everybody hugs so you can have sweet dreams."

Mike pushed his chair away from the table and followed Virginia and the children upstairs. While his sister was busy with the children's baths, he stood by the open door to his bedroom and listened to the rise of discordant family voices debating what he should do about life without Amelia, or how the children would fare without their mother. His face flushed and his heart raced as the noise downstairs wrestled upward.

Virginia shepherded the children into the bedroom, dressed them in pajamas, and tucked them in. She walked to Mike, who was standing in the doorway, lifted his chin, and looked into his sad eyes. "I'll be downstairs." She turned off the light switch, and hazy amber moonlight streamed through the curtains, settling in the room, leaving Mike alone with his children.

Henry and Kate were under the bedspread singing the alphabet to Claire. "Okay, you Hagerty kids. Let's go to sleep." He pulled back the makeshift canopy of their covered wagon and sat on the edge of the bed. "C is for church, and that's where we're going tomorrow. Sweet dreams." Each of his good-night kisses was followed with a whispered, "Love you." The melody of Amelia's bedtime prayer song suddenly washed over him. Closing his eyes, he joined her voice to lull the threesome asleep. "*Che Dio vi benedica, benedica mi familia.* May God bless you, bless my family."

He walked downstairs and was confronted by the tribe of relatives. Amelia's oldest sister pursed her lips and looked directly at Mike. "Well?"

"Well, what?" he answered.

"We think it's best for the kids, and you too, if we take custody of them. Better than some busybody church lady thinks you can't take care of them the way they're supposed to be taken care of . . . you know, with a mother and all . . . and she calls the county and the next thing that happens is that they're in foster care. They should go with us." She continued rambling, "The girls can stay together with one of your sisters. We're not sure which one yet, still figuring that out. Henry can come and stay with me. I'm his godmother."

Mike exploded from his reverie. "What?" It wasn't a question or even a rebuke. It was a challenge. The smoldering ashes in his stomach caught fire. "County? Foster care? Splitting my children up like what?" Mimicking an auctioneer, he bellowed, "Okay folks, here's what you've been waiting for. Two fine heifers there, lot twenty-two. Oh, and look here, we got us a nice little bull calf in lot twenty-three! Let's start the bids..."

"Stop it Mike, please. Just stop!" Virginia said.

He tried to calm his dizzying heartbeats pulsing out of synch. "I'm sorry. Your hearts are in the right place, but your heads aren't." His focus renewed, he continued. "It's been a tired day in this journey for all of us. Let's get some sleep and pray tomorrow. He stopped at the bottom of the stairway. "Good night."

Sunday morning broke dreary. Three of his brothers had left earlier for their farms, promising to return for the burial. Other brothers were stationed on the porch with suitcases lined up. The women put dishes in the cupboard, arranged chairs and cleaned. Soon, because there was nothing left for them to do, the wives joined their husbands. In a tight-knit convoy of pickup trucks and long sedans, they drove off to church.

Virginia had neatly combed the girls hair, and had dressed them in their best outfits–a pink hand-me-down for Kate and a yellow one for Claire. Despite the heat, Henry wore a long-sleeved shirt with his father's cufflinks and an 'I Like Ike' button pinned on the pocket. The stair-stepped children sat on the davenport, and waited for their father to walk with them to church, away from the empty house.

The eleven-thirty mass at All Saints was well-attended. Several churchgoers in the rear pews recognized Mike and the children as they walked down the aisle. A few leaned forward behind their hymnals and whispered to their neighbors.

The priest, Father Sullivan, walked up to the candlelit altar and intoned the opening prayers with reverence. Mike mouthed automatic responses, first kneeling, then standing, and finally sitting for the sermon. He was startled by words from Ecclesiastes—'There is a time to be born and a time to die, a time to plant and a time to uproot.'

The service was brief, and the parishioners were quick to file out, row after row, moving to the organ's recessional hymn like devout dancers. The Hagerty's and relatives emptied their pew and walked up the aisle in single file, then gathered outside on the church steps, briefly acknowledging sympathetic nods from churchgoers.

A few of the parishioners had surrounded Father Sullivan, listening to him recount a tale from his wartime stint as an Army chaplain. He straightened his shoulders and stopped talking when he saw Mike and the children. Smiling, he walked towards them. "Mike, may God have mercy on Amelia, you, and these youngsters." He corralled the children in his arms and blessed them before he turned to face their father. "Trust in the Lord and God will provide. Don't call retreat, Mike. Your family matters."

Mike thanked the priest and joined the rest of his waiting family. All that needed to be said had been said. They embraced one another and assured Mike they would return for the funeral and the burial, and left him on the sidewalk at the bottom of the church steps. Virginia was scheduled for that afternoon's shift at the hospital, but she had promised Henry and the girls that she would take them to the park before she left for work.

Mike walked home alone, with the burdened steps of a widowed parent, thinking about Amelia and her faith in him. *Faith. Why had his prayers for recovery gone unanswered? How could he believe in a God that took away the love of his life? Would a God help him raise three children? Watch over them when he went back to work? Walk with them to school?*

As he neared his quiet house, he took a deep breath and shook his head, as if to dislodge loose debris. A nearby sound caught his attention. He noticed Mrs. Flynn in her yard, humming a tune, lost in an old widow's solitude. He quickened his pace, turned into his yard, and sat on the porch steps.

With the children in tow, Virginia appeared around the corner of the block and joined her brother. "Mike, I need to go to work. Dinner is ready in the refrigerator and just needs to be warmed up. The milkman will be here in the morning and there's cereal in the pantry for breakfast. Oh, and I did laundry.

It's on the clothesline drying but we're supposed to get a shower later, so maybe you and Kate can keep an eye on it? I'll check in tomorrow if I have time after class." She frowned, kissed Mike, and hugged the children. "Love you all."

The afternoon passed quietly. Raindrops started to bounce on the roof and the family hurried outside. Claire was lifted up so she could unpin the clothes, and Henry and Kate rushed the baskets of laundry into the house. Mike gave the children folding lessons until they got tired and went upstairs to play. He opened the stack of mail piled on the kitchen table and set the bills aside, staring blankly at the envelopes addressed to 'Mr. and Mrs. Mike Hagerty.'

Dinner was early, a relief of sorts. Claire was fussy, Henry was teasing Kate, but Mike managed to settle them down long enough to eat. He looked at them looking at him between mouthfuls as they slurped spaghetti strands and splattered sauce on their chins.

At bedtime, Kate knew the routine and was glad to help with pajama tops and bottoms, a book, and toy animals. Mike opened the window in the bedroom just enough to keep the rain outside. There was room in his bed for all of them. He managed to squeeze in between arms, legs, and a fuzzy, stuffed elephant, then began to read the next chapter in the story about the family journey across the plains. Soon, the gentle power of a child's love, his memory of Amelia and her faith in him began to restore his dormant optimism. He paused reading as tears washed his face.

"Daddy, please don't cry," Kate said. She took a handkerchief from her pajama pocket and gave it to him. Henry followed his sister's example, took his handkerchief from his pajamas, and offered it to his father. Both handkerchiefs had been embroidered with a delicate, careful touch. Embellished with verdant tendrils, a bright yellow thread encircled the stitched outline of a red heart. A royal blue capital letter had been darned in the heart's center.

Claire began to whine. "I don't have a handkerchief for you, Daddy." Kate and Henry began to cry. Mike gave them their handkerchiefs, took one from his pocket, and offered it to Claire. "Here, honey. You can have this one. See, it's just like Kate's and Henry's."

Claire sniffed and took the handkerchief. She looked at it and started to howl. "But it's not like theirs. Look, it's the wrong letter. It's an 'I' and not an 'H.'"

Puzzled, Mike looked at the handkerchief in Claire's hand. The 'I' was stitched on the left side of the heart, not in the center. Amelia had begun the embroidery but had only sewn the first part of the letter before her stroke.

Suddenly, a new moon breeze billowed the curtains. He took the handkerchief and wiped away all his young family's tears. Smiling at them, he looked into their eyes.

"Tomorrow, we'll begin to finish what Mom started. Together."

13

THE DEATH DEFYING LIGHT BULB

JANICE COY

"Ha! Listen to this." My mother taps her iPad. Her voice brings me back to the kitchen table from the small examining room where my mind had been wandering, picturing the mostly flesh colored nodule the doctor removed from me yesterday. Was I imagining the dash of red?

"A light bulb in England finally burned out after seventy years," my mother reads. The morning sun angles through her reading glasses highlighting an unexpected smudge on the upper edge of one lens. "It says here they used the same light bulb in the men's restroom since the fifties. Hope they cleaned the urinals once or twice since then. Ha. If that bulb had been in the women's restroom, it would have burned out at least sixty-five years ago from use."

My mother doesn't wait for my response. Her eyes shift to another article. I would have asked her how they knew the bulb was seventy years old. Did the same person clean that bathroom all those years? Did he or she come in every day, a new light bulb handy, just in case? God, I hoped not. Seventy years.

A long time. For a light bulb. And for a bathroom cleaner to keep track.

I look up at the canned lights in my kitchen ceiling. I would be lucky if I didn't have to change them again in a month.

After the doctor removed the nodule – "This won't hurt" - doctor pinches always hurt. She asked if I wanted to see it. I struggled to a sitting position, the paper liner on the table crinkling beneath me, sticking to my sweaty legs. She held up a test tube, and there the bugger was, floating in some sort of clear liquid. It was the same size as the tip of my baby finger.

"Mother," I say. She holds up her index finger; I wait for her to finish.

When I was a child, she read an article about teaching children to respect their elders. After that, she made me address her friends as Mr. or Mrs. So and So. I was to call her mother. The phase passed but I was used to her new name and never switched back to Mom. Now, when mother looks up at me, I ask, "How old were Grandma Betty and Grandpa Hal when they died?"

"Why?"

"Just curious." I sip my coffee, the liquid bitter on my tongue. I haven't told her about the biopsy, yet. She doesn't know my doctor will be calling today with the results. She just happened to come to town for a short visit and I took the day off to recover. I didn't mind. We have an extra room and no children. I don't keep many secrets from her. But I've never had a secret like this before. Things could get serious. I don't want to explore the possibilities with her right now. I could hardly talk about it with my doctor and my husband. And somehow, it would seem more real if I told my mother – the person who has known me the longest.

"Let's see." Mother takes off her glasses, and chews on the end of the earpiece. I raise my cup to my lips again. "Grandma was fifty- eight; she died of cancer. She suffered terribly." My mother grimaces. "Grandpa didn't last long after grandma passed. Of course, he had always been bothered with heart troubles." Mother looks sad.

"What type of cancer did she die of?" I ask. She has never told me. And before now, I had no reason to ask.

"I don't know," my mother says. She nibbles on her glasses, then clears her throat. "Some female type, I think." She returns to her online newspaper, but I persist.

"Cervical cancer?"

"What? Oh yes, I think that was it."

I bite my toast and work the dry piece in my mouth. Her words unnerve me.

"What about the other grandparents?" I ask once I've swallowed the dry lump of bread. "Grandma and Grandpa Collins?" I know I need to ask about them too to keep my mother from guessing.

"You've never been interested in this before," she says. She lowers her reader to the table; sets her glasses on top.

"New insurance at work," I say. "This one wants family medical history."

My mother stares at me, quizzing me with her eyes. She's good at it. I usually cave, but not today. I drop my eyes to the table. I set down my toast and pretend to be absorbed in sweeping crumbs into my cupped hand.

"Well, Grandma and Grandpa Collins lived fairly long," she says. "I think they were in their late sixties when they were killed in the car accident."

Grandma and Grandpa Collins were my father's parents. My mother lost touch with that side of the family when she and my father divorced. I would have asked my father, but he died of a heart attack at fifty- nine while cleaning the gutters of his house. He smashed his head pretty good when he hit the concrete. He didn't exercise much and didn't like heights. I never knew why he was up on that ladder. Probably because he was too cheap to hire someone. Like those people who kept using the same light bulb for seventy years.

After a moment of silence, my mother returns to her reading while I pick at my toast. Grandma and Grandpa Collins got close to seventy years old. If only their car hadn't wrapped around that tree, and instead bounced off onto the golf course, wheels spinning into the deep sand of a trap. If it wasn't for that extra martini at the clubhouse, they could still be alive today and in perfect health.

I can't stop thinking about that seventy-year-old bulb. How could a light bulb, which is simply a thin layer of glass surrounding an even more delicate filament survive intact for nearly a century? All it would take was one good slam of the restroom door or one careless swing of the mop and the bulb would shatter - splinter into useless shards. Was it possible to verify the light bulb had worked for that long? My cell phone trills. It's not the doctor.

I drain the last of my lukewarm coffee, push back my chair and stand.

"I'm going for a walk." I'm desperate for fresh air.

"Want me to come?" my mother offers.

"No. I mean, you just had surgery, can you walk far?"

"That was two months ago. I'm perfectly fine. I'm supposed to walk." My mother removes her glasses again. She refused my help after her knee replacement. "Don't waste your vacation time on me," she had said. Now, I want to be alone, but I'm not as good at refusing her.

"I'm not sure how far I'll go," I say instead. I rinse my cup and plate in the sink, swirling the last of my toast down the drain. My mother did seem to have recovered well from the surgery; she looked good. Everyone said she was a young sixty-seven, and with her stylish haircut and clothes, I could see why. So far, she seemed to have escaped the family curse of dying young. But still...there were three more years to account for until she was seventy. I would be lucky to make it that long. Maybe I would be the one in the family who died young. The thought depresses me.

I grab my cell phone. "You relax, and I'll be back soon. We can walk together later." I leave the room before she can answer. I pull a fleece from the hall closet, the hangar still swinging as I rush out the front door.

My jacket billows in a sudden gust of wind, flying out behind me like a cape. I shiver and zip it closed. Leaves litter the sidewalk. Only a few stubborn ones cling to the tree limbs. Leaves come and go with the seasons, but don't trees live hundreds or even thousands of years? I search the block as if I could find one of those ancient giants preserved among the rows of houses. Leaves crunch under my running shoes; I don't see any trees older than five years, the same age as the subdivision. I keep walking, my cell phone silent.

At the neighborhood fire station, a man in navy pants and a navy t-shirt polishes the chrome on the fire truck. The sun glints on the silver. I pause and watch, shading my eyes with my hand. The man whistles, taking his time with a rag. I wonder how he can concentrate on water spots knowing his careful wiping is at the mercy of the fire alarm. Some of those blots might have to come with him as he careens off to a catastrophe. I cradle my cell phone in my jacket pocket and move on.

Back home, I slam the door open so it bounces against the wall. The light bulb in the entry doesn't even rattle in its glass fixture.

"You scared me!" exclaims mother. She's on the couch working a cross-stitch. "Was it really necessary to fling the door open like that? I bet you marked the wall." A drop of blood wells on her little finger where she pricked it with the needle. Before it can fall and stain the cross stitch, my mother blots it with a handy tissue.

"I'm sorry," I say. I move closer to get a better look at her project, a wall-hanging of a nursery rhyme for a friend's daughter who's expecting a baby in March. Maybe this nodule has something to do with my inability to produce children. I realize for the first time that my mother hasn't asked about grandchildren for at least a year.

"Hickory, dickory, dock, the mouse ran up the clock" is stitched in blue. The body of the clock is complete, as is the mouse. All that's left is the clock face and hands. My mother likes to work ahead.

I retreat to the entry with my jacket. I'm careless in hanging it up, shoving it in so that the shoulders slouch. I return to where my mother is sitting. "I had a nice walk. It's a beautiful day out." Thank God for the weather. Without it, I might just tell my mother why I'm on edge. I might just fall apart.

"You have some color in your cheeks," my mother comments. "I wonder how long this weather will last before the truly nasty stuff sets in?"

My mother lives in Phoenix in a comfortable condo close to her golfing friends. She doesn't visit in the winter. This will probably be the last time I see her until spring, unless we make the trek to the desert. Does she talk about the weather with her friends when she wants to avoid a subject? Could they talk about the weather with any real conviction? Maybe they discuss how much hotter it is than the day before.

I hear a muffled ringing. I've left my phone in my jacket pocket. I scramble to the entry, tripping and almost falling on the rug. "Important call," I say. I yank open the closet door and paw at my jacket.

"Is this Cara Stearn?"

"Yes, yes it is." I'm on my knees in the closet; my jacket has slipped to the floor by the vacuum.

"Birth date?"

I stare at the vacuum. My mind a blank.

"Birth date?"

"Um..eight..twenty nine...eighty four."

I inhale a deep breath to clear my head catching the faint scent of pine sap from our last camping trip on the sleeping bags rolled in the back corner.

"I have good news for you. Doctor wanted me to call you right away. The tests came back negative."

"Thank you. Thank you very much."

"Have a good day."

My chest is swollen with relieved tears. I suck in a few more deep breaths, and nearly choke on vacuum dust. After my coughing fit dies down, I pick up my jacket sliding the hangar under the shoulders. I back out of the closet, straighten the hall rug with the toe of my shoe.

"Everything all right?" My mother's looking at me with concern. Her needle and scissors are put away in a cloth bag.

I float to the couch and plop beside her. She has missed some stitches on the "H" in Hickory, and the bottom of the clock is uneven where the stitching is too tight. I kiss her soft cheek. She smells like roses. She always has.

"Maybe we'll be the first to outlive that light bulb," I say. My voice cracks. Mother holds me while I sob at the vagaries of life.

14

THE TOAD WHO KNEW IT ALL

MARGARET HARMON

There was once a toad who went to the city and learned all about the world. While he was there, he learned *everything*.

It was so important that he wrote it all into a large book which he carried with him wherever he went. The toad carried his book pressed against his heart so he would never forget what he had learned and would always know precisely what to do.

One day the toad was crossing a river on a fallen log. With his enormous book pressed against his heart, he could not see where he was walking, and he tripped over a knot in the log. The toad made one anguished squeak as he slid off the log and into the river.

The current was running swiftly, and the toad needed both hands to save himself by grabbing the edge of the bank. But he dared not let go of his book of everything.

The toad with his book tumbled down the river, head over binding. At last, the book became waterlogged and sank; and the toad, clutching it against his heart, drowned.

15

AFTER MIDNIGHT: ROLL THE DICE

RICHARD PETERSON

Prologue
Harriet Palmer, a retired San Diego homicide detective, has recently created her own firm called Argus Investigations. James Powell, her former boss, also retired, is now her part-time colleague. This is their second case.

Mid-May 2023, a San Diego casino, 9:11 p.m.

A figure appeared on Harriet's right side. She looked up to see a well-muscled, twenty-something young man with curly r ed hair. She didn't hear his approach because of the chimes and dings of the slot machines and the ever-present back-ground music. She asked, "So Walt, how's Mr. Lucky doing?"

Walt shrugged. "Nothing new. With blackjack he's always one step forward, two steps back." He shook his head. "The same with most of the games he plays."

Harriet stood and stretched her back, groaning. She watched as Walt sipped from a plastic cup. Probably iced tea. The kid loved his iced tea.

"This guy hemorrhages money," Walt continued. "But

where does it come from?" He paused. "You said his wife was a hard-nosed business type—degrees in IT, computer science, and all that. Why didn't she find anything wrong in their finances?"

She replied, "Clearly, she failed to tell me about his gambling problem. She just wanted to know if he was cheating on her. She couldn't find anything awry in any of their financial records." Harriet whooshed out a tired breath. "You and Dana have been invaluable, analyzing this guy's play."

"So how much longer—"

"Not much longer at all," Harriet said. She stared over Walt's shoulder at their subject, Sergio Flores Meza. He was seated at a semicircular blackjack table and wearing, once again, a tropical shirt. This one was decorated with green and dull red palm fronds. "We've done enough observation and photos," she said. "This is our last night, thank goodness."

She left Walt and strolled across the room to a roulette table. She casually positioned herself beside a tall black woman in a pale blue pantsuit. Harriet inhaled the sweet scent of golden mimosa with a hint of musk. L'Eau Papier, as usual. Harriet touched her forearm. "Dana," she whispered, "I'd like you to go and stand next to Mr. Lucky. Try to strike up a conversation. Get what information you can. Don't be obvious about it."

The woman nodded and left without a word. In a casino, security had eyes and ears everywhere.

Harriet pretended to watch the roulette action. Good kids, both of them, she thought. Dana and Walt were up-and-coming actors who were moonlighting for Argus. They'd been referred to Harriet by her good acquaintance, Samantha Brin. Samantha, a Rancho Santa Fe philanthropist, had numerous, high-level connections at the Old Globe Theater.

After a bathroom break, Harriet settled herself at a different slot machine. She was so sick of surveilling Mr. Lucky at various county casinos, she could punch holes in a wall with a baseball bat. Adding to her frustration, their four-person team had to work within the confines of a casino's sophisticated security apparatus—both human and electronic.

A hand squeezed Harriet's left shoulder. She flinched.

"He's heading out," said Jim Powell, his mouth close to her ear.

She looked over. Sure enough, Mr. Lucky had quit the blackjack table and was walking toward the casino's main entrance. *Why so early?* She broke away from Jim and headed that way as well. Then she remembered: Sergio Flores Meza had left early at a different casino five days ago.

Was he going to the same place?

I SHOULD'VE ASKED BEFORE," Dana said, "but wouldn't it be easier to use some kind of vehicle tracking device?"

Harriet, who was driving, smiled. "Hah. If only. But without consent of the vehicle owner, we'd be committing a misdemeanor. That's California penal code. No can do, kiddo."

"So that's why you've been using two cars to do the following."

"Yep. Less obvious that way. And I suspect Mr. Lucky is en route to a Chinese restaurant he went to a few days ago. The Blue Sapphire." Harriet relaxed her shoulders. Jim and Walt had taken the primary station behind Mr. Lucky, so she just had to follow Jim's Toyota. "What happened last time," she said, "was that he went inside for a while—this was before you and Walt joined us—and then left with some takeout. He went straight home."

Harriet sighed. *No infidelity. Case closed.*

"Mr. Lucky was like a sphinx, talk-wise," Dana said. "But he's carried off his disguise pretty well," She crossed her arms.

"Just a pair of glasses and a mustache. He did okay, for an amateur."

Harriet chuckled. "You're the expert. But these casino security folks weren't fooled. I'm sure they come across such people every day. You can bet they were keeping an eye on him." Ahead, Jim's turn signal flashed as he moved onto a freeway off-ramp leading into Mission Valley.

"Just as I thought," murmured Harriet. They drove west on Friars Road, a route she knew would take them to the Blue Sapphire.

She glanced at Dana. "Another takeout," she said. "Give Jim a call on your cell, will you? He and I are gonna follow this guy inside this time."

Soon she and Jim were climbing a short series of steps leading to the restaurant's glass double doors. Two fearsome-looking, stone guardian lions flanked the doorway. Inside, the restaurant was half full of customers. Sergio Meza's tropical shirt was easy to spot. He sat alone at a corner table, unfolding a newspaper. Harriet and Jim requested an upholstered booth with a good view of both the area and Meza. After they sat, Harriet surveyed the attractive black-and-red interior, then glanced at the menu. She looked over at Meza.

"No more glasses and false mustache," she muttered to Jim. "Of course his mustache isn't as handsome and debonair as yours."

He gave her a lopsided grin. "Debonair? Sure, my wife tells me that all the time . . . I wish." Leaning toward her, he asked, "Is this really necessary? Haven't we seen enough?"

"Just curiosity," she replied. "Making sure the case has no loose ends."

He laughed. "Loose ends? My God, this was child's play compared to the investigations we used to wrestle with." He sank back against the red cushions and ran a hand over his buzz-cut hair. "Geez, Harrie, we had some tough nuts, didn't we?"

She grunted. "Tough? *That's* an understatement. I still get flashbacks from—"

"Holy shit," he hissed.

It was almost comical. Jim's upper body had gone rigid, as if he were an English Pointer freezing at a hidden quail. She followed his gaze. Meza, still seated, had put down his newspaper. He was chatting with a slim woman who towered over the table. She was holding a medium-sized, reddish paper bag with handles. Meza smiled up at the woman.

Harriet focused on her. First impressions: straight, jet-black hair, inverted bob; waist-length ivory coat; pale-blue slacks. The woman shifted her weight and turned slightly. Harriet glimpsed several gold buttons on the coat front. *Screams chic.*

Jim lifted the menu to cover his face. "Damn, Harrie, that's Min Kuo-feng. It's her, *the* Min Kuo-feng." He spoke fast and low. "She owns five or so Chinese restaurants in Southern Cal and one in Las Vegas. Very successful, big money. Two years ago Canziani and Dobbs were working with LAPD on possible murders of one restaurant owner and a restaurant manager in Los Angeles. One suspect was brought in. Min's name popped up during interrogation." He frowned. "No solid connection, though. Nothing could be proved. If I remember right, two competing restaurants caught fire. Early morning stuff. Total loss."

"Arson?" she asked.

Jim lowered his menu. "Damn," he said. "In person. *Here.*" He paused. "Oh, yeah. Uh, arson was the official conclusion. But man, her showing up like this is way out of character."

The woman placed the bag down on Meza's table.

A plan of action flashed through Harriet's brain like an electric jolt. *Why not?* "I'll be back," she said, gathering her purse and sliding out of the booth. She walked toward the bathrooms. *Slow down, act normal.* She pulled her cell phone from her purse and called Dana.

"Dana here."

"Hey. Didn't you tell me once that you enjoyed doing improv?"

"I sure did."

"Super," said Harriet. "This is your chance to prove it."

HARRIET WENT BACK to their booth. The scenario had changed. Now Meza was standing and the tall woman was disappearing into the kitchen. Harriet bent down toward Jim. "Partner, I need your help," she said. "There's one more thing I gotta do. But I need you to keep Meza here in the restaurant for twenty more seconds."

"What? What the hell are you—?"

"Twenty seconds. Humor me. Go over there, keep him talking."

"Really? How?" he asked.

"Flattery," she said. "He's a politician, Jim. Flattery." She straightened. "Do it now. Please." She turned and sauntered away. After a few moments she glanced back. Jim was crossing the room. *Good man.*

She flagged down a waitperson and told her they had to leave. She looked again. Jim was shaking hands with Meza. *Super.* She pushed through one of the glass doors and stationed herself beside a stone lion statue. Seconds later Walt and Dana emerged from the parking lot. When they stopped at the bottom of the stairway, Harriet gave them a thumbs up. They did the same.

Seconds ticked by. Then more. Harriet took deep, regular breaths to control her pounding heart. She was ready to give the signal. Her plan had to be well executed, like the last few plays of a tied football game. Then a glass door opened. In her peripheral vision she glimpsed a tropical shirt, red bag. She quickly brought her cell phone to her ear, giving the signal.

Meza started down the steps.

Harriet stuck the cell phone into her purse, adjusted the purse strap on her shoulder, and carefully followed.

"I don't need *you* to help me get my license," said Dana from below. She and Walt were facing one another. A little louder, "Besides, you don't know *jack* about real estate."

"Oh, I know plenty," Walt shouted. "And you need a lotta help, honey."

Meza slowed as he watched the couple. He moved to one side, his right hand coming out to grip the handrail.

Harriet quickly scanned the area. Three people were approaching from the center of the parking lot, but they were far away. She snapped her attention back to Meza and increased her pace to get behind him.

"You're drunk!" shouted Dana. "Again! Whadda waste of time this is."

Walt shouted back, "Hah! *You*, getting a *license*. Man, that's a bad joke."

"I don't need insults," said Dana. "You're an idiot. Get outta here. *Now*." She pushed Walt's shoulder and his upper body twisted.

"Wait a minute," said Walt. "Are you serious, bitch? You gonna hit me?"

"Don't you touch me!" she shrieked.

Harriet moved even closer to Meza.

"You bitch! You freakin' bitch!"

"Go away, go away!" Dana pushed Walt hard this time and he shouted as he staggered to his right. His feet tangled, he spun around, and fell into Meza in a clumsy embrace.

Now. Harriet stepped down to Meza's side and grabbed the carry-out bag with her left hand as both men collapsed to the ground. She pulled at the bag. *Get it, get it.* Seconds later the bag tore free. She pushed herself up and away from them, then tucked the bag into her left arm like a football.

She pivoted and began quick-walking down the sidewalk. The bag felt strangely heavy. *Gotta find time, find time.*

A waist-high wall was on her left, and the tall lights in the parking lot only gave a pale wash of light. Harriet thrust her right hand into the bag and fished around inside. She felt several cartons, but below those, something she couldn't identify.

"Stop! Hey, you!"

She glanced back. A dark figure, clearly male, was running after her. Fast. She had hoped to take photographs of the bag contents, but that was no go. Harriet stopped and set the bag atop the wall. Opened it. She tilted the bag toward the parking lot lights for a better look inside.

Daaamn.

"Wait! Stop there!"

Harriet turned. The man was coming up on her, his feet pounding. She wasn't too concerned. She'd gained a high level of confidence from her self-defense lessons at Athena Martial Arts Academy. But confrontation? A last resort. Leaving the bag on the wall, she turned and trotted down the sidewalk. Slowed and looked back. No one. She hurried over to a long row of tall bushes and small trees, then crouched in a dark shadow between two bushes. Amid the pungent odor of vegetation, she took her cell phone from her purse and called Jim.

A few minutes later a car pulled into that corner of the parking lot and stopped beneath one of the tall lights. Harriet pushed herself up, walked to the car, and got in.

"Dang, you're one crazy lady," exclaimed Jim. "You okay?"

"Super. Where's Mr. Lucky?"

"The last I saw, he was headed toward his car, bag in hand."

"I'm not surprised. He wouldn't wanna make a scene."

"Oh?" said Jim. He began driving. "Dana's waiting in your car, with Walt. I recommend we go to Denny's on Mission Gorge Road. We're hungry, after all."

Harriet exhaled hard, then said, "You got that right."

He gave a quiet laugh. "All right, Harrie. Cut the mystery crap. What was in that bag?"

She inclined her head toward him. "Partner, I saw a whole lotta trouble for Sergio Flores Meza."

TWO DAYS LATER, *western Balboa Park, 9:55 a.m.*

With a loud, high-pitched whine, a blue-and-white airliner passed over downtown buildings on its glide path toward the airport.

Shielding her eyes with a hand, Harriet peered into the bright sky. Alaska Airlines. Then she walked a few more yards and stood to one side of a statue. *This feels strange. I'm like a character in a spy novel, waiting for a rendezvous.* But Jim had said these were the instructions, direct from police Captain Joyce Seidman. The captain had conferred with the local Drug Enforcement Administration to set up this meeting.

Harriet smiled to herself. Although retired, good ole Jim still had plenty of pull with the captain.

"The Mother of Balboa Park, huh?"

Harriet jumped, startled, then looked over.

A woman had quietly appeared on her right side and was gazing at the statue. She had a Pug with her on a black nylon leash.

"You're, uh, right." Harriet composed herself. "Yeah, that's what she's called. Kate Sessions: horticulturalist, scientist. Like the plaque says."

They both stood in silence as they stared at the bronze statue of a somber-faced woman wearing a hat and long flowing skirt.

"See?" Harriet pointed. "She's holding a seedling in one hand and—what's that?—sorry, I'm not a gardener." Smiling, she scanned the woman. *About my age, average height, broad-brim straw hat, Italian features, blue-tint sunglasses, tan pants. Nothing that would attract attention.*

"Me, neither. But I think she's holding a trowel."

Code word. Bingo, DEA contact.

Just then a young woman jogged past, her blonde ponytail swinging, dressed in a black sports bra and tight blue yoga pants.

"Jonnie Drake," whispered the woman.

"Harriet Palmer. Glad to meet you."

"And this is Hegel." Drake nodded toward the dog, which seemed content to sniff around nearby blue lilies. "He's my husband's, not so much mine. But Hegel and I have an understanding. We agree to tolerate each other."

Harriet chuckled, then gestured with her arm toward a broad sidewalk. "Shall we?"

They fell into a slow pace. In a large grassy area on the right, a tiny white dog scampered after a thrown yellow ball. Watching, Hegel strained at his leash. Drake held him back. "No, you don't, Hegel. You stay with me."

Harriet said, "I don't know how much Captain Seidman told you, but my investigation involves Min Kuo-feng. What can you tell me about her?"

Drake tucked a few wayward hair strands behind her ear. "We'll get to that. For now, though, just tell me your story."

As Harriet related the Meza case, Drake would occasionally nod or ask a question. At one point Hegel started barking at squirrels and Drake said, "I didn't quite get that. What was in the bag?"

Warm sun pressed on Harriet's shoulders. "Nothing exotic," she said. "Just small, bound stacks of US currency in 50s and 100s."

Drake remained quiet while a plane descended over the park toward Lindbergh. Then she said, "Min Kuo-feng has been on our radar for some time. We're trying to prove she's the brains behind the distribution of Calico, that cocaine variation you ran across a while back. I read the report." She glanced at Harriet. "Kudos for your curiosity. Anyhow, Kuo-feng's restaurants are legit, but we believe they're a money-making front for whatever criminal activities she's into."

"So why bribe Mr. Lucky?"

Drake stopped and gazed at the high-rises across Sixth Avenue. "Mr. Lucky . . . quite a nickname for the honorable Chair of the San Diego County Board of Supervisors." They resumed walking. She went on, "I'll work that angle. I know some politically savvy people. There could be upcoming votes on the Board that affect Kuo-feng's businesses. Maybe that's why she needs Meza in her pocket."

"Right," said Harriet. "We need to know the why." She bent down, picked a long stick off the pavement, and tossed it onto the grass. "But what if you could turn Meza, use him to your advantage?"

Drake grunted. "The captain said you were a bright spark. Sure, we'll approach him and see if he wants to play ball. If we can prove that Kuo-feng's been bribing a public official, that would be good." She nodded. "Yeah, more than good."

They were now strolling past the Sessions statue. Harriet slowed. "One last thing. Feel free to contact me if any other questions come to mind."

"Understood," said Drake. "But do not get yourself involved with Min Kuo-feng. Stay clear." Wind gusted, and she grasped her straw hat. "I've only surveilled her from afar. Sure, she comes across all smiles and charm . . ."

She removed her sunglasses and gave Harriet a hard look. "But make no mistake. The lady keeps her knives sharp."

∽

THREE DAYS LATER, *Harbor Island, Tom Ham's Lighthouse restaurant, 12:40 p.m.*

Samantha Brin lifted a spoonful of black bean soup. She stopped it in midair. Her reddish-brown eyes widened. "She really said that?" she asked. "'She keeps her knives sharp'? Goodness, that's dramatic."

Seated across the table, Harriet recalled that moment and felt a brief tremor of nerves. "Yeah, dramatic. But it's for real." She bit into her turkey avocado sandwich and watched as a white sailboat cruised by. The restaurant's tall windows offered a sweeping view of downtown and an overcast sky; across the grayish-blue water sat the moored hulk of an aircraft carrier.

Jim, seated on her right, said, "Joyce is my conduit." He turned to Samantha. "Sorry, she—Captain Joyce Seidman— was our boss in Homicide. I found out through her that Drake heads a task force focused on the Calico drug. The DEA is working with the district attorney to hammer out a deal for Mr. Lucky. Once that's done, they'll approach him. They'd like to use him as a DEA informant." He plunged his fork into his plate of mixed greens.

"I see," said Samantha. She gazed out the window for a moment, then turned back. "All right, then. Well, fill me in. How did Dana and Walter do?"

"Excellent," Jim said. "A top-notch job."

"Ditto," Harriet said. "I told them they were at the top of my list if a future need arises."

Samantha's face brightened. "I'm so pleased. There's such a wealth of talent in our local theaters."

Just then their server appeared and set down three old fashioned glasses.

Harriet smiled. "My treat," she said. "Mai Tai's. The name means good in Tahitian."

Jim put down his fork and leaned back. "Do I sense that this is becoming a ritual?"

Harriet held out her hands, palms up. "Could be," she said, then gave Samantha a wink. She lifted her glass. "Now, I propose a toast."

Jim sighed, frowning. "If we must . . ."

Harriet went on, "A toast to those talented actors, Dana and

Walt. And to my partner, Jim, who once said that this case was child's play."

"I retract that statement," Jim said quickly.

The two women laughed.

"Finally," said Harriet. "To the continued success of our small but mighty firm, Argus Investigations."

They raised their arms and clinked glasses.

"To Argus!"

16

COVID LOCKDOWN REVELATION

JR STRAYVE JR

Imposing fire trucks lined the circular driveway. Their strobing red and white lights flashed, illuminated the dark night. Firefighters manhandling mammoth snaking hoses sprayed water on smoldering wooden beams and glowing cinders.

Speaking into a cell phone, the fire commander said, "No, ma'am. Yes, we checked inside the house, no sign of him."

Thirty-six hours prior to the fire, Jon lay in bed on his back, arms extended above his head, fingers interlocked, staring at the ceiling. He couldn't help but feel content, relaxed and hopeful after the sex with his wife the previous night. Jon sighed, just thinking about it. He grinned.

A gentle breeze rustled the curtains, keeping the morning sunlight at bay. An occasional prism of light snuck in, dancing on the walls and the sheet that covered his naked body below the waist.

He turned his head to the left and studied his wife's uncovered back. It fascinated him with how beautiful her toned muscles and porcelain skin looked together. She had taken excellent care of herself. He wished he had done the same.

Sharon was disciplined and intensely goal-oriented in every aspect of her life.

He felt himself getting aroused thinking about the intimacy they had had the night before. It had been the first time they'd been intimate in weeks, maybe a month. Certainly, since before the COVID lockdown.

He turned to his side and wrapped an arm around her and pressed up against his wife. *If only every day could begin like this,* he thought.

Sharon squirmed away and got out of bed. As she wrapped a thin wool robe around herself, she said, "I'll go make breakfast."

Jon watched, lustful, frustrated, as she left the room and walked down the hall. A door closed; he clenched his teeth. Once again, she had gotten as far away as possible from him and used the guest bathroom.

"Well, so much for that idea," he mumbled, "rejected again."

He rolled over on his back and returned his gaze to the ceiling. "Fuck it!" Moments later, he pleasured himself, thinking about the most recent young 'model' he had been with in his studio.

Jon showered and joined his wife in the kitchen. Sharon had finished her breakfast and placed her dishes in the dishwasher.

She hadn't prepared his breakfast.

Jon erupted, "You aren't even going to try, are you?"

He watched her body tense, her back to him. "Try? We had sex last night. Wasn't that enough for you?"

"It isn't just about sex. It's about us, damnit!"

"About us? There is no 'us.'"

His stomach flipped. He took hold of a kitchen chair and sat down.

Sharon turned around and said, "If I hadn't had an extra glass of wine, last night would not have happened."

He thought, *who is this woman? I really don't recognize her anymore. I know I'm not perfect, but jeez, this is unreal.*

"So, Sharon, there is no 'us?' And you don't want there to ever be an 'us?' It's over?"

"Don't act so surprised," she snapped. "Think for a change. You're an artist. You're not an idiot. Don't confuse the two."

Jon's eyes blinked.

He tried to process what he had just heard. *Christ! Why does she shred me when she speaks to me? She cuts so deep, so cruelly. Honestly, I've tried to be a good husband, lover. Why does she have this contempt, this disdain for me?*

Sharon snarled, "I'll be in my office. Don't bother me."

She tossed a dishcloth onto the counter and walked out of the kitchen.

He wrapped his arms around himself and whispered, "This just can't be. I don't understand. What is happening? I don't get it."

Emerging from his mental fog, determined to quit whining, he thought, *I'm not a victim, damnit!* He got up and made a cup of coffee. Having no appetite, he sat in the breakfast area, gazing out the bay window.

His coffee cup empty, he got up and walked over to the counter and slipped a pod into the Keurig. As he waited for the machine to do its thing, he thought back to the beginning of the lockdown. The first weeks found them adjusting to being around each other all day long. Day after day together had strained their patience.

Like many married couples, their daily habits had, over years of marriage, developed into a routine. Prior to the lockdown, she would get up early, catch an early train to the city and return home after 8:00 p.m.

The past few years, he'd remain in bed. He was not a morning person. Early in their marriage, fighting the grogginess caused by denying his circadian rhythm, he would get up to make their breakfast while she dressed for work before she caught the train. *That was then.*

Months prior to the lockdown, he'd acknowledged she had become more of a housemate. Not a wife. A housemate with occasional, very occasional, benefits.

These days, after rising from bed and grabbing coffee and a light breakfast, he found his way to his art studio in the remodeled garage at the far end of their vast park-like backyard.

This morning he followed the serpentine walk leading to his studio. He paused occasionally to admire the Flemish Bond brick pattern he had insisted upon, and to take in the expanse of lawn and the fragrant blossoms swaying in the gardens. Now and then he wondered what had gone wrong with his marriage. Strolling through the yard, coffee in hand, Jon felt a sense of calm wash over him, preparing him for the day ahead and perhaps even paving the way for his creativity to flourish.

Jon wondered if Sharon felt the same about her day when taking the speeding Acela into New York City every morning.

This morning, he faced reality. He realized his daily walk to the studio was an escape from the harsh truth of his struggling fifteen-year marriage.

Instead of continuing to the studio, he took a seat on an ornamental wrought-iron bench and stared out into the yard.

Until the lockdown, they lived separate lives, able to deny their deteriorating marriage. Now, Sharon and Jon were physically close to one another, but remained emotionally distant. She hid herself in her office and he worked in the studio.

He took a gulp of his coffee and, finding it cold, spewed it out onto a nearby flower bed. He shook his head and wiped his mouth with his sleeve. "Yuck!"

Sharon had always been ambitious. She thrived at her high-pressure job in the city. A series of promotions had come rapidly and required her to spend more time at work.

For five or six years, they'd worked hard to make up for her time at the office, but candlelight dinners and weekend getaways were now things of the past. Her career had become the most important part of her life, canceling plans and consuming weekends in her home office or the city. Instead of spending time with him.

Jon resented his partner's work schedule. To accommodate her, he hired a housekeeper and started preparing their dinners. However, she would arrive later and later, claiming to be too tired to eat, or she had eaten elsewhere. Eventually, their dinners together ended.

He ate alone.

When the lockdown began, he'd thought it might be a good thing. Maybe the Covid lockdown could bring them back together.

Who am I kidding? We haven't had a thoughtful conversation in weeks, maybe months. It feels like both of us are biding our time, me in my studio and her... Well, he paused his thoughts, then said to himself, *we had sex last night. I wonder if it was the last time. Didn't see that coming.*

He got up from the bench. He pushed the clouds from his mind the further he walked from the house. Jon took a moment to inhale the cornucopia of fragrances wafting about the yard and then toss some fish food into the koi pond.

Jon brushed fish food from his hand, smiled, and turned back toward the house. He lifted his gaze to Sharon's office window. He thought he caught sight of Sharon's silhouette, partially concealed by drapes. He gave a nod and mouthed, "Have a nice day."

Late afternoon, invigorated by having unleashed his creativity in the studio, Jon thought, *be positive, see if we can have an enjoyable evening together. Surely, after eight or nine hours apart, things should have simmered down a bit.*

Sharon's breakfast comments still stung, but masters of compartmentalization, as they both were, perhaps they, he, could deal with it.

He entered the kitchen. It appeared to have been untouched all day.

Well, he thought to himself. *I wonder if she has even been down stairs. Who knows?* He bit the inside of his cheek. *The koi are warmer than she is. God, why did I think that? It is no way to patch things up. Maybe she's right. I am an idiot. Or did she say artist? Shut the fuck up, Jon. Be positive. Rise above this. Ha! I'll make her favorite dinner.*

Thirty minutes later, he had combined chickpeas, quinoa, cucumber, bell pepper, red onion, parsley, and cilantro. He then tossed in avocado and pumpkin seeds. He drizzled a dressing of lemon juice, olive oil, salt, and pepper on it and placed the bowl in the refrigerator.

As he prepared the meal, he heard sounds of activity, obviously Sharon, moving about at the other end of the house. Muffled sounds of doors and drawers opening and closing occasionally reached the kitchen.

He put a bottle of chardonnay on the kitchen table he'd set for two; he smiled.

Returning from the refrigerator with the salad, the pièce de résistance, he placed it on the table.

A nearby door closed as Jon lit a candle centered on the table.

"Well, at least I know she's still alive," he said. "Hope she's hungry."

"Who are you talking to?" Sharon asked.

Jon looked up from the flickering candle.

Sharon stood in the kitchen entry dressed in a dark navy suit, crisp white blouse, her hair pulled back in a chignon, and wearing red soled pumps.

Jon's heart sank. *She's going out,* he thought as he stared, his hands now dangling at his side.

He forced a cheerful voice, "I made dinner. Hungry?"

She looked at him, expressionless.

He grinned wide, gesturing to the table. "C'mon babe, how 'bout a glass of wine?"

She replied in a flat tone, "I have something to say to you, Jon."

He pulled out one of the kitchen chairs for her, then stepped back.

Without looking at the chair, she sat. She reached over and grasped the bottle of wine snuggly wrapped in a red and white plaid towel and poured generously into a glass. Sharon returned the bottle to the table and, lifting the glass to her nose, breathed in the bouquet. "A Vermentino, right?"

Jon nodded, "Yeah, good guess!" He filled his glass. "Salad?"

"No, thank you."

"Okay."

Sharon placed her glass at the table and stared at Jon. "Neither of us is happy with our situation. Like I said, there is no *us*. There hasn't been one in a very long time."

"Sharon, uh, there could be."

"No, there cannot be. We have to move on, divorce."

"But why? We haven't even talked about it. Counseling, how about a marriage counselor?"

"Maybe a couple of years ago—. Our lives diverged and forked into separate paths years ago."

"When did you decide we couldn't save our marriage?" He looked at his glass as he twirled it, thinking, *where the fuck is this coming from? Fuck, she's right. I'm not letting her off the hook so easily. She should at least try.* Jon sipped his wine and said, "Not even try to save it?"

She leaned forward. "It's been a long time coming. I have had counseling. Years of it."

Jon's voice shook. "Without me? Without including me? Without telling me?"

Sharon refilled her glass and sat back in her chair. "It had been my intention to include you, but I wanted to *fix* me first. I knew I was a big part of the problem. Certainly not all of it."

"When? How long ago did this happen?"

"About the time you started playing those passive-aggressive games with me by first getting up to fix breakfast, then pretending you were too tired or ill. Then you ramped it up by no longer making dinner and getting resentful about my schedule. I understood. Your feelings were hurt. Life wasn't as picture-perfect as you wanted, not an Ozzie & Harriet or Leave it to Beaver sorta thing. It was difficult for us both, so I sought counseling."

"Why didn't you tell me, or confront me?"

"You were angry, deeply resentful. You hollered at me when I came home from work. You threw things. When you were mad at me, you were mean to the dogs. I lost count of how many glasses you broke in the middle of one of your tantrums."

Her voice shaking, she said, "I was—. I am afraid of you!"

"Afraid of me? You're exaggerating."

"Right, I'm exaggerating. And the studio fire, the one before we refurbished the garage."

Jon shuddered. "What about it?"

"I hired an investigator to look into it."

"Why?"

"You were so angry that morning. You slammed the bathroom door hard enough to damage the door frame. Remember?"

"An accident," Jon retorted.

"Right, an accident. Back to the studio fire. You don't smoke, there were no open flames. It's always neat, and you paint with watercolors."

Jon quipped, "What did your private dick conclude? That I caused the fire?"

"Who else could it have been? You were the only one here, right? We don't have any neighbors nearby. No evidence of an intruder, right?"

Jon folded his arms across his chest and stammered, "Ree, er, ridiculous!"

"After years of my going to counseling and efforts to pull things together, and our growing apart, I'm tossing in the towel."

"But we haven't been given the chance to work it out. Work it out together!"

"I just don't want to be anywhere near you anymore. You scare me."

"There is more to this than you are telling me, Sharon."

She stood. "I'm going to the city. Staying in the city for the foreseeable future."

"Where?"

"My boss is stuck in Europe. He's offered me his place for the duration."

"Your boss?"

She snapped, "It's none of your business."

Sharon left the kitchen momentarily.

She returned after having donned a jacket and said, "You know, in all the years we were married, all those years you were painting other people, particularly women, why didn't you ever ask me to sit for you?"

He opened his mouth to speak—.

She held up her hand, silencing him. "It was a rhetorical question. Don't bother to answer, it won't matter to me. But you, you think about it."

Sharon walked out of the room.

Moments later, the sounds of suitcase rollers running across the tiled foyer floor; the opening and closing of the front door signaled she'd departed.

Jon heard the resounding slam of the car trunk and the subsequent thump of a door closing shut. Soon the fading sound of tires crunching on the crushed stone driveway loomed ominous.

He thought, *how many times have I heard that? Hmm.*

Jon finished his second glass of wine and poured what they'd left in the bottle into his glass and gulped it down.

Jon leaned across the table and picked up the empty bottle. He threw it, sending it crashing through the breakfast bay window. "Bitch! I've never been good enough for you!"

He sat back, grunted, and looked at the table. "Well, I can't let good vino go to waste." He downed Sharon's wine.

He got out of the chair and, in an unsteady gait, made his way to the wine refrigerator. "I'll have another one of them Italian wines." Jon pulled out one, then two more bottles. He retrieved one of the cloth bags from a nearby drawer. He belched as he placed the wine in the bag. "No plastic for me! Damnit! I'm one of the good guys!"

"I'm hungry, and I sure as hell don't want any salad."

"Where are the chips? Some cheese and prosciutto would be nice." A couple of minutes later, the bag bulged with wine and snacks.

The sky had begun to darken, taking on shades of blue, purple, and pink. Several large yellow moths fluttered about the yard. Snow crickets helped fill the silence as Jon, laden with the overfilled bag, made his way along the brick sidewalk toward his studio.

Ah, yes, he thought, entering the studio. *Let's get this show on the road.*

Unpacking the cloth bag, Jon hummed a tune he'd picked up traveling in Spain with Sharon. He prepared a charcuterie board of sorts.

Jon pulled out his phone and tapped on Spotify. He dialed in the wistful and romantic Brahms Symphony in D major and put it on loop. The music filled the studio with its soaring melodies as he completed prepping a 32 x 40 inch canvas.

He took out his pencils and drawing pad and placed them in front of the canvas. His hand moved across the pad, drawing quickly without pause. Once he had completed his sketch, he gave the pad a kiss. "Now, there. That is a great start."

Well into the second movement, *Adagio non troppo*, he transferred his sketch to the large canvas.

Jon timed his brushstrokes to the rhythm of the symphony, adjusting his movements to match the tempo. His strokes varied in length, intensity, and direction, following the music's cues, creating a harmonious blend of color and sound.

Sometimes he would stop and reflect on his subject, completely engrossed in the music. He delved deep into every aspect, wasting no brush stroke and carefully placing every drop of color. As he painted, he advanced at a faster rate, completing the piece in less than an hour.

"Now you sit there and dry."

Jon refreshed his tray of food and placed it and the three bottles of wine and a glass on a low table next to an easy chair. Next, he located a pack of cigarettes he'd kept hidden. "Why do I hide these, anyway? Guess I don't need to do that anymore."

He dimmed the lights, plopped himself in the chair, and lit a cigarette.

Jon woke ten hours later, the rising sun striking his face full on.

His head pounded. Three empty wine bottles and a half bottle of bourbon stared at him from the table. "Ouch." He paused, placing his palm against his forehead. "Part of the plan. Deal with it, kiddo." He got up from the chair and walked over to the now dry painting. "No frame for you."

Jon held the painting in one hand, let himself out of the studio, and walked to the house. Taking note of the glass from the broken bay window scattered across the lawn, he mumbled, "Hmmm. Wonder who'll be cleaning up this mess?"

Entering the house, he made his way to the formal living room. He removed the seascape hanging above the fireplace and replaced it with his latest project.

A Regency-era dress made of muslin and silk draped loosely and flowed around a young woman as she sat on a swing. Multi-colored pastel ribbons encircled her wide-brimmed straw hat, causing it to appear as if the ribbons were being playfully tossed by the swing's undulating movement.

Jon stepped back from his portrait of Sharon. He couldn't help but admire her beauty. The painting captured his ideal image of her, particularly Sharon's flawless porcelain skin tones. It portrayed her long blonde hair in delicate tendrils, cascading down and dancing about her shoulders, framing her deep aquamarine eyes and radiant smile.

Jon threw the portrait a kiss. "I love you, I'm sorry. Yes, I wanted, had to have, the perfect marriage. I wish we'd tried harder."

He returned to the studio carrying four bottles of wine, rubbing alcohol, and three bottles of bourbon.

Later, in the early evening, the studio burned to the ground.

Days later, Jon's remains were discovered in the debris.

17

OH, BARBRA!

KEN YAROS

Late one morning, Richard, my dental school flatmate, tapped on my bedroom door complaining of a headache and seeing double. He stood there holding his head. "I think we need a breather."

He was right. We needed a break from our graduate school studies, being exhausted from long hours of reading, preparing for exams, and completing laboratory projects. We had been sharp with each other for days.

"What did you have in mind?"

"I'll let you know after the aspirins kick in," he shouted after slamming the door.

Well. At least he's talking, I thought.

An hour later he tapped again and suggested we could visit the Philadelphia Museum of Art even though it looked to be a miserable day past our apartment's filthy windows.

"Didn't know you were the museum type," I said, frowning. "But okay. If you want."

We left after lunch for a bumpy, grimy, ear-shattering subway ride that Sunday in April 1966.

A late winter rainstorm taunted us as we exited near the

museum. My umbrella wouldn't stay open. Two bleary-eyed, disheveled students splashed through the puddles and jogged up the many steps toward a bank of tall glass and bronze doors. We pushed them open to enter the warm spacious foyer.

Happily, they accepted our student IDs. I slid a dollar through the window, took my ticket, checked my umbrella, and stuck the ticket in my wallet. We took a moment at the base of the staircase to review a visitor's brochure, which contained the museum floor plan, to determine where to head to see a grouping of newly acquired Italian Renaissance paintings.

Richard and I climbed the magnificent marble stairs with its spacious open balconies to the third level, figuring to work our way back down to the visitor center's gift shop. Despite the gloomy day, the oversized domed skylight illuminated the foyer flooding it with natural light. It took us about an hour to explore the medieval gallery.

We then decided to head back down the stairs to the second floor. Looking down at the lobby, I noticed people coming through the front doors, but thought little of it. Sometime later, a guard gave us our first warning.

"The museum will be closing at 5:00 p.m. today," a kindly older gentleman tipped his cap. His uniform appeared immaculately pressed and his black shoes polished to a patent leather finish which suited his professionalism.

"But the ticket says ten to six," I said.

"Sorry, sir, we're closing at five today for a private function. They'll stamp your ticket so you can come back for free tomorrow if you like."

"Damn, only thirty minutes left," I moaned to Richard.

We made our way to some Roman statuary to discuss the best use of our time. The guards, now more noticeable, roved the near-empty corridors every few minutes. I suggested we should head to a remote section of the exhibition, hoping to remain as long as possible.

Soon after, I observed lighting for some of the larger

displays on the second floor was being switched off. The guards began ushering us toward the staircase along with other visitors. I paused for a few moments near the stairs to observe the foyer and the entrance below. A large sign which simply said "Barbra" had been set up by the ticket booth.

Activity at the front doors had increased as some museum goers left. Others who appeared quite well dressed for a dreary weekend afternoon, streamed in through the massive doors. Bright lights now illuminated the entrance.

"What do you think's going on?"

"Don't know." Richard huffed. "You're the smarty."

"You're the one who suggested we come."

"Yeah. Brilliant, wasn't it?"

We stood for a few moments longer to contemplate what was developing on the main floor when I observed at least a dozen workers pushing their way in carrying long folding tables and bulky boxes.

The foyer flooded with even more workers. Uniformed servers worked quickly to set up the tabletops and lay white tablecloths. In the middle of the floor other workers converged, then went their ways directed by uniformed caterers barking all sorts of instructions. Billboard-sized signs and decorations such as balloons and streamers were carried in and set up on the perimeter. Then, I spotted a large sparkling silver sign, "Happy Birthday, Barbra," set up by the front doors.

"Wow," I said. "This is going to be some birthday party. Maybe it's for some debutante from ritzy Main Line, or a daughter of a bigwig benefactor to the museum? Hope they didn't pay the printer too much. Looks like he goofed her name."

Richard started to laugh and shook his head. "Rich people. Don't know what to spend their money on."

Minutes later, others brought in dishes and cutlery, a silver fountain, trays of hors d'oeuvres, and a six-foot-high white cake on a dolly.

We were now among the few visitors left in the museum. I looked up to see the museum staff had turned off the lights on the top level. I assumed that soon our floor would be darkened as well.

Finally, Richard spoke up. "This is too good to miss. Let's move somewhere out of sight."

Twenty feet away I spotted a maintenance closet. We ducked into it, switching off its light, and leaving the door cracked open. The closet proved to be a good vantage point to view the entrance. No one could see us.

Just before 5:00 o'clock, a noisy crowd gathered outside the front doors. I could see nearly everything below, right through to the front of the museum.

Four musicians, lugging their instrument cases and folding chairs, pushed their way in through the outside congregation to set up just inside the grand doors. They positioned their seats to face the doors and started tuning up. Within minutes, rich notes from their stringed instruments calmed the chaotic scene.

Then, as if directed by some invisible maestro, most of the workers disappeared, leaving a handful of smartly dressed servers to light candles in the silver candelabras and pour gallons of chocolate into the fountain.

A few minutes after 5:00 o'clock, a shiny, pink bus with extra lights on its roof pulled in front of the doors. The driver honked repeatedly after it stopped. An enormous cheer outside erupted which dissolved into chanting, "Bar-bra, Bar-bra, Bar-bra!" The remaining guards upstairs went to the railings to view the circus below.

Museum workers pulled the entrance doors open to allow the crowd in.

"Damn. Would you look at that?" Richard said.

I still didn't know quite what to think.

Echoes of the mob's footsteps and loud conversations shattered the normally hushed hallways. My eyes fixated on the entrance. Several minutes later, the front door of the bus opened. A tall gentleman wearing a black tuxedo and top hat exited the bus and opened his umbrella. Out stepped Barbra, I supposed.

Richard started to laugh.

"I bet you're glad we came now," I whispered. The escorted woman made her way through the open doors into the foyer. The guest of honor appeared to be about five foot five and slender. She wore an enormous white fur stole which nearly covered a shimmering tinsel dress slit up the side and matching shoes with the highest heels I had ever seen outside a movie screen. The string quartet rose to their feet and switched to a snappy tune to enhance her arrival.

She paused for a moment inside the doors and bellowed, "Hello, Philadelphia!"

"It's Streisand," we both said simultaneously.

"Holy shit," I said.

Richard burst out laughing again.

The birthday girl sashayed into the foyer, paused to adjust her bangs, blew kisses toward the quartet, threw her hands into the air as if royalty, and got immediately mobbed. Pandemonium ensued. Soon clatter and screams of delight nearly drowned out the quartet.

I'm guessing the closet door must have squeaked as we tried to get an even better look. A nearby guard turned and spotted us. "Hey. You two! What the hell you think you're doing?"

"Err, just watching, sir," I said, hoping to placate his ire.

"This is an invitation only event. Out of there, now. Both of you."

Seconds later, several guards escorted us brusquely down the back stairs and out a side entrance. We didn't have time to button our coats.

"What about my umbrella?" I said, hoping maybe we could somehow still join the festivities.

"Pick it up tomorrow."

The grumpy guard stood outside the door, arms folded. "And don't try to come back."

The evening's darkness and cold drizzle thwarted us as we made our way back over soggy ground to the front of the museum. Remnants of the crowd along with a half dozen museum guards lingered by the front doors. We stood with them for a while to share their excitement. On the side of the bus next to its front door a small plaque in polished chrome read, Miss Streisand. What a day to leave my camera home.

"Wow," Richard said, beaming for the first time in a week. "Can you believe it? We were that close. Wonder if she's going to sing?"

Neither of us spoke on the long ride home.

In the years since, we graduated, married, built practices, had kids, grandkids, and retired. Richard and I remain best friends, although we live on separate coasts now and only get to talk on the phone.

Through the decades, I've followed Barbra's amazing life, watching her perform for presidents and royalty, star in and produce motion pictures, and win more music awards than almost any performer in history.

I doubt Barbra Streisand remembers much of that gloomy April day in Philadelphia, but I'll never forget the excitement I felt from my near encounter with a budding international celebrity that came for the price of a museum ticket—and an old umbrella.

18

THE COPPER WIRE

CAROL HEASLEY

The September sun hadn't warmed it, yet it looked hot coiled in the pungent sage that flooded his senses. Kenny bent down and picked it up, then straightened his toned fifteen-year-old body. He slid his finger around the coil of bright copper wire and dropped it on the ground before he walked away.

The dry hot summer in southern California's high desert was about to give way to breezes and the dropping of leaves. Along the roadsides, ripened helianthus seeds were popping out of their pods. In early spring, he'd driven a neighboring farmer's new '65 Ford tractor loaded with sprinkler pipes in the alfalfa fields, positioning the heavy cylinders in rows, strengthening his body.

He swiped back his brown hair drooping over his blue eyes. Tanned facial features formed a resolute expression.

A month ago, his father had returned home from a two-month stay at the Veteran's Hospital due to a psychotic break. Now Kenny believed his mother depended on him, depended on her half-grown boy to bring home money—money she desperately needed.

He continued his pace to the house. His mother had a request for Kenny to help her today, but he would rather be riding his Triumph in the hills and exploring the old reservoir.

"Kenny," his father called from where he was welding a trailer. He pushed up his face guard. "Where are you going? You left your motorcycle in the driveway. Are you taking it to school?"

He stopped. Before he turned to his father, he thought carefully about what he would say. "No, I'm not taking it to school." He wanted to say something defiant, but seeing his older sisters get hit had taught him better. He too had been slapped in the past when his father was angered.

"What did I tell you at least a dozen times? Someone will steal it from the school because there isn't any reliable security. Get it back inta' the shed right now."

"Yeah, yeah, yeah," Kenny muttered.

"What did you say?" his father asked. "For goodness' sake, don't you ever listen?" His father stepped closer with extended arms like a swooping great-horned owl, embracing the back acre where the copper lay. Kenny stepped back. "Out there are several jobs I gave you. After school, come out here and get them done." His father returned to working on his project.

Maybe he was unconsciously looking for signs of his father's illness, because watching his father now, he clearly visualized what his father did leading up to his hospitalization. He'd driven the truck pulling his welder erratically over the fields, up and down ditches, leaving it in a ditch. Then he'd walked to town, his speech incoherent—a series of words no one understood. "The cops in Riverside say Alice is ratting on us, let's hope she can make it to the meeting, the place the church is at is coming at me and Satan is not okay, I will get the people responsible for Social Security, they say my medication isn't for schizophrenia, they said I don't have it, it's the government that planted a device in my head."

The whole family had been numb and frightened. Kenny

recalled that when the doctor came to the house to give his father an injection, Dad quieted and stared at them blankly until aides from the Veteran's Hospital came to take him away.

Kenny continued on to the house but made up his mind to come back and pick up that roll of copper wire his mother wanted him to sell. In the kitchen, his mother in her flowered housecoat was preparing bottles of milk in a steamer on the gas stove while his shrieking baby sister straddled her hip. "Kenny," she said, "I think you can sell that wire. It has lain there for two years." She tilted a bottle into the baby's mouth, then instructed his older sister to put the margarine and the blue ceramic plates, topped with hot pancakes slathered in syrup, on the table. Kenny's mouth watered. Pancakes reminded him of the Aunt Jemima commercials he saw on Grandma's TV.

Mom raised her voice above the raucous chatter of the other children. "Somebody, grab some glasses and pour the milk. The bus will be here soon. Eat and get out front so the driver doesn't have to wait—books and clarinet with the science project are by the door."

When Kenny looked at her, he smiled and thought her furrowed brow and long dark hair pinned in curls made her look cartoonish. For a few minutes, he felt her observing him. He could always break out in a sudden disarming smile, tease her, and make her laugh. It was seldom she laughed right out loud. Kenny knew she was aware he must face his father's tough commands and expectations, just like they all did. For his mother, there was no time to play her accordion or write music. If his father saw her taking time for herself, he insisted she do chores: Wash my paintbrushes, make me coffee, repair my shirts and pants—a litany of demands.

But Kenny often wondered if his dad's harshness was truly his own—or if it was the schizophrenia speaking. His illness had started showing itself more frequently, and it scared Kenny. Dad demanded more of him than he did of the girls, which aggravated Kenny. Was he demanding because he wanted

Kenny to be a man? Or were the voices of demons in his head forcing him to be cruel?

Kenny pointed to where he wanted his sister to put his plate. Happy for her to serve him, he sat down. "Another glass of milk please," he added, taunting her with a grin. Fork in hand he turned to his mother and lowered his voice. "Mom, I'd have to skip school today to make that sale happen. You know that, right?"

"Yes, I realize that you would need time to find someone."

"Okay then. I'll do it. I'll be back, ah, probably late." He ate up the pancakes, then pushed himself away from the table. After placing his baseball cap on, he went out the back door to his motorcycle.

It was his decision to help his mother who struggled to put food on their table. There was encouragement in her gestures, like the language between their mother goat and her kid, a natural intuitiveness guiding the young one. But it was dangerous. His father had told him to leave the wire alone—not take it. Kenny knew there was a buyer for the copper wire, valued by electricians far more than other metal Dad collected for welding jobs.

At times he felt he was not yet prepared to figure out who he was and found it his role to mimic his father. Sometimes he felt like they were silhouettes—one inside the other—their broad hands moving over the same terrain. His hands on the tractor steering wheel were the contours of his father's hands, like the shape of his father's body captured in his mind.

Kenny tied the shiny copper roll to his '50 Triumph with twine and silently pushed the motorcycle onto the road. A friend had helped him adjust the carburetor since the bike had been difficult to start and backfired. *Let's see how this goes.* In one fluid motion, he swung onto the seat of his motorcycle, pushed the starter, twisted the throttle, and revved the engine. He sat a few moments, listening to it run smooth—his torso absorbing the gentle vibrations. He felt for a pocketknife in his jacket and pushed his hat down tighter before he lifted his foot off the ground to kick the stand up. He zipped onto the road.

Negotiating the low-lying hills that hemmed their small valley, Kenny headed toward the house where Mr. Hooper, an electrician he knew, lived, but first he made a small detour and checked out the reservoir where granite boulders were scattered like bumps on gourds. At the reservoir, he parked the motorcycle and decided to climb in. He thought *this will be a mental and physical challenge*. Empty, it was at least four times larger than a standard swimming pool and deeper.

Clutching onto protrusions—bumps and knobs in the concrete—he eased down alongside skinks navigating the terrain. At the bottom, he breathed deep and exhaled. Kenny stood still for at least ten minutes in solitude—a space that provided him adventure and quiet unlike any other place in his life. The cool air in and out of his lungs smoothed the day's demands and paved the way for inspiration. He reflected on onthe brown-haired girl in English Lit and the poem she wrote about him. Overwhelmed, his face and neck tingled at the memory. Realizing how she felt about him caused him to shudder. He sat down and enjoyed the sensations.

His trance faded when he remembered his promise. He needed to leave. To hoist himself, Kenny grabbed for a solid protuberance, but after several attempts, he failed to find one. Exasperated to the point that his short-sleeved shirt was soaked with sweat, he feared that he might not be able to get out of this trap.

In a last attempt, he faced a corner and spread his legs to scale the grainy sides. Balanced on his right leg, he placed his left foot flat against the wall above a small protrusion, trying to hold onto the concrete with his hands. He lifted his right leg to feel for a place to anchor. He could only pull himself up a little way and had to drop down.

Above him, the blue sky and white clouds filled the squared edges. He watched several overhead passes of slate grey B52 bombers nearing the Air Force base of the strategic air commands for landing. The behemoths' loud rumblings were deafening. Time slipped away, and the temperature turned chilly. Many times, Kenny called, "Help! Help me. I am down in the reservoir."

The tangerine glow of the sun setting in the sky turned faintly smokey. Then grew dark. Soon it was so black he could not see his own hands. The brilliant stars twinkling in the black blanket of the sky made him feel even more alone. For now, it was only the cold night air to breathe, and without a jacket, he huddled against the warmest side of the concrete. He heard packs of adult prairie wolves howling from over the hill, and the yipping echoes of their youngsters. *Even if they discovered me and ventured close, they can't get down in here.* Kenny was sure Dad would start looking for him if he didn't show up for dinner.

He didn't know the hour when at last he heard his father's voice calling him.

"Kenny, Kenny, answer me. Are you up here?"

"Here, Dad, down in the reservoir. I'll keep answering so you find me," Kenny's anxious voice rose.

His father's voice grew louder as he reached the edge of the reservoir. "How'd you get down there? Why can't you climb back up the way you went?" His flashlight shone on Kenny. The back glow revealed the worry in his father's brown eyes.

"I've tried, believe me, but I can't find any places to grab. They must've broken off."

"All right. I'm going back to the car for rope."

I knew Dad would come looking. I'm so glad he isn't mad.

"Kenny, watch for the rope. I will anchor it. See it now?"

"Yes. But I'm slippin'. It doesn't seem to be holding on your end."

"Right," his father said, "hold on while I tie it around a boulder . . . tight now?"

"Yes, that's it. I'm coming up. I'm almost at the top. Finally."

Kenny lay on the ground to catch his breath. "Thanks so much." After a few minutes, he got up and said, "Dad, hey listen, I will see you later at home 'cause I have something I need to do."

His father wrapped the rope around his shoulder and gave him a quizzical look.

Kenny rushed over to where his cycle was parked by a patch of night-blooming cactus before his dad had a chance to see the roll of wire. The moon now visible provided some light.

He rode about six miles through the hills. The Triumph's headlight helped him navigate the rutted dirt roads where it dipped hard and bounced the bike. Nearer the electrician's home, he slowed and prayed to the Guy above that Mr. Hooper wanted his cache. *It would be easier if we had had a phone to call ahead,* he judged. Kenny made his way to the top of a low dry bank where a fenced, leaning wood house stood. With no lights, it appeared empty.

Without warning, two missiles, an Alsatian and a Doberman, tore from the darkened porch, barking and heaving their muscular bodies into the chain link fence. The red-hot end of a cigarette or cigar glowed in the dark held by a man as he exited the house. His sturdy body appeared middle-aged. "Hello, there. They can't tell friend from foe, young feller. Heh, aren't you Frank's son?"

His voice is raspy, Kenny thought, *kindly, with an accent like my godparents from Oklahoma.*

"Domino, Chester, go lie down with your pups." Mr. Hooper waved his dogs away. He ground his cigar stub into the dirt with his cowboy boot, then used a key on a retractable belt cord to unlock the padlock on the gate. He approached Kenny by a large tamarisk tree all illuminated by the shine of the moon. They shook hands. "So what cha' doin' way up here? The last time I saw you was out at the go-kart track at Gavilan Hills." He smiled. "A while back I saw your older sister racing a kart on the road out at your place."

Kenny didn't waste time shooting the breeze. "Mr. Hooper, I've got some copper you might be interested in buying. Take a look." Kenny used his pocket knife to cut the twine from the wire and handed him the roll.

"Good, it's bare wire. Sure, I can use it. What'cha askin' for it?"

"Fifty dollars."

He seemed to be considering. After a few moments he said, "Okay, I'll take it."

Like a copper wire connected to electricity, every synapse in Kenny's body fired, infusing him with a sense of relief. Fulfillment spurred him as he rode down the hill to the highway, ignoring the coming-to-Jesus he knew would come from his father. Out on the highway with no warning the cycle's motor cut off. As the bike rolled to a stop, he gripped the handlebars tighter, hopped down, and pushed the bike off the paved road. Not one car passed. Though stressed that not even the lights were working, instead of leaving it there he forced it along toward home.

Abruptly, over the dividing line a car poked its headlights at Kenny, then swung back into the lane and drove away. In a sudden turn, the car circled, approaching from behind, spotlighting him, and sped up seemingly in a game of hit and miss. Kenny darted aside. As the car turned back, Kenny saw passengers in the back seat. This time the vehicle slammed into him with a baseball batter's accuracy. The crunching impact sent horrendous pain through his leg and lifted him into the air. His body arced and then slammed down onto the cold hard plate of tarmac.

~

THE ROOM WAS COMING into focus, and he could feel a painful aching all over his body. His senses were steeped in antiseptic scent. He heard his mother and father talking, then saw it was to a woman in a white coat.

"Doctor, we just heard," his father said, "from the policeman who came to the house, that the young men who hit him, picked him up and brought him in here."

The woman in the coat answered, "Yes, that's correct. Kenny was unconscious, but while we were examining him, he woke. It will take some time for him to recover fully, but he will be okay. Come back tomorrow."

"Where is my motorcycle?" Kenny murmured.

His mother rushed to his bed and kissed him on the forehead. "Kenny, look at me," she said, "Thank God. I am so happy to hear your voice. The doctor just told us you will be fine."

"They took it to a garage," his father informed. "It's not repairable. The motor was crushed." His father clasped his hand. "Just a little while longer here for observation and you can come home."

"Don't you worry. You'll be okay." His mother whispered in his ear. "That is all we are concerned about. I have the stuff from your pockets and your wallet," she tapped her purse, "with everything still in it." Their eyes met and they both looked over at his father.

Kenny came home the next evening. The doctor told him to stay away from motorcycles. He sat on the back porch and brooded about being without a motorcycle. There had been no predicting his father's hospitalization and that his mother would need him to help provide. Nor could he ever have imagined surviving the accident on that darkened country road. He looked closely at his hands that chose the copper wire like he was seeing them for the first time and felt a sense that everything would be all right. He could not predict what might happen next, or exactly what his father would do when he discovered the wire was missing, but it didn't matter. Kenny was no longer afraid.

19

OKRA

JANET TRAVERS

E very day at three o'clock in the afternoon, Suzanna became tired, but today she was tired *and* angry. Fortunately, she was alone. She yanked a dishtowel off the hook below the kitchen sink of the restaurant in which she worked and wiped down a counter. The tip of a paring knife was sticking out of one of the utensil drawers. She pulled the drawer open, pushed the knife back into place and saw a yellow legal pad and a red grease crayon. She took the pad out of the drawer, sat down on a stool, and with sloppy, manic handwriting, jotted down ideas of what she saw herself doing for the rest of her life, a practice she performed frequently.

The culprit that triggered her frustration this time was...okra. She had just cut ten pounds of okra into one-inch pieces. Okra was also known as *lady fingers,* a name she found creepy and disgusting. But they *did* look like lady fingers; smooth and tapered without knuckles, miniature unblemished appendages. Nothing like her large, strong, bony hands with protruding knuckles. For some inexplicable reason, today she got mad at that okra and hurled two fistfuls of it against the white kitchen wall. The routine of the okra, its consistency, its predictability, irked her. It has five perfect cylinders of seeds. Vegetables need to be cut uniformly to cook evenly. She was sick of evenness and routine and uniformity.

Yesterday, she became outraged at the *irregularly* shaped bell peppers she was preparing. Some of them had huge clusters of seeds, some had a few, some had four bumps on the bottom, some had three. Some were contorted and looked like abstract art sculptures and were difficult to slice.

She knew she had better learn how to meditate (or medicate) soon or change her life entirely *again,* if *vegetables* could piss her off, especially okra, a vegetable she thought probably had a good sense of humor. Okra...Gumbo...New Orleans. She scrawled on the yellow pad:

NEW ORLEANS...WORK *in the French Quarter, small restaurant...the smell of coffee and beignets in the morning, gumbo and fried catfish at night.*

Note to self: Learn French and find out the meaning of Mardi Gras.

SHE DIDN'T LIKE the taste of okra very much on its own, but it was an excellent thickening agent in gumbos and stews. She thought it was funny that there were things you don't like but use or keep because they hold it together. She thought okra got the last laugh. Not everybody loved it, it had to be doctored up to taste good, but it was needed. Those diehard pieces of okra probably laughed at her when they hit the wall. Bell peppers wouldn't have laughed. Bell peppers weren't that smart and didn't have much of a sense of humor. Bell peppers didn't get the joke.

Suzanna took this sous chef job a year and a half ago not long after her divorce. She wanted to work alone and chop and cook and think. She had done this at home by herself for years, but now she was working in a restaurant and getting paid, which felt good. She wasn't ready to work with and talk to new people.

She'd told the owner she specialized in soups, stews, gumbos, and bisques; dishes that could be made ahead of time. This type of cooking had worked for her family. A pot of chili or soup simmering on the stovetop made meals convenient with everyone's busy schedules. She had run her household and raised the children until they were up and running and gone.

Her husband had made the money and as time went by, they had less and less in common. With little to talk about, they stopped going out to movies and restaurants and the television took over her husband's spare time. Their marriage that was once a primary color was now variegated. If she was out and came home in the evening, she'd pull into the driveway and the glow of the television screen was visible through the glass panels of the front door. She couldn't bear seeing that glow of television every night for the rest of her life, so she asked her husband for a divorce.

He would have preferred her to stay because she was useful, but for a change, he didn't argue, and it wasn't messy. He didn't fight for the marriage, nor did he fight against the divorce. She had enjoyed being a mother and the backbone of the family and had worked hard at becoming a good cook. Food brought people together. Food makes you feel good. Food creates conversation. Food was paying her back.

After she cleaned the slimy green okra off the wall of the kitchen, she began to cube potatoes for clam chowder. She could smell the cream, bacon, and tarragon she was going to put in later. She stopped and wrote down another idea:

. . .

MOVE TO NEW ENGLAND, *maybe Vermont. Work in a small restaurant specializing in chowders. Wear thick gray sweaters with wooden buttons.*

Note to self: buy thermal underwear.

CHOP, chop, chop. Suzanna peeled and cubed potatoes for Irish Potato Soup.

MOVE TO IRELAND. *Get a job in a restaurant in Kinsale. Live in a little white house with shutters overlooking the sea. Get a goat, some chickens, and a sheep dog.*

Note to self: wear ivory wool Irish sweaters.

A FEW YEARS BACK, one of Suzanna's friends named Nina stopped returning Suzanna's phone calls. Nina was from Russia and was new to the United States. She was a single mother who was highly educated, a pleasant conversationalist and financially independent. The two of them had gone to parks and playgrounds with their children and sometimes got together and drank wine in the evenings. When Suzanna ran into Nina in a grocery store, she asked her why she had stopped returning her calls.

"Because," replied Nina, "you seem to need me too much, and I don't think I'm capable of giving you what you need."

Suzanna froze. She was humiliated and embarrassed and at the same time couldn't help but admire how blunt Nina was.

Nina continued, "You are a lovely person, an interesting person and I like you very much. You have been a good friend to me. You have so much that I would like to have but still you complain about things you do nothing about. I had to work hard and make sacrifices to improve my life. I am sorry if this hurts you, but you don't seem to appreciate what you have and you don't do the things you say you want to do. You don't leave your husband, or travel to Italy, or write your book. Perhaps we will see each other in the future. I hope so. You have to do things for yourself first before others." She kissed Suzanna on the cheek, walked to the cashier and was gone from her life.

Life to Suzanna seemed to be a process of identifying flaws and fixing them. Doing this had become tedious, and she didn't have the energy, or perhaps the desire to fix problems anymore. Why didn't someone else fix the problems? How much had she wanted to straighten out her marriage? Could it have just stayed crooked? Could someone else please pick up a nail and swing the hammer? She hadn't thought that making things easier for her family, teaching and helping them, would leave her empty. Drip by drip the last vestiges of what had one time made her interesting had made her a bore.

The cannellini beans floating in the pot of water looked like miniature inflated neck rest pillows. She prepped everything she needed for Ribollita, the Tuscan bean and vegetable soup she liked that was easy to make and kept well. Ribollita translates into "reboiled" in English and Suzanna proceeded to reboil the beans and make something new, the way she was trying to make something new out of herself with what *she* had leftover. Cubes of bread, thick rich soup, parmesan...Tuscany. She made a note:

TUSCANY. *Great olive oil. I can live near the water.*
    Note to self: more stylish reading glasses in Italy. Learn Italian.

SHE DRAINED THE BEANS, put them in a pot of water to boil then simmer, and left instructions for the nighttime sous chef to take the pot off at six o'clock. She Googled Tuscany on her phone but typed in Tucson by mistake. Tucson, Arizona. Southwestern cuisine...chili...tortilla soup, albondigas, pozole. She made a note:

TUCSON, Arizona...I love turquoise! Fresh masa.
   Note to self: Brush up on Spanish

SUZANNA FINISHED her work half an hour early then sat on a stool at the counter in the kitchen with a steamed artichoke and a cup of melted butter. The soups were simmering, and the kitchen was clean. She smelled comfort and accomplishment. She thought her kids were going to walk in the door the way they used to and ask what was for dinner, when her cell phone rang. It was her sister Leah.

Suzanna hadn't returned any of her phone calls in the last couple of weeks. Suzanna had more money than her sister, had traveled more and had gone to college. She'd always wanted more in life and marveled at how content Leah was with her life.

Leah didn't go to college, always had money problems, hadn't traveled more than five hundred miles from their hometown, and was cheerful and fun. For all the formal education Leah hadn't pursued, she more than made up for with her intuitive common sense. She said she got it from their grandmother, a lovely woman who was always there for them, who often gave them advice. Leah had listened to her but Suzanna had not because she said their grandmother spoke too slowly. Suzanna hesitated, scraped the flesh off an artichoke leaf with her teeth and answered her phone.

"You're picking up! Why haven't you returned my calls?"

"I've been busy here at the restaurant." Suzanna ate a little more artichoke.

"You've been working there for more than a year without a vacation...what's that noise...what are you eating?"

"An artichoke."

"I'm glad I'm not there. I've seen you scrape the meat off an artichoke leaf and it's not a good look. Can anyone see you?"

Suzanna smiled and replied, "No one else is here. At least I don't lick my plate when I'm finished like you do."

"That's acceptable if no one is watching. I do it in front of you because you're my sister and you don't count. I've been calling you because you need a break. Come for Thanksgiving! I'll make the turkey. You won't have to cook anything. It'll be fun."

"Leah, I'm working on Thanksgiving. Sorry. Listen, I have to go. The rest of the crew is going to be here in a few minutes."

"Yeah, well, let me tell you something. I've had enough of your self-imposed exile and you're beginning to annoy me. You don't sound good. You were depressed before you left Paul, and I can tell you're depressed now. What do you want? If you'd ever talk, I'd listen. If you won't come for Thanksgiving, then I want you to listen real hard—bend over and pull your head out of your ass and rejoin the world. I love you. I'll never abandon you. You've got to snap out of it."

Suzanna broke into a sweat and dropped her artichoke leaf. She was jealous of her sister's happiness. She whispered her reply because she knew she'd cry if she spoke in a normal tone of voice. "Leah, I feel like I haven't done anything with my life, and I don't know if it's too late to do something new. I don't know if I have the energy to go out on another limb. I feel like I haven't done...enough."

Leah let out a woop. "You're talking, Suzanna!"

"Leah," Suzanna said slowly, "you always seem to be okay."

"I'm not always okay. I just don't let things or people bother me that much."

"I threw some okra at the wall a little while ago."

"What?"

"I heaved a bunch of okra at the kitchen wall."

"Why?"

"Because they made me angry."

Leah burst out laughing. "Okra...made you...angry?"

"Do you think that's weird?"

"Yeah, it's weird. Did it feel good to beat up a defenseless vegetable?"

Suzanna paused. "Yes."

"Good for you. Listen. I've seen therapists, tried acupuncture, read too many self-help books..."

"You never told me all this."

"I did tell you, but you weren't listening. I also exercise and make kale smoothies then I eat four Little Debbie Banana Pudding Rolls a day."

Suzanna groaned. "That's disgusting!"

"I know!" Leah sighed.

"How are you so happy?" Suzanna whispered.

"I have low expectations and I *work at* being grateful for what I have. Everybody has doubts, Suzanna. You already made a huge change in your life by getting divorced and finding a job you enjoy. You've got good things going on that you created. *You* did it!"

"What should I do now?" Suzanna had never asked Leah for advice.

"Finish your artichoke. Come for Thanksgiving. Go home and have a drink or three."

"That's it?" Suzanna asked with a smile.

"That's it," Leah said.

"Alright."

Leah feigned a gasp. "Did you say *alright*?"

"Yes, Leah. Goodbye. Chew with your mouth closed."

"Laugh with your mouth open. See you at Thanksgiving."

20

THE FLASH

C.H. CURRIER

The vortex, created by my motorcycle, swirled fallen leaves behind me as I sped north on Madre Street. I had fifteen minutes until my shift began at a local gas station. I was eighteen years old in 1972, and this was to be my first day at a real job. Hal, the owner, had given me a warning, "Don't be late." With no delays, I'd make it with time to spare.

Uh-oh, I missed the damn light, I thought, as I approached Del Mar Blvd. Being stuck at this intersection could be a problem. I grew up in the neighborhood and knew this traffic signal only changed when a vehicle larger than a motorcycle rolled over its magnetic sensing device buried in the pavement.

With my destination still two miles away, I had to decide what to do. The flow of cross traffic was too heavy to consider running the light, plus I already had one moving violation. If I took a right turn, I'd have more traffic signals to deal with before I could double back toward the station. I'd have to wait. I checked my rearview mirror. Madre Street was deserted.

I shifted the motorcycle into neutral then leaned back with my feet on the ground and arms crossed. Several times I checked behind me and pleaded under my breath, "C'mon, c'mon, someone please, trip the switch."

This intersection was by an elementary school I had attended years before. I stared at a section of the sidewalk that made me uneasy. It was the same spot I found myself in a recurring dream when I was in second grade. A boy darts out between two cars and although someone yells, "Watch out," the child is hit. Then I'm floating above the child looking down. When he's turned over, it's me.

I'm shaken from the disturbing memory by the sound of a VW bug pulling up behind me. The traffic light facing Del Mar switches to yellow. On my left, a semitruck slows to a stop in the right lane. Still rattled, I tell myself, *Okay, that was just a dream and now you're late*. I lean forward and grasp the handlebars.

The light facing me goes from red to green. I rev the engine and release the clutch. The motor roars but the bike doesn't move. *Idiot, you're in neutral*. I pull in the clutch, downshift into first gear, let the lever out, and accelerate headlong into a new understanding of life and death.

I'm SEEING a newborn suckling its mother's breast, and a towheaded boy kicking a ball in the backyard, and a slender teen thrilling at his first kiss. Wait, they're me. I'm loving my wife and holding my first child. My God, I'm an old man writhing in pain but also feel the release of that pain as I cross into a bright light and welcomed by loved ones long dead. I am in all these experiences and millions more. Every moment of my past, present, and future envelop me, not in measurable time, but in a single instant.

I HEAR A VOICE. "DUDE, YOU OKAY?" Shaking my head, I realize I'm straddling the stalled bike in the middle of the intersection. Confused, stunned, but unhurt, I get off. With unsteady legs, I push it to the opposite corner and sit on the curb. The truck driver and the woman driving the Volkswagen park their vehicles then run to see if I'm alright. They exclaim, mostly to each other with eyes wide, how lucky I am not to have been killed. The car that ran the red light was doing at least sixty miles per hour as it blew through the intersection inches in front of me.

Once my initial shock subsided, the two go on their way. I remained sitting with my head in my hands trying to make sense of what happened. I thought about how odd it was for me to have neglected to shift into first gear before the light changed, an unusual mistake. I had been riding for years. But without that one second delay, I'd be dead. Was it only good luck or had this experience revealed that something or someone was watching over me?

I couldn't recall the make, model, or even color of the car that ran the light. Then I thought, maybe I hadn't actually been there. Perhaps my *being* knew better than to stick around for the probable carnage. Had my soul fled my body an instant before, and as it bailed out, revealed my entire life? *The Flash*, as people call it, can't be easily understood, only experienced.

I STARTED the bike and made it to my new job twenty minutes late. Hal, a big burly man, growled that he was disappointed, but softened once I explained about the near accident. He admitted that as a Marine in Korea he had also experienced *The Flash*. An enemy grenade had landed in his foxhole. For some reason it didn't explode. He sighed, shook his head, and smiled. After all those years, he had never told anyone that story. He assumed people would call him crazy.

Ding, ding. He looked at me. "Okay, rookie, go pump some gas. And don't forget to check the oil."

21

A SIMPLISTIC TRUTH

FRANK PRIMIANO

s a reflection of the late twentieth century's cynicism that carried over into the twenty-first, a saying circulated: "Life's a bitch, then you die." Contemporaneously, a less severe version expressed comparable futility: "You're born, you buy a boat, then you die." Harland Jarvis, III, having been born, was destined to put the second adage to the test.

Although his name might have suited a pretentious person of wealth, Harland was, instead, of modest means. He'd completed all the preliminaries: secondary education, marriage, fathering twin boys, and achieving a modicum of professional success, having risen to just below his level of incompetence as assistant maintenance engineer of the local high school. He was a janitor.

A model citizen, Harland led a Thoreau-disparaged life of quiet desperation. He lived nowhere near Walden Pond. The Atlantic Ocean, however, teased him from the other side of New Jersey. This slowly upset the inner tranquility of his otherwise serene existence.

For almost five decades he took the world as it came. But

when middle age caught up with his psyche, it hit hard. Crisis time. Not normally a cerebral person, Harland took stock of himself. Was he going to continue in his not-too-unpleasant, humdrum lifestyle, or would he, could he, break out, do something daring? And if so, what would that something be?

A deep-sea fishing TV program suggested the answer. It revived long abandoned daydreams from his youth. He could buy an ocean-worthy boat and be the captain of his destiny, at least on weekends and holidays. He'd have adventures out on the open seas pitting his skill against tuna, swordfish and barracuda or whatever else still survived out there.

But two minor obstacles loomed. Or, maybe not so minor – money, and convincing his long-suffering wife and eventual – he hoped – first mate, Mamie, that this was a good idea.

The money problem might be overcome by managing his expectations. A yacht was out of the question. A new craft was also. It had to be "pre-owned," perhaps only 20 or so feet long so it could handle at least the ocean's swells. He had lots of studying and preparation to do. His enthusiasm overcame his lack of talent or experience in researching an unfamiliar subject. In addition, he applied his full brain power to devise a plan he hoped would bring Mamie on board.

ONE EVENING while they were cleaning up after dinner and the boys were in their room studying, Harland said to Mamie, "You work hard cleaning houses, for us and other people. You deserve to have some fun."

Mamie looked at him sideways as she continued scraping leftover food from a dish.

"So, I been thinkin'. Now's the time, before we get too old and before the boys move out – if ever – to do something we can all enjoy together."

Mamie put the plate in the dishwasher and picked up

another from the counter. "What do you have in mind?" she asked.

"Maybe I could buy you a boat. The boys will love it ... going out on the ocean on days off, and vacations. Cool breezes when it's hot and humid here. Fishing. It'll be great."

Mamie blinked. Visions of more work – cleaning fish and the boat, packing for weekends away, especially on her days off – cascaded across the display screen of her mind. "Buy *me* a boat? Where'd you get an idea like that?"

"We always wanted to live near water. This would be the next best thing. We could drive to the shore in an hour and cruise in your boat. I saw a program on it on the Discovery Channel."

"You're serious, aren't you?"

"Yes. It'd be your toy. You could invite your girlfriends to join us. And if you ladies get tired of the boat, you can gamble in the casinos between cocktails while the boys and I haul in fish."

"That idea is ridiculous. Boats are expensive. Where would you get the money? You could lose your shirt."

"The house is nearly paid off, less than a year to go. Since the boys opted for community college, a lot of what we saved in their college fund is available. We can get a small loan for the rest. I'll shop for a bargain."

Although his wife's response that evening was negative, her asking how they could afford a boat meant to Harland his cause was not completely lost. Several months of not letting the topic die at last yielded success. Mamie reluctantly agreed to let her husband buy her a boat for himself ... on one condition. It had to have a bathroom.

"It's called a 'head'," Harland corrected, showing off his newly acquired knowledge of nautical terms.

～

ANTICIPATING EVENTUAL VICTORY, Harland kept an updated list of acceptable prospects gleaned from ads in boating magazines, online listings, and conversations with brokers. Prices ranged all over the place. A flyer nailed to a post in a boatyard he visited at the shore advertised the least expensive one he'd seen, just within his budget. He considered himself lucky to have found it.

The seller, Joshua Swindler, a pleasant fellow, several years older than Harland, immediately apologized for his name and assured his potential customer that it didn't describe his business practices. It was just an embarrassing family heirloom.

The boat he was selling was a 20-foot, cuddy cabin ideal for fishing because you could walk outside around the small, carpeted cabin that had two seats and housed the controls. Harland never heard of the manufacturer in his self-schooling on seagoing vessels. The boat had a fiberglass hull, a plywood deck, and a 125 horsepower Evinrude outboard motor. Electronic gadgets in the cabin included a VHF radio for when out of range of cell phone service, a depth finder and a GPS position locator. Various antennae, lights and a horn protruded from the roof. Below deck were crammed two narrow bunks and the mandatory head.

The deal included a trailer. Harland's three-quarter ton pickup – the family's "car" – could easily tow the boat. Swindler's story was that he'd owned it for eleven years and was ready to move up to a larger vessel. It was easy to handle and never gave him any trouble. Everything was being sold "as is" with no warranty.

Harland was curious about the name on the transom, "Pee Sea," one word on each side of the motor.

"It's from what's become a pet peeve of mine," Swindler said. "The story's a bit long."

Harland, and the boys, who were with him to observe the transaction, sat along the boat's rail. "We have time," Harland said.

"The name is to show my displeasure with Political Correctness, by phonetically spelling its initials that way."

Harland was confused.

Swindler explained. "Traditionally, sailors refer to their vessels as female. I felt comfortable referring to my honey that way. Then along came the politically-correct vocabulary that refers to everybody and everything as plural and genderless."

Harland had run into misunderstandings caused by this a couple of times, and nodded.

"My friends, especially their wives, began riding me for my 'old fashioned' attitudes. Even my daughter wanted me to 'get with it.' I got sick of the harassment. I resent the nonsensical alteration of our perfectly good language by substituting something worse in an attempt to correct perceived problems. Remember Garrison Keillor and his radio show, "A Prairie Home Companion?"

Not being an NPR dilettante, Harlan was unfamiliar with the show.

"Well, one of his recurring bits was to mock English majors by implying the only jobs they'd land were those requiring proper spoken English. For example, when asking, 'Would you like fries with that?'

"However, they are actually trained to maintain and improve verbal communication via a modern, clear vocabulary. But what did the academics, editors, and writers do when some yahoos decided new pronouns were needed? They allowed politicians, the 'often wrong but never in doubt,' self-serving know-it-alls, to usurp their authority in the matter."

This explanation wasn't making things any clearer for Harland.

"All they had to do was come up with a few, new – or old – gender-ambiguous pronouns. Instead, they permitted plurals to be substituted for singulars and imposed them on all people and things, not just those intended to be referred to by new pronouns. Uncertainty in number is now used to produce ambiguity in gender in our previously precise language because fine arts faculties demonstrated a lack of imagination and creativity, as well as cowardice, in not pushing back against the bastardization of the English language.

"So a boat or ship is no longer feminine: 'She handles great.' It's 'They handle great,' even though you're talking about only one craft.

"As far as I'm concerned, the whole exercise is a pissing contest and, to be politically correct, we should acknowledge we're over our heads in a big sea of pee. So, I temporarily christened my neutered boat the "Pee Sea" hoping that reason and ingenuity will someday return, and appropriate, gender-ambiguous pronouns will be developed so I could rename them. But now that I'm selling them, you can rename them anything you want. I bet you didn't realize you were buying a fleet and not just a single boat."

Harland got the gist of Swindler's logic. It was sort of funny. The boys chuckled. Harland decided the name could stay, mostly because he knew his limitations as a painter. No reason to pay a professional to change the lettering.

Swindler took Harland and the boys for the obligatory test cruise through the calm water of the bay. Harland manned the helm for a while. Holding the wheel, and in control of the motor's power, he felt like a real captain. Exhilarated, he was sold, especially for the price. They signed papers and money changed hands.

Swindler offered to help Harland load the Pee Sea onto its trailer but Harland wanted to take it out once more with his sons before he drove his ... er, Mamie's ... beauty home. So, he and the boys received only verbal instructions.

∼

HARLAND ADMIRED the Pee Sea out of the water, resting majestically, high on its land transport. The trailer-boat combination glided even at the speed limit. Smooth sailing on land.

Until the loud, smashing noise.

"What was that, Dad?" the boys shouted in unison.

Harland rode the brakes to the berm. Walking around the truck and trailer, he saw that all tires were intact. Nothing obvious under the truck. The grill and bumper were undamaged. He hadn't hit anything. He looked at the boat atop the trailer. His eyes glanced upward. Something was wrong. The several antennae once protruding from the top of the cabin were reduced to splintered stubs.

"Crap," Harland muttered. Swindler hadn't warned him about lowering the antennae before driving under bridges. The problem hadn't occurred to inexperienced Harland. Unforeseen expense number one – probably to be followed by many more.

IN THE SUBSEQUENT MONTHS, the neophyte sailors enjoyed the boat whenever time and gas money permitted. Mamie warmed to the notion of being a boat owner, if in name only. She delegated its maintenance and navigation to Harland and his crew of two, and gladly assumed the role of passenger.

The family couldn't afford to rent a slip so they dragged the boat to launch sites along the Jersey shore, then back home. They learned that channel markers are to be taken seriously and must not be ignored, especially at low tide. Several times Harland ran aground and had to be towed off sand bars. More frustrating, he often fouled the propeller in seaweed beds lurking invisibly just below the surface. Suffering through a minimum of one calamity every excursion became routine. Conclusion: boating isn't for sissies.

A fishing outing was considered successful if at least one

substantial, edible creature, usually a hapless flounder, were pulled on board. The fresh seafood was delicious and precious. Based on their total haul, by the end of the first six months the family owned the Pee Sea, the fish they consumed cost over $115.00 a pound before filleting. Harland considered it a bargain.

He attempted to explain his attitude to the boys using a politically-correct description of one of the Sunday funnies with which he identified. "A man dressed in a captain's cap and blazer gets into their long, black sedan and drives to a dock. They take a bushel basket from their trunk and walk to their boat. The basket is filled with twenties, fifties and hundreds. The man dumps the bills onto the boat and into the surrounding water. They return to their car and drive away, whistling."

The only differences Harland saw between the man in the comics and himself were that Harland drove a pickup, and he carried his spare money in a single trouser pocket in the form of nickels, dimes and quarters. If you own a boat, nothing's cheap.

～

THE DENOUEMENT of Harland's midlife fantasy came in his ninth month of boat ownership.

It was a beautiful spring day. He and the boys started late and were in a hurry to get to a spot that had been productive in the past. Having launched the boat and parked the truck and trailer, Harland eased from the ramp, then rammed the throttle forward. The Evinrude gave a thunderous roar as it strained to meet the demands placed upon it. The boat accelerated, pushing the boys deep into their seats in the stern, and Harland hard against the back of the captain's chair.

Two events occurred almost simultaneously. First, the half-dozen screws at the base of the pedestal supporting Harland's chair lost their grip in the plywood deck. The chair tipped backward, almost dumping Harland onto his back. His grip on the wheel was all that kept him and his seat from landing flat on the deck.

This was followed almost immediately by what proved to be the infamous "Last Straw," a loud clang and sudden silence as the aged motor expelled a rod. The boat came to rest after coasting about thirty yards parallel to the shore. Harland tossed the anchor line to a sympathetic onlooker on land so the Pee Sea could be pulled back to the ramp.

An inspection revealed that the wood of the entire deck was rotted to varying degrees throughout, a process that must have been underway for, perhaps, several years. Most likely Swindler had known this when he sold the Pee Sea to Harland. In the cabin, the rot under the captain's chair may have been intentionally hidden by the carpeting. Despite his protestations, Swindler apparently lived up to his name. "As is" means "as is."

The motor and deck were beyond repair, at least for Harland's limited resources. Mamie's boat was sold for scrap. Besides some good and bad memories, its legacy was just enough cash for a delicious, inexpensive-by-comparison, fish dinner for the family ... at a multi-star restaurant. Maintaining her silence on the subject, Mamie resisted reminding Harland of her warning about the expense of boat ownership. What could she say? He still had his shirt.

After the meal, Harland walked between his sons on their way to the truck, He draped an arm over the shoulders of each boy and said, "When you're my age, remember what the loss of the Pee Sea taught us:

"You're born, you buy a boat, then they dies."

22

THE THING ABOUT LYING

WENDY MATTHEWS

Evan Corless thought he had an excellent memory. And he probably did, but not good enough to remember all the variations of his lie that he told to different people. This made lying very complicated for him. The thing about lying is that you must have a very good memory because you probably lied about the same thing to others. Maybe embellished a little more with some. Pretty soon, you can't remember which version you said to who. But let's give Evan the benefit of the doubt and say he lied the same to everyone. His lie was plausible. No one thought him to be an outrageous liar. He studied the subject of his lie so thoroughly that he sounded like he was telling the truth. Let's face it, when confronted with an extraordinary experience someone shares, you don't say to yourself 'He's lying.' No, you say the usual things like 'Wow,' or 'Really?' Evan counted on this. It showed that people were impressed by his lie and therefore, in his mind, with him. Only they didn't know he had done no such thing.

It was an inferiority complex that started back when he was a child. The first born in his family, Evan enjoyed all the attention from his parents, grandparents, aunts and uncles. Being first is a wonderful thing until someone else comes along to be second. Now, the attention is diverted away. For Evan, this meant finding creative ways to get the attention back to him.

When he was six years of age, his baby sister, Yvette, was born. He allowed time for all the newness of this crying creature to settle down. Being in the spotlight is where he wanted to be, but baby Yvette now commanded that position. Evan made sure whenever someone tried to take a picture of this new arrival, that he too was in the picture. But enough was enough.

"Who wants to go outside to play catch with me?" he asked the latest round of visitors. The adults just stared at the baby. There were no takers.

"Who wants to see how high I can bounce on my pogo stick?" he then asked the group. Again, no takers. So, he went outside and pretended to fall from the porch where he wailed in pretend pain, cradling his arm. Hearing his cries, his dad raced down the steps to pick up poor Evan. After examining the arm though, he pronounced it was just fine, then walked back to the house.

"Play catch with me, Dad."

"Maybe later son."

Once Evan came back inside, he could smell clove-scented ham, baked beans and other tasty aromas that drifted through the house. His aunts and a few of the neighbors had brought food. Evan ate some of this meal his grandmother prepared for him, but he didn't want the rest of it. His stomach and brain were computing what it meant to lose his standing as the number one child in the family. The taste of that adjustment didn't sit well with him.

Over the course of ten years, his mother came home three more times with another bundle wrapped in a pastel-colored blanket. Two blues, and a pink. Each arrival pushed him farther away from the spotlight. Evan was sixteen now. His family lived in Livonia, a suburb of Detroit. All the houses on his block looked the same. Built for returning veterans of World War II. Brick houses with a small front porch three bedrooms, one bathroom and a basement. The addition of all his siblings made for a very crowded house. It was after the last baby brother was brought home that Evan was given the basement as his bedroom. He liked not having to share a room with anyone except his dog. He smiled at the thought of having all this space to himself.

The basement was where Evan and his pals hung out together. They had all become NASCAR race fans and watched the races on the small screen television in Evan's room. Evan told his friends about his favorite part of the race. He loved watching as the driver wriggled out the window of his car and was showered with abruptly opened bottles of champagne. Lots of pretty girls stood around clapping and cheering the winner. You could practically see little hearts dancing around their heads as they applauded. Evan wanted that type of adoration too.

When he watched a race, he memorized details like the lap times, the sponsors, and the names of the drivers. Cale Yarborough was his favorite. Evan checked out a book in the library that described what racers went through when the G-forces slammed their bodies against the doors as they careened around a course. He also learned about a heel-toe foot pedal technique. This allowed a racer to angle his foot over both pedals. He re-checked out that book many times, practically memorizing the entire thing. His dad thought his son's interest in racecar driving was a passing thing, but it wasn't. It became Evan's desired persona.

On a hot and steamy August day in 1969, Evan begged to borrow his dad's car and he and his buddies jumped in. They all chipped in for gas to go to the Michigan International Speedway. This would be the first time the boys would be able to see a race in person. Cale Yarborough would be driving in this race. The thought of seeing him race sent a small but thrilling tingle from Evan's neck to the top of his head. This was going to be amazing, he thought. He was going to listen to the sound of Cale's car, hoping to detect the heel-toe foot pedal techniques the book described.

To the delight of the boys, Cale won that race, with the lead changing thirty-five times. On the drive home, each of them recounted their favorite portion of the race. Evan tried to practice what he thought was the heel-toe technique, although it wasn't as easy as the book described. Still, it made him feel like he was practicing like a real racecar driver.

The year Evan was a junior in high school, his father's company relocated the family. They moved to Stockton, California, where Evan knew absolutely nobody. His last year in high school and he had none of his friends with him from Livonia. Instead, he graduated quietly from Lincoln High. His parents, brothers and sisters were there, of course, but he felt deflated. It would have meant a lot for his buddies to be with him. The diploma in his hand seemed hardly worth holding. He wanted more but wasn't sure what it was or how to get it.

It was the next year when Evan began practicing his alter ego. There were a few disingenuous stabs at working, first at an industrial laundry, then selling subscriptions door-to-door for encyclopedias. He talked to his co-workers about his racecar driving background. No one he met knew a thing about racing, although his new friend Henry knew a little about NASCAR. Evan tried on the persona of a former racecar driver and enjoyed the way people were amazed at his stories. Eyes wide open, shaking their heads in disbelief. He even felt emboldened enough to embellish his lies with a few more details.

His latest job was as a local gas station attendant. Still, he was adrift. A girl who graduated with him drove into the station for a fill-up. Her name was Angie, and she was driving a butter-colored Mustang. Angie flirted with him a bit then invited him to a party that night. Evan smiled and accepted the invitation.

At the party, Angie introduced him to two other girls, Stella and Marcie. They had also graduated that year, but from another school across town. He was glad to get to know some more people. Things were looking up. He decided to try on his new persona as a race car driver with these girls. He had been practicing in his mind for months. Something told him now would be a good time to try it out. These girls would never question his story.

Stella and Marcie could hardly take their eyes off him. He was good looking, with slicked-back dark hair and ocean blue eyes. Another girl, Lizzie sat down with them as Evan began trying on this new role he'd been practicing.

"When I lived in Michigan," he began, "I was a grease monkey. I loved working on cars and had a job tuning up a race car for a local guy. I was good at it, and the car owner asked me if I'd ever consider being a driver."

"A driver?" Marcie asked. "Wow, how exciting."

"Of course, I jumped at the chance. I knew everything about that car and couldn't wait to put it to the test," Evan said, enjoying their rapt attention. "My first time on the track was almost as good as the track record. So, the owner offered me a job driving on his team."

"Oh my gosh, you were so lucky," Marcie said.

"Lucky and talented," Stella said, trying to compete with Marcie.

Evan liked this persona. He slipped into it so easily and liked being the center of attention with these girls. None of them knew anything about race car driving. They were eating up his story, so he decided to keep it going.

"Were you ever in a crash?" Lizzie asked.

"Me, nah," he said. "I've always had a sixth sense about when a crash might happen, and I just stay high on the track to avoid them. That works for me."

"Did you ever win a race?" Marcie asked.

"I came in second once, that's as close as I came," he said, not sure if he could carry off a lie so big that he had actually won a race. Evan watched the girls' faces, trying to determine if his story was being believed. He decided it was and boldly said, "But I did outdo Cale Yarborough's course lap record one time."

The girls all perked up because they had heard about Cale Yarborough.

"You did?" all three girls asked in unison.

"Yeah, and Cale was there. Afterwards, he came up to shake my hand and congratulate me. Told me I was a natural and knew he hadn't seen the last of me."

"Where are you racing now?" Stella asked.

"I'm looking for my next sponsor, it's just a matter of time," Evan said.

At this point, Evan felt his own heartbeat racing and he decided it was time to refresh his drink. "Hey, can I get you guys anything? I'm going to get another drink."

All three girls declined. They leaned into each other as Evan walked toward the beer keg on the patio. The thrill he felt at being believed was exhilarating. He liked playing this part. He also knew he probably wouldn't see these girls again, so it felt safe tossing in the Cale thing. In the backyard, he had a brief encounter with his friend Henry. Henry was repeating the lies Evan had told him about being a race car driver and some of the other kids leaned in to hear the story. Evan relished the attention but decided it was a good time to leave. He had run out of tales to tell for the night.

The next morning, Evan went to work at the gas station. He took his lunch break down the street at the A&W Root Beer. There was a concrete table open where he sat down to eat his burger. It was a surprise when Stella and Marcie walked up.

"Hey, imagine seeing you here," Stella said. "Mind if we join you?" They both held their trays with their burgers and cokes.

"Sure," Evan said, pointing to the bench for them to sit down.

"We loved hearing about your racing stories last night," Marcie said.

Evan nodded and smiled. He decided to continue the lie by telling them about the time when he drove race cars at the Michigan International Speedway. It was in 1969 at the Wolverine 4-hour Trans Am Race. In reality, that was a race he had only watched on television. Once again, he had their rapt attention. As he began his story, another girl brought her tray over to sit with Stella and Marcie

"Evan, this is Brenda," Marcie said, "she just moved into our neighborhood a couple weeks ago.

"Hi," Brenda said to Evan. To her friends she said. "Sorry I took so long. They messed up my order and had to start over."

"This is the guy we were telling you about at the party last night," Stella said to Brenda. "The one who is a race car driver."

"You drive, huh?" Brenda asked. "What kind of car do you drive?"

Evan wasn't quite prepared for a girl to ask such a question. How would she know what kind of race cars there were?

"The last one I drove was the usual Trans-Am model, but my crew worked hard to trick it out, and we were able to win that day," Evan said, making up details as he went along. Their attention was intoxicating.

"Tell us more," Brenda said, biting into her burger and reaching for some french fries.

It was the adrenaline rush he liked about lying. None of these girls were going to question his story. Brenda had sort of caught him off guard. The lie further blossomed in his mouth as he exaggerated the telling of a near fatal crash that he was able to avoid due to his driving skills.

"Knowing how to drive with the heel-toe position so I could accelerate, or brake as needed, is what saved my life," he said, looking to see who was the most impressed with this comment.

"Oh my God," both Stella and Marcie said, practically in unison. Then they looked at each other with odd expressions on their faces.

"When was this you drove?" Brenda asked looking agitated.

"1969, just over a year ago," Evan said confidently.

"That was the year Brian Bocchio died in a car crash at the Michigan Speedway, right? Maybe the one you narrowly avoided?" she asked.

Evan didn't know who Bocchio was and wondered if she just threw that out there. His cheeks flushed red. He desperately searched for a way out of this line of questioning and began gathering up his burger wrapper and napkin.

"Did you know Brian?" he asked Brenda.

"He was my step-brother. Probably about your same age, maybe a little older," she said.

Evan felt trapped. He couldn't believe his dumb luck. It was only the third time he tried to impress someone about being a race car driver and he had to pick someone who had a brother who died in the race he said he had won.

Stella and Marcie both looked shocked. They immediately hugged Brenda to show how sorry they were to hear this story. "That's so sad," they said to her.

After a pause, Marcie said to Evan, "I thought you said last night that you hadn't actually won a race."

Now, all eyes were on Evan. He couldn't say he'd forgotten a race that he won just a year ago. Not only that, but he would surely remember a race where someone was killed. He was flummoxed, not knowing what to say. A crash would certainly leave a huge impression on you. Especially if you had been to the one to avoid a crash that Brenda's brother had not.

"It's, a,..." he stammered, "bringing back a memory I thought I had put away," he recovered, scrambling to find a way out of this mess. "That was your brother?" he asked Brenda, swallowing hard.

"Yes, Brian loved racing," Brenda said. "So, do you still race?"

"No, no, I do not. That was enough of a close call that I decided not to tempt fate. I talked it over with my sponsor and he agreed. I didn't get a new ride with his crew." The lies came so easily to him. He was feeling a possible opening for how to get out of this conversation. "In fact," he said, "just talking about it gives me the shivers."

Stella looked at him with her head cocked slightly. "But you're the one who brought up the subject of being a race car driver."

"Big mistake on my part," he said. "I need to get back to work. Sorry this conversation brought up such sad memories for some of us." He stood up and waved goodbye to the girls.

"I don't understand how you could be in a race where someone was killed, and not remember it or the driver," Brenda pressed on, not letting him go.

"I told you...I quit racing because of it," he said defensively. "I've gotta go, see ya."

After he was gone, Stella asked Marcie "What do you think that was all about?"

"Huh," Marcie said, "and before Brenda sat down, he said he was looking for a new sponsor," Marcie reminded her.

"Ladies," Brenda said, "I think what we have here is just another guy trying to shine us on with a fake story, to impress us." She shook her head and smiled. "I don't even have a brother, but I did have a cousin who used to work on a crew at that raceway in Michigan. Nobody died in that race. If this guy really did race there, he'd know that. I just thought I'd toss that out there to see what he would say. Sometimes you need to catch these guys in their lies before they do further damage."

Stella and Marcie just looked at each other, shaking their heads.

"Anyone want some of my fries?" Brenda asked smiling.

23

THE LUNCH LADY

SHUJEN WALKER

The oven beeped for the third time.

"Mom," Emma called out from the living room. "The cake...the cake!"

"I know. I know," I said, stretching the last bit of wrapping over the back of the gift to cover it completely. The tape finally stuck, and I leaned back in the chair, taking in my masterpiece—lopsided and bunched up on the sides, but wrapped well enough to hide the train set from my birthday boy's eyes.

I entered the kitchen and slipped on my oven mitts. The timer beeped for the fourth time as I pulled out the chocolate cake and placed it on the counter. My eyes took in the moist center, then wandered to the edges, cracked and charred. An aroma of cocoa butter and burnt crust overwhelmed the potpourri bag hanging by the window. I stepped back, mumbling expletives on why I didn't listen to my husband and order a store-bought cake. I checked the clock hanging on the wall, thinking I might have time to run to the market for a replacement. However, the party was less than an hour away, so I sucked it up and Googled "How to save a burnt cake."

After watching a YouTube video, I followed the instructions by trimming away the burnt sections, cutting out a number six, and slathering the entire thing with fluffy chocolate frosting. As I finished the decorations, Emma strolled into the kitchen, eyeballing the cake but sniffing the air.

"You burned it."

"I didn't," I said.

"Let me see." She swiped at the frosting and licked her finger. "Well..." she said, smacking her lips. "Doesn't taste burnt."

She tried for another sample, but I waved the spatula at her. "I just made it perfect."

"Okay, okay." She smiled. "Wanted to tell you I hung the balloons up on the patio, placed the plates and napkins on the table, and now I'm going to put the party bags together. How many should I make?"

"Well..." I put the spatula down. "Let me think. There's Ivan and his mom, me, you, Dad, and Ken. So six."

"What? That's all that's coming to the party?"

"Some people couldn't make it."

"That's boring." Emma frowned. "We should have invited my friends, Eva and Brandy and Jordan. I can call them now."

"No. This party is for Ken. His special day with his friends."

"One friend, you mean."

"It doesn't matter. One friend is plenty. He'll be happy. And when it's your birthday, you can invite whoever you want."

"Whatever." Emma rolled her eyes and stormed out.

I leaned against the kitchen counter, contemplating what Emma said and convinced myself I'd made the right decision. Ken's day. Ken's friend. Even if it were only one person. Ken didn't need a bunch of screaming older kids taking over his party, like last year.

I finished up in the kitchen and placed the cake on the table with the Spiderman party horns, lollipops, and bubbles. With everything set, I went upstairs to change into my sundress. As I brushed my hair, the phone rang. It was Ivan's mom, Jessica.

My eyebrows lifted and face beamed at the thought of talking to another mom with a kid on the autism spectrum. We had met a few weeks ago at the school awards ceremony when Ken and Ivan both got *Most Improved* certificates.

"Hi," I said. "How's it going? Are you almost here? You can park in the driveway since you're the only ones coming."

There was a long pause on the other end of the phone, followed by an exhale. "I'm sorry, but we can't make it to Ken's party. Ivan woke up with a cough, and he..."

Jessica's words flowed into my ears like a steady stream of howls from an agonizing breakup song. They entered my body and jumbled my insides, preventing my lips from forming words. I fought hard and managed a "you're not coming?" whimper.

"Again, I'm sorry. Ivan was looking forward to it, and I know how kids are when their friends don't..."

Every syllable she uttered dropkicked my heart like a game of hacky sack.

"We got Ken a gift." She continued. "My husband will drop it off later, or I can give it to him at school. Again, I'm sorry."

She hung up before I could respond. Or maybe I responded before she hung up. Or maybe I stood there in the stale air, swallowing the letdown like every other blow to our lives since my son's autism diagnosis four years ago. The disorientation pounded in my head, and I couldn't tune out the constant reminders.

He's different. He's in the special needs class. He's not that social. He doesn't have any friends.

My dream of finally chatting with another mom about the ups and downs of raising a child with disabilities faded like the numerous faces of my son's rotating therapy squad. I slumped forward, arms resting on the counter, body sagging like an imaginary sack dangling from my neck, collecting tears.

The bedroom door burst open with Emma rushing in and screeching about Ken raiding the party bags and messing up her perfect decorations. "He's eating all the Reese's."

I kept a straight face until I could no longer hold in the frenzy. It poured out in a roaring laughter that made my daughter jump.

Ken has no friends coming, and she's worried about candy.

My laughter grew louder until my eyes found Emma's confused expression. I didn't have the guts to tell her she was officially the only other kid at Ken's party or that her decorations would go unseen by anyone outside the family. So, I faked a smile. "It's fine. It's his birthday. He can eat whatever he wants. All the candy in the world."

Her mouth dropped open. "Are you okay, Mom?"

"Yes. I'll be down in a minute." I motioned for her to go out the door.

When she left, I gathered myself together and ambled down the stairs, passing by my son's birthday flyer hanging on the wall, the one I made for him to hand out to his classmates. Thirty flyers, I recalled. Thirty flyers I'd handed out, and not one friend coming to celebrate his birthday.

My hands shook as I glared at the calendar next to the flyer, the one with all happy faces marking the days till Ken's birthday. I grabbed the Sharpie, ready to scribble a frown face on his special day, when Ken rushed up yelling my name and hugging me. He buried his chocolate-covered face into my dress.

I chuckled. "How's the birthday boy?"

Ken pointed to the front door and said, "Go, movies."

I let out a deep sigh. Movies. Movies. Movies. That's all he talked about since encountering the Minions trailer on TV. "It's your birthday today." I reminded him for the ten millionth time.

"Movies."

Ken only knew a few words, and *movies* was one of them, so I couldn't help but feel grateful. "Okay. Where's Daddy?"

Ken pulled me onto the patio, where my husband and daughter danced to the "Baby Shark" song. Ken joined in, bobbing his head and waving his arms.

"Honey, can I speak to you?" I motioned my husband away from the kids and into the living room, where I vented my frustration for all the cancellations and for not inviting our extended family and Emma's friends. He managed an *oh* before I continued. "Let's go to the movies. That's what Ken wants anyway."

As we went onto the patio to tell the kids, the doorbell rang. We looked at each other.

"I wonder who that could be?" I rushed over to the door and opened it.

Standing on the front porch was a woman, a man, and three kids I didn't recognize.

"Hi," the woman said. "We're here for Ken's party. Are you his mom?"

My eyes widened, and I stood there, speechless, trying to comprehend, *people for the party?*

"I'm Janet. This is my husband and my kids." She held out her hand to shake mine. "Sorry, we're late. We couldn't find the place, but we're here now. Where's the birthday boy?" She glanced past my shoulder into the house, while her kids shuffled about, appearing eager to get in.

I took in their smiles with a look of bewilderment until I realized this was the lunch lady at Ken's school. She'd texted me a few days ago, asking about Ken's party. I remembered thinking, *autistic kids only*, as if it were some special club her kids couldn't attend. However, I couldn't remember my response, or if I even responded at all. Before I could build up enough courage to motion her in, Ken appeared in the doorway, eyes wide open and yelling, "Friends!"

He pulled the kids inside, tossed them chocolate bars, then dragged them into the backyard to jump with him in the bounce house. Afterward, they had water balloon fights, played basketball and hide-and-seek. Ken whacked the piñata, and when they sang Happy Birthday to him, his eyes lit up, and I knew that he knew it was his birthday.

"Thanks for inviting us," the lunch lady said. "My kids had been looking forward to it all week. Ken is great."

She talked about all the wonderful things he'd do in the lunchroom, like hug her and say *please* and *thank you* whenever she handed him a food tray. Every compliment she paid my son chipped away at the deserted feelings that had been festering within me.

Nighttime came, and the party ended. Ken didn't want to let his new friends go. I didn't want to let the lunch lady go. She might not have a kid on the spectrum, but she showed up to support Ken, even staying until he fell asleep.

I finished cleaning up, then headed to bed. On the way, I stopped at the calendar. Marker in hand, I drew a smiley face on Ken's birthdate. His first *real* birthday party, and the beginning of many on this journey through his autism diagnosis.

Thank you, lunch lady. Thank you for not only making his day, but for showing me he's no different than any other kid.

24

STRAYS

SUSAN CARTER

Holding a cup of steaming coffee in one hand, Sam pushed open the kitchen door with the other and stepped onto the porch. It was his second cup, but he was anxious to get started so brought it outside with him. His father drove the truck to his job at the salt mine, so Sam had the place to himself. He walked down the back steps followed closely by Stray.

The scruffy dog had shown up at the farm last year, dirty and shivering from the cold. His gray fur was matted and covered with burrs, his ribs starting to poke through his sides. Sam cleaned him up, fed him, and gave him the name Stray. From then on Stray was devoted to Sam and never more than a few feet away from his new owner. Sam had hoped that he could train Stray as a hunting dog, but it looked like Stray was not a birder and didn't show much interest in running through the woods after rabbits. He did enjoy the occasional romp chasing their goat, Maud, around her pen. That usually ended up with Stray splashing through puddles and getting exiled from the house for a while. Sam did not want to share his space with an animal that smelled like...well, like wet dog.

Sam and Stray walked side by side down to the shed. At the shed, Sam put his cup on the ground so he could use both hands to remove the heavy lock on the shed door. "Don't you dare touch that," he warned Stray. Stray sat on the ground waiting patiently. Sam picked up his coffee cup and pulled the door open. The hinges squeaked loudly in protest. *Those hinges could use some grease*, he thought. *I'll get to that later.* It was dark inside the shed. A few streaks of light were slipping through the cracks in the east wall boards, but there was not enough light to begin working even with the door open.

Sam stepped carefully across the wooden floor, watching for hazards. His father was the worst for leaving stuff lying around everywhere in the shed. Sam was wearing his heavy boots so he knew nails would not be a problem, but he didn't want to risk another bruise to his shin like the one he got from stepping on the long-handled shovel. He made his way over to the kerosene lamp on the back shelf, struck a match, lifted the glass globe, and lit the wick. The lamp flickered to life and then threw out a harsh yellow light that lit up the inside of the shed. Sam preferred working in natural light, but the sun would not be all the way up for a while longer.

Stray followed Sam into the shed, began his slow walk in a tight circle to make his bed, and then plopped down to sleep while Sam worked. Sam loved the solitude in the shed and the quiet of the early morning. A slight breeze picked up outside, and Sam could hear the low hum from the tops of the tall popular trees as the wind passed through them. He heard a wagon coming down the road, hooves clomping on the packed dirt and the driver calling, "Git up there now." The only other sounds were the hiss of the kerosene lamp and Stray's soft breathing. Sam didn't have any deliveries that day, and Lucy was not coming by, so he had all day to work in the shed before tending to the animals and garden. He tugged on the suspenders that looped over his blue denim work shirt to hike up his pants. After standing at the workbench and surveying the items on the table, he walked around the shed and picked up the equipment he would need for today's project—a six-foot length of copper tubing and two black rubber stoppers.

Sam enjoyed working with his hands and looked forward to making the coil. He loved the smooth, slick feel of the copper tube when he ran his hands over it. He pulled on his leather work gloves, inserted one end of the copper tube into the bench vise and tightened it securely in place. He gripped the tube tightly with both hands and slowly leaned forward using his weight to coax the copper tube into the first loop. He adjusted his grip so he could pull the tube toward himself at the correct angle to complete the loop. Then he started the next loop. He released the tube from the bench vise and repositioned the tube for each loop. The angle and distance between loops were important. The loops could not be spaced too closely together or too far apart. Copper tubing did not tolerate constant re-bending so getting the spacing right the first time was a priority.

Sam carefully repeated this process until half of the tube was bent into a coil, finally stopping to give his arms a rest. He took off his gloves, walked over to where Stray had made his bed, bent down and scratched the eager dog behind his ears. Stray had one pointed ear that stood up straight and one ear that flopped over. When he looked at Sam with his head cocked to one side, it looked like he was concentrating very hard on whatever Sam was saying to him. He was certain that if Stray had words, they could have some great conversations.

Stray turned his head to lick Sam's hand affectionately. For Sam, the feeling was mutual. Sam never had a dog growing up. He always wanted one, but it was dangerous to keep a pet who might end up getting a swift kick in the ribs when Sam's dad was on a bender. It was better not to get attached to a dog. Now that Sam was older, he was taller and heavier than his dad, and the dog's safety was not an issue. Sam was sure his father would not bother his dog. "There you go, Stray," Sam said softly as he scratched the dog's head. "You're a good dog. Aren't you glad you came to live with us?" Stray smiled up at him. Or, at least, that's what it looked like to Sam, who was convinced that Stray smiled at him all the time.

The sun was coming up now and penetrating the shed with sufficient light, so Sam turned off the lamp and returned to the workbench to continue bending the copper tube. His mind drifted to thoughts of Lucy. He found himself thinking about her all the time. He had never met a girl like Lucy. She was down-to-earth, so happy, so full of adventure, so willing to look for fun.

At 18 years old, Sam had his share of past girlfriends. He knew girls were attracted to him, and it was never hard to pick up one. But most of the girls he met seemed superficial to him. They flirted with him and wanted his attention, but they were only interested in him until they figured out that he didn't have a lot of money to spend on them. Why girls expected you to buy them expensive presents was lost on him. Some girls were clingy or pushy or bossy or, worst of all, only wanted a way to escape from a rotten homelife. Sam was not willing to be anyone's ticket to "get out of Dodge" as he liked to say.

But Lucy was different. She was cute, of course, but that wasn't why Sam was so smitten with her. She laughed at his jokes. She listened carefully to him when he talked. She asked him questions about his own interests without judgment. She told him how great his ideas were, and she never criticized or belittled him. Being around Lucy made him feel strong, capable, maybe even invincible. He loved that about her, how she made him feel. It filled his heart with joy when he thought about her.

Sam made two coils that morning, fed the chickens, and collected fifteen eggs. He knew his father would be late if he came home at all. It was payday for his dad, and Sam never knew where he might take off to when he got some money in his pocket. He hoped his father would be gone for a few days, which was usually long enough for him to dry out. It wasn't unusual for his father to show up at the house with dried blood on his shirt or with a black eye. He never explained anything to Sam, and Sam never asked. Back in the kitchen Sam scraped the remains from his breakfast of eggs and fried potatoes into Stray's dish, washed the dishes and sat down at the kitchen table with another cup of coffee.

He reached into his shirt pocket with two fingers and removed an envelope folded into thirds. The envelope was smudged and worn at the seams of the folds. He took a paper from the envelope and placed it on the table smoothing it flat with the butt of his hand. Although he knew the contents of the letter by heart, he reread each word scrawled in that recognizable, uneven, and loopy script.

Sam

I'm sorry about this, I really am. I just can't do this no more. Taking Luke and Louisa with me. You are big enough to make it on your own. Them not. Were going away with Fred Duckett. Member his wife died last spring? Hes a good man and needs help with those three youngins. Don't try to find us or tell your dad. It could be bad. I love you and always will. Mom

Sam knew there wasn't anything he could have done to stop her. He just didn't understand why she didn't want him to go with them. His mind drifted back to when he was just a kid before things got bad. They didn't have much money and moved a lot, but the fights were mostly just the yelling back then. He thought about when his mom would ruffle his hair with her coarse, gnarled hand when he walked past her. He wanted desperately to conjure up what his mom smelled like when she hugged him. In his mind she smelled sweet and clean, not at all like she looked. She always looked tired, worn out. *What did she smell like?* Sam wondered. *Why can't I remember?*

The kitchen was starting to feel cramped, like the walls were closing in on him. He folded the letter, slipped it back into the envelope, and returned it to his shirt pocket. He always carried the letter with him. He could not come up with a good hiding place in the house and did not want to risk his father finding it. Sam knew he had to get out. He wanted to get away from this place. That's why he was working on a plan. A real plan. A plan that would get him enough money to go someplace else and have a good life. A plan that included Lucy.

SECTION TWO - ESSAYS

25

A COMPARISON OF MY EXPERIENCE WITH KÜBLER-ROSS'S MODEL OF GRIEF

PENNY PAUGH

Swiss-American psychiatrist Elisabeth Kübler-Ross created a model originally based on her observations of terminally ill patients as they faced imminent death. The model has been adopted by mental health clinicians and is regarded an authority on grief. Because I've outlived my parents, a stepson (who I raised since the age of nine), three dogs, and multiple cats, I discuss my experiences as the basis for discussion of Kübler-Ross's findings.

I suggest the standard model receive some adjustments: add a few stages and alter descriptions of three phases to better describe the grief experience. Additionally, I propose that a viable model of mourning not just label stages but include ways that promote the healing process.

My Personal Experiences

From the Swiss psychiatrist's list of stages I have experienced three: denial, bargaining, and acceptance. Those I haven't undergone include clinical depression and anger. However, I know people who have experienced those two stages. Therefore, for all five stages, I can attest to the model's accuracy as defined by Kübler-Ross.

People I Have Lost

Grief can be an all-consuming state of mind. For me a loss requires that I make a physical adjustment as much as an emotional one. I have to acclimate to not seeing, hearing, or touching that person or animal. With my parents' deaths, I swam in intense feelings. To stay afloat, I comforted myself, and if anyone expressed any interest, I talked about my loss. On each occasion, a black and white image of the parent's face flashed across my mind. In the next moment, panic rippled through me. I'd be living without them for the rest of my life. Feeling helpless without their protection and support, I envisioned being crushed over and over, akin to experiencing recurrent rainstorms of boulders. I curled up inside myself and cried to find relief from the austere picture I made of my future. I will call this the **Bleak-Future** stage. All my grief experiences have initially featured this stage.

When I was 32, death paid my father a visit as he cross-country skied with his girlfriend. They were miles from help when he had a heart attack. Later, she told me he was very frightened in his last moments as he lay in her arms on a mountain covered with thick snow. At the time, I believed in an afterlife, but no matter how deep my faith in something, I'm never above questioning my belief when I lack concrete proof. I could easily imagine falling into a dark and frightening place when facing death.

Since Dad's body had been cremated and I never saw his body, it took a while to fully feel he would no longer be in my life. Physically, I was in shock (what the model calls denial). When no longer emotionally numb, I kept thinking about Dad's last moments and imagined being in his shoes. Hours from help while experiencing his third heart attack, he would know he had little chance of survival. He had stated many times that there was no such thing as a spirit or soul. Of course, his last moments had been terrifying. I wanted to comfort him, as though I could go back and erase his fears. This experience is not mentioned by Kübler-Ross. I will call what I felt **Empathy-with-the-Deceased.**

Dad had been emotionally distant and critical of me as I grew up. His death left me craving a relationship I would never and could never have. Fortunately, I had several close friends and concerned people at work who were very sweet. Because of this support, my period of mourning lasted a few short months.

Ten years after Dad's demise, minor strokes wracked Mom's brain every six weeks. Each event destroyed parts of her personality. By the fourth event, she no longer resembled the person I had known. Abandoned, I tried to negotiate with God. I begged for the return of Mom's intelligence, independence, and humor. My reaction fit the model's stage of bargaining.

Mom seemed to die in pieces. In six months, the strokes transformed her into a child I fed, bathed, and dressed. After each attack, it took time for me to adjust to her altered personality, as well as to the expansion of my caregiver duties. This I will call a **Multi-Staged Grief.** The process completely absorbed my energy and emotions. While it's not mentioned by Kübler-Ross, I have talked to others whose loved ones died in stages, like my mom, and they reported they felt as I did.

Being newlyweds, my husband and I took care of Mom at home where she wanted to die. Steve's presence and assistance during her last days helped make this possible. When she became bedridden, her friends, also elderly and facing the end of their lives, made demands. I had known these people for most of my life. None thought of me or my struggles. Most insisted I treat Mom like a queen, telling me to let her stay in bed and cater to her every demand. When I tried such an approach, the following morning, Mom lay rigid, eyes filled with terror while gazing at the ceiling. I felt certain she was staring at some image of death. I cajoled her and insisted she get up, change clothes, and come downstairs for breakfast. Her fear seemed to dissolve and her face radiated as I helped her change to day clothes and assisted her downstairs for her favorite meal of peanut butter on toast.

Of course, Mom's friends didn't believe she had been consumed with fear after I claimed to have pampered her. They all quit talking to me when they visited Mom and snubbed my invitation to her wake. These were people who had played family-like roles for me and my parents. I felt guilt for disappointing them, and their rejection added to my sense of loss. I also grew angry they dared to make demands when they never offered any assistance. Yes, I experienced anger, but not as the model defines it. The grieving person thinks, "Why me?" and "Life is not fair." They may have bouts of anger about their loss. I didn't feel sorry for myself and didn't think life was unfair. I had feelings toward specific people for how they had treated me during a trying time. At the same time, I felt guilty for not being able to comply with demands made by Mom's friends. Feeling both put me through inexplicable torture. I call this **After-Death Guilt.**

Kübler-Ross's model says the stage of acceptance happens when the grieving person emerges from their loss. I did get to the point of moving forward with life; however, I never stopped feeling Mom was irreplaceable. Forty years later, I don't yearn for her company but treasure the unconditional caring and enduring friendship she offered me during her life. I am now grateful I enjoyed close to forty years with her in my life. But I know plenty of people who look back years after a significant other died, and they have regrets, anger, guilt as well as fond memories. I will call this **Late Reflections.**

The next person I lost died last summer. Josh, my older stepson, had been a tough child to raise. He was severely learning disabled and alcoholic with a tendency to be out of touch with reality. For example, we bought him an electric bass. Without any lessons or skills, he tried to join a band. Even after the group rejected him, he would slide the bass over his shoulder and pretend for hours. I would hear him brag to friends that he was in a band. Needless to say, he didn't adapt to the real world easily.

He went through jobs and was unemployed most of the time. In his late thirties, Josh chose to be a tow truck driver and stuck with it. Being part of the first responders at accidents, he expressed pride in his choice of profession. However, the job hardly kept him afloat. Working six-day weeks, and twelve-hour days, he only earned $30,000 a year. He never could afford a car or health insurance.

At age forty-seven, Josh fell ill with several ailments and, without effort, he shed pounds. He had weighed over three hundred pounds most of his adult life. Josh loved his new thin appearance. I said I was pleased for him, though I felt certain his weight loss meant something was seriously wrong. For several months, Josh remained too weak to go in for follow-up tests. Just when he finally had the strength to schedule appointments, he had a major stroke. Within hours doctors declared him brain dead.

Early in his illness, his father, Steve, and I divided Josh's bills and exchanged our worries. Being retirees, neither of us could care for Josh if he needed prolonged treatment. Also, Steve shared something Josh kept from me—X-rays of Josh's liver and lungs showed dark spots. Josh smoked and drank, but I had no idea how much. He certainly had a worrying cough. When I received a call from the hospital, for selfish reasons, I experienced relief the stroke had not left him maimed.

He'd been a source of worry and pain all the time I had known him. For the first two weeks, I walked around in shock. His death had been sudden, and I was on the other side of the continent. When I accepted the loss, I grieved very little. Instead, I had an **Empathy-with-the-Deceased** moment— feeling thankful he would know freedom from a hard life while living in our less-than-humane American economy.

Loss of Animals

My most traumatic loss was more painful than any before or after—even the loss of my mother did not compare. My younger stepson, Dan, when nine or ten, wanted a dog. We found a yellow lab mix. I suspected Sander had some deer in his family tree. He didn't run but sprang forward as he leaped in the air. When Dan became socially active in high school, Sander became mine.

Following me everywhere, the dog was my dearest love. In his tenth year, he developed seizures. The vet drugged him to the point the poor dog walked like a drunk. However, he continued to fall over, shaking from head to toe. I asked the vet to put Sander to sleep. With the dog's demise, death took a part of me too. It was the most painful time of my life. The sorrow didn't flow through me, it surrounded and engulfed me.

By then, my twenty-year-old marriage had turned harsh. Without the dog's trust and love, I withdrew from the lack of kindness and support at home. Dan had returned angry after a tour in Iraq. Fearing being the object of his son's anger, Steve joined Dan. Becoming their target, I moved into a separate bedroom and worked long hours. To save our marriage without actually changing his behavior, Steve suggested we go to an animal rescue gathering. We met a trained Labrador. Though more independent than his predecessor, Coda dulled my sense of loss. He ran after Frisbees, adored other people, and loved long walks, but when I left the room, he didn't follow unless I called. Since home life remained unkind, in 2007 I divorced my husband, taking Coda with me. We went to doggy parks and made new friendships together.

In 2013, I moved to San Diego. For the road trip, I brought Thor—a black, white, and brown tabby. I needed an affectionate companion to help me adjust to a new city. When we got settled, I worked at home on a computer most of the time. Thor found ways to be nearby wherever I labored. During breaks, he'd stick his chin out and I'd find myself petting him.

In seven years, the sweet animal developed a stomach problem. His doctor prescribed special food. Nevertheless, on a Friday afternoon, Thor stopped eating. He spent the weekend perched on a side table and didn't respond when I petted him. On Monday, I called his doctor. We agreed it was time for a final goodbye. When I took Thor on his last trip to the clinic, the look of trust in his eyes shredded my insides. By putting him to sleep, I was betraying his trust. I experienced agonizing **After-Death Guilt.** Later, I talked to a friend who convinced me that by relieving Thor's suffering, I had done the cat a favor. The pain of my loss lessened after guilt no longer had a grip on me.

Stages to Add

In summary, I experienced several stages that could be added to Kübler-Ross's model. I am sure a broad survey of people in mourning would reveal even more. Here are what I discovered:

Bleak-Future when the loss seems so large, the one in mourning can't imagine living without that person or animal.

Empathy-with-the-Deceased is felt when the loved one who died had lived a hard life or had a harsh time before they died.

Guilt-after-Death occurs when the mourner holds him- or herself responsible for actions or inactions before their significant other passed.

Multi-Staged Grief happens when the person dying endured a slow decline before they died. Their loss is experienced incrementally by family and friends.

Late Reflections occur when the person has recovered and their loss is a distant memory, when they have thoughts and feelings about their loved-one years later.

Terminology

Of the five stages mentioned by Kübler-Ross (denial, anger, bargaining, depression, and acceptance), I criticize the terms denial, anger, and bargaining.

Denial: Alcoholics Anonymous (AA), developed in 1935, used the word *denial* long before Ms. Ross created her model in 1969. In no way does the word denial connotate shock. Using a word adopted for entirely different conditions must create confusion. The AA member shatters his/her denial by confessing to a weakness of body and character to overcome their addiction. Clinically, treating a person suffering a major loss requires an entirely different treatment than someone fighting dependence.

Kübler-Ross's definition of denial describes three distinct stages—Shock, Fantasy (or Wishful Thinking), and Break-with-Reality. Shock would cover the initial numbness when reacting to a loss. Fantasy would, for example, be when a person imagines that their lost one, though cremated or buried, will nevertheless walk in the door at their usual dinner hour. Break-with-Reality describes when the grieving person is so devastated, they are unable to recognize their loss. I would use these labels in place of denial when treating a person in mourning.

Anger: The description of this phase needs to be expanded. People in mourning can be angry at the person who has died for a wide array of reasons. The standard model states the grieving person thinks, "Why me?" and "Life is not fair" or they may have outbursts of anger without stating any specific cause. I suggest using a wider definition of anger.

Bargaining: Generally, bargaining means to cajole God into changing all sorts of life conditions. Janis Joplin's song "Mercedes Benz," where she pleads with God to buy her a Mercedes, reminds us how frivolous we can be. Kübler-Ross's definition contains negotiations the person in grief makes with themselves, people around them, or with a higher power, to lessen intense bereavement. Negotiating would be a more apt term to apply to this stage.

Recovery

I think a viable model of mourning should recommend ways

to promote the healing process. My mourning, caused by the loss of both my parents, was eased by loving support and tender care by the people around me. From that experience, I incorporated that kindness and now give it to myself. Though Dad's tendency to be hypercritical kept him alive within me, I now tend to be resilient when I experience loss. I also bounce back from moments of self-criticism. In addition, experiencing loss has helped me to see we are all temporary. I now regard the people who are close to me as precious. When younger, I pretended that I would somehow escape death's clutches. Now, I accept it is part of life.

Conclusions

Apparently, a person facing their own death has similar but not identical reactions as someone who has lost friends or family members. Kübler-Ross suspected this would be true. She suggested her model be tested with healthy persons grieving over lost loved ones. Based on my experience, I have suggested some stages that could be added to the existing model. Two phases, denial and bargaining, I propose be relabeled to more accurately fit the grief experience. One phase, anger, I recommend be redefined. Last, I think the model should include findings that promote recovery from loss.

Facing One's Own Death

Kübler-Ross studied people who were revived after death. Subjects reported consciousness after death. Some were met by family and friends, others by guardians and religious figures. She also reported that the divine light was described by many as a source of unconditional love. Her findings gave me some hope for a peaceful afterlife.

However, I can't create faith in something just from reading about it. I need some form of evidence. I believe Josh visited me soon after his demise.

My new cat would cry to be let in during her lunch and dinner hours. I am almost completely deaf. Yet, several days in a row, Josh's voice cried, "Meow." Each time, the cat stood on the other side of the door, wanting to be let in. However, when I asked Josh to stop, the meows ceased.

I am optimistic that Death will hold back for a few more years; however, when my moment comes, I hope I won't lose myself in a state of fear. Instead, I am determined to remember Josh's meow and search for the light.

26

TRAVERSING LIFE
PATRICIA DALY-LIPE

For me, "traversing life" translates as travel across the years. To express my life over time, I am using the surf as an analogy. When watching the ocean waves surge, I hear the sound of the surf as it thrusts foam over the rocks and pounds the sandy shore. Life can be like that, surging through episodes. Events and experiences can break the pattern. We can wail, whine, or whimper. Or, we can come to accept change and grow as a result.

As a child growing up in La Jolla, the ocean was my refuge. Was I escaping reality? No, I was a child enjoying nature's gift. The smell of the surf, the salty air, the rocks, the shells, the tidepools, the sand were all mine to enjoy. That love of the Pacific has never left me. The ocean is a gift. The sound, smell, and sight of the surf have, over the years, inspired me both as a writer and an artist.

History is another wonderful example as a source of inspiration. We can learn from the past and, as a result, create something new in the future. This life we lead is a voyage of discovery. It is a journey, destination unknown. This is the path

I have taken, never forgetting my childhood, but allowing that love of nature to express itself via creativity.

Remember that sense of wonder I experienced watching and listening to the sound of the surf. For me, sitting on the sand, toes in the sea, ignited my imagination. But, for you, it could be watching the sun set, or the moon rise, or the stars twinkling brightly in a vast universe above. It might be walking through the woods, listening to leaves being tossed by the wind as the birds tweet to each other. Nature in all its forms is a gift for us to appreciate and enjoy. As we feel and absorb the world around us, let imagination take root. For the artist, author, or musician, the beauty of nature reflects clarity and order. For me, it inspires, and that inspiration leads to creativity.

Traversing life events happen inside as well as outside each of us. As the years pass, our emotions, our reaction to our surroundings, and our experiences show how much we share with nature. And, recognizing how close we are to our surroundings can inspire us. This recognition and under-standing can and should be shared.

What I learned as a child, enjoying the sea and surf, has enriched my life. It has caused me to respond to that feeling, the wonder and the delight of watching and smelling and feeling the ebb and flow of the surf. These memories have manifested in writing and painting. Consider the word *recognize* which translates to *re-know*. As an example, you can *re-know* your past through the written word. And what a surprise when you to read what your memory allowed you to write. For the writer, it is an emotion that has found and translated its source. For the reader, it is a gift.

As a child, I was closer to nature. As an adult, I need to remember those feelings I had. I need to take time out from the constant strain of activities. Go outside. Watch the birds flying out of the trees. See the clouds as they form patterns and shapes. Feel the breeze. Smell the perfume of the flowers. Appreciate nature in all its forms.

To express my reactions to nature, I rely on my imagination and translate creatively. Art of any kind brings order out of chaos. It finds meaning in all aspects of life. For me, the medium is words or paint. "...now and then a man's mind is stretched by a new idea or sensation, and never shrinks back to its former dimensions." (Oliver Wendal Holmes) Hopefully, my mind will continue to stretch just as the waves will never stop pounding the shore.

This is what traversing life means to me. It is my trip through the years as I absorb, appreciate, and share the beauty and fluidity nature has to offer. That is what I wish to share.

In sum, as we traverse life, we must aspire to inspire before we expire.

A POETIC MEDITATION

On this earth, there is oneness.
A rhythmic flow, a great symphony that is life.
Trees with roots, stems, and leaves
Shells, fins, furs and wings, all living things.
Each has a purpose and to each, an end
And then...a new beginning.

Let us recapture the imagination of a child
See once more the mystery, beauty and joy of God
Playing within and behind, beyond and above.
Unite with the intimacy of commitment.
Trust takes time
But the gift is there...waiting.

27

CITY FACE
TIFFANY NOEL FROESE

G rowing up, my only true ambition was to live abroad. The Southern California beach town where I was raised felt desperately provincial, and I yearned to immerse myself in unknown people and languages. By my early twenties, I'd already had more opportunities to travel than many of my peers, and these experiences taught me how to navigate uncertainty and have confidence in my ability to get along in the world.

Cities were my favorite places, especially ones with subways. I liked the feeling of hurtling through tunnels underground with a bunch of strangers, headed to different places, but traversing life together, if just for a few minutes.

Those few minutes are microcosms of life in general. Most of the time, they are ho-hum, but every now and then something happens on the subway that is scary, or exciting, or comforting. Every now and then something happens that changes the way you move through the world.

In 2004, I was living in Vienna, a city I love for its contradictions, taking the subway, or U-Bahn as it's called there, to daily language classes. One Sunday, after I'd been there about three weeks, I set out to meet a friend at a church service. I waited on the U-Bahn platform, still rubbing sleep out of my eyes. Only one other person waited with me, a stocky, decently dressed man who I didn't give much mind to.

The wind kicked up and the rails of the track began to hum, announcing the approach of our train. I ambled forward as the train slowed to a stop and opened its doors. The car was empty inside except for a young man leaning against the window in slumber, hugging his backpack to his chest. Something in the tender angle of his forehead against the glass gave me the impression that his day was ending just as mine was beginning. I smiled at this thought as I took a seat on the other side of the car. The man from the platform had entered the same car from the opposite direction and we briefly made eye contact. Before I knew it, he appeared in the seat directly facing me. He leaned close to say something, his knees just inches from mine.

His proximity and the way he leaned in to talk softly was not normal U-Bahn behavior. Like every other subway system in every other metropolis in the world, people generally don't talk to each other unless it's to say "excuse me" as they pass through crowded cars. They sit in their seats and stare straight ahead. If you make eye contact with someone, they look blankly through you. This had driven me crazy the previous year when I'd spent three weeks in Vienna with a group from my college. I thought that if you accidentally made eye contact with someone, you could give some acknowledgement that you recognized them as humans. But on that trip, I'd had to come to terms with the distance between my expectations of Vienna and the reality of it.

I first laid eyes on the city when I was fifteen, during a layover on the way to Turkey and Greece. It was my first time abroad and I had spent my whole young life dreaming of going to Europe. Our layover in Vienna was brief, but long enough for a tour of the city center where we saw *Stephansdom*, the cathedral at the heart of the first district, and the *Staatsoper*, the state opera house.

As we gathered in front of the *Staatsoper* on a late summer evening, city lights twinkled in the twilight and opera goers, whose show had just finished, gathered in the square in front of the renaissance revival building. They were all impeccably dressed, and the men were the most beautiful my young boy-obsessed eyes had ever seen.

From that moment, Vienna lived in my imagination as a kind of gold-drenched heaven: clean, beautiful, romantic, safe. In the eight years that passed between this night and the trip to Vienna with my classmates, I had traveled many times across four continents. I knew Europe wasn't perfect. Yet that fifteen-year-old's idealized vision was hard to shake.

With my classmates, I saw parts of the city that I hadn't seen during that one-night tour. *Karlsplatz*, the park that surrounded the beautiful baroque *Karlskirche* and a major U-Bahn hub, seemed to also be a hub for homeless young people, punks, and beggars. We visited the old Jewish quarter, where synagogues had been bombed and innocent people murdered as Hitler took over Europe. We learned of the Viennese disdain for *Ausländer*, foreigners, despite hosting the headquarters of the United Nations. Despite my new perceptions of Vienna, I seldom felt unsafe as I mostly traveled in a pack with my classmates.

On this current trip, a year later, I was alone, but I still felt confident in my ability to safely navigate the city. I've always felt emboldened by the bustle of people and businesses in cities, and I prided myself on knowing how to move with purpose and blend into new places.

The daily commute to a language school in the city center from the district where I lived with a host family made me feel like I was part of the fabric of Vienna instead of a tourist. To fit in, I tried to adopt what I'd observed to be the stony silence of the natives, simultaneously ignoring people and remaining aware of my surroundings. In some ways, this was a coping mechanism, too. I barely spoke the language and understood little of what people said. The effort to understand people on the street was exhausting, so to blend in and not look like a foreigner, I ignored them.

But this tactic backfired about two weeks into my solo trip to Vienna, when a young, sloppily dressed guy had approached me on the crowded platform at *Karlsplatz* station. Based on the way he was dressed and the way other people on the platform shook their heads at him, I assumed he was begging for change. As he neared, I looked away, hoping to make myself less of a target, but he approached me anyway. All I could think to say in response him was "*Nein,*" no. He kept talking and I kept saying no. After a few moments he became enraged. He shouted a string of words I couldn't make out until he said one word, "*Ausländer.*" He finished his tirade and walked away as my train arrived. But that word haunted me. Could I have avoided escalating the situation if I'd made more of an effort to understand him?

Now, on my way to church with this man's knees a breath away from mine, I thought back to my previous experience. Ignoring this man wasn't an option. Other than the sleeping boy, I was essentially alone on the train with him, and didn't want to risk his anger. My confidence in my language skills had greatly improved after another week of German classes, so I leaned in to hear what he was saying over the creaks and moans of the subway car as it hurtled through the dark tunnels of the underground system.

"*Ich glaube er arbeitet spät.*" I think he works late, the man said, referring to the guy sleeping across the way. I agreed and he immediately noticed my accent and asked where I was from. He was from Egypt, and we communicated in the simple sentences of second language learners. I liked that I could understand his simple German and that I was able to respond, but I was still uncomfortable with how closely he leaned into me and the way his palms seemed to hover above my knees. His questions got more personal: Where did I live? Did I have a boyfriend? I knew that how I responded could determine how aggressively this man pursued me.

"Yes, I have a boyfriend," I said, as an image of my friend Johannes popped into my head. Johannes was living in Norway, and we communicated regularly while I lived in Vienna.

"Here in Vienna?" the man asked.

"In Norway," I responded without thinking. I kicked myself for not saying that Johannes lived in Vienna with me. I wasn't used to lying.

The man then asked me to dinner at his place, and I saw where this had been going all along. I began to panic and looked up to see where we had stopped. Good, only one more stop until I changed trains.

"No, thank you," I said curtly. He continued to try to persuade me by mentioning wine and music.

"I have a boyfriend," I said.

"But he's in Norway." He rested his hands on my thighs.

I jerked my legs to the side and threw my hands up, palms facing him. "*Entschuldigung*," I said firmly. "*Das ist nicht ok.*" That is not ok.

He withdrew his hands and began apologizing but did not back off. Fear lurched from the pit of my stomach to lick my racing heart. My thighs felt like someone had taken a branding iron to them where his hands had been. I was afraid to stand up and move, thinking it would betray too much of my fear. I looked him in the eyes and saw he had no intention of backing off. This was more unnerving than the fact that he'd had the audacity to put his hands on me.

I was desperate for an escape. I looked to the door and saw that we were pulling into the station. My connecting train was stopped across the platform, and hope of salvation sprang me towards the door. But the timing of Vienna's underground transport system is cruel. Just as the doors of my train opened, the connecting train's doors closed and the train moved out of the station.

I ran out of the train, hoping that would be enough. I was wrong. He was behind me, shouting, "Wait, wait." I looked up and down the empty platform. My mind raced. People, I needed people. I ran towards the escalator to the street and took the stairs two at a time. I was hoping to find an U-Bahn security office, or at least a tobacco shop at the top of the escalator. A huge sign saying *Sicherheit*, security, came into view as I ascended. But where I was hoping to see the lights of TV monitors that signified a security office, I was met with a dark gray fiberglass wall. My hope for a tobacco shop or newsstand was also thwarted by the sudden realization that it was Sunday and the shops would be closed.

I knew the street was likely to be as empty as the station but thought I could lose my assailant there. I didn't think he had followed me up the escalator, but I exited the station quickly anyway and ran around the side of the building. I waited there, looking in every direction, taking comfort in the cars, buses, and scattered pedestrians that went by. I must have looked insane: trembling, jumping at every noise, eyes darting side to side. I didn't know how to get to church, or even to the next station, using above ground transportation, so after I knew that at least two trains had come along, I went back into the station, scanning the shadows for him.

My train came just moments after I reached the platform. I boarded quickly, still paranoid the man had managed to follow me. I kept looking all around for him. My mind replayed the scene over and over. *What could I have done differently? Did my demeanor or body language give him the idea that I was interested? It all started because I smiled at that kid sleeping. But I was smiling at the kid, not at him. Well, he did say that he was Egyptian, didn't he? Maybe Egyptian men just interpret smiling as a come on, no matter where the smile is directed. But that look in his eye. That predatory look. That wasn't "cultural;" that wasn't normal. God, I can still feel his hands on me. Thank God I got away. What if he finds me again? I mean, he did get on the train at my stop.*

The dialogue in my head continued all the way to church. By the time I sat down for the service, I was exhausted to the point of tears. My body felt stiff and cold except for heat radiating from the spots where the man had touched my thighs. For the first time in my traveling life, I wished I could go home.

Even as I wished for comfort, a voice inside me said, "Come on. Suck it up, girl. You're fine; you got away. You don't need to go home. You maneuvered your way out of it. Just get over it." My desire for comfort warred with my desire to be tough and independent.

The church service didn't calm me. I didn't find my usual solace in the familiar hymns and passages read from the pulpit. I could still feel his hands on me. I didn't tell my friend what had happened. I was afraid I might fall apart if I did, and I didn't feel like I had a right to fall apart. After all, I had gotten away.

Later, I told a family friend, who lived in France. She told me that I was too open and that I couldn't move around cities the same way I moved around my hometown. I had to wear my "city face." It wasn't exactly comforting, but it confirmed what I had already observed in the people around me and what I had been trying to practice. So, I doubled down on my city face. But I also left the apartment where I lived less often. It took days for the burning feeling on my thighs to go away.

One day, a couple of weeks after this incident, I was sitting on a crowded train, heading to the city center to attend my German class, city face intact, lost in my own thoughts. The train stopped and a guy who looked about my age entered my line of sight as he searched for a seat. I noticed his belt buckle first. A giant metal contraption that looked like an eagle, or maybe an angel, with its wings spread. Two sharp points led my eyes upward to a face that looked like one of the Greek gods had just incarnated on the train—large, wide set green eyes in a broad face and full lips a naturally reddish color. He was the first person I'd seen in Austria who reminded me of the beautiful men of my first visit to Vienna, but something about the way he carried himself looked hard. I wondered if he was one of the punks from *Karlsplatz*, but he looked too clean for that. I remembered myself and averted my eyes, staring blankly into the middle distance.

He sat in a seat facing me on the opposite side of the aisle, a few seats away. Despite my doubled-down effort at city face, my eyes slid towards him. I found him staring at me. It wasn't predatory, the way the man on the way to church had been, but there was a challenge in it. It made me mad. Didn't this guy know to keep his eyes to himself on the U-Bahn? Isn't that the respectful thing to do?

So, I stared back, unsmiling, hard; and it turned into a standoff. All the frustration and anger I felt about being a vulnerable young woman alone in Vienna was channeled into that stare. Everyone else in the train disappeared as we locked eyes. At some point, our intense staring contest struck me as absurd.

As if he'd read my mind, something in his eyes shifted and suddenly we were both smiling, silent laughter lighting up our eyes and connecting us across the crowded train. Pleasure pulsed through my body and the train felt overwarm. The sudden attraction I felt at the moment of our mutual amusement was even more intense than our standoff had been. I desperately wanted to meet him, but at the same time, I wondered what would happen when we figured out we didn't speak the same language. What then? Would we have some groping tryst in a dirty U-Bahn bathroom, using touch to communicate where words had failed us? The thought was equal parts titillating and revolting.

The dour old woman sitting across from me harrumphed as if my thoughts had skipped naughtily from my mind to hers. I glanced at her, and her eyes darted away from me, utter indignation on her face. When I looked back at the guy, he was still smiling at me.

My stop was approaching, so I got up and moved towards the exit with the other people getting off. He got up and moved towards me through the crowd. The ferocity of our connection unnerved me. While part of me wanted to see what would happen next, that spark felt more dangerous than the man who'd put his hands on my thighs. Like if I gave into this desire, I would unravel, or be spirited away from everything familiar.

So, I did the only sensible thing I could think of. I ran. I pushed my way through the crush of commuters and tourists, up several flights of escalators into the cold, damp air of *Stephansplatz*.

Even as I ran, I looked behind me, hoping he'd followed, or that some force would draw me back underground, back to him. So what, if he was some modern day Hades bent on trapping me in his world. Persephone was allowed to leave the underworld for half the year. I could live with that arrangement.

I moved slowly through the square, keeping my eyes trained on the mouth of the U-Bahn station. But he wasn't there. It was almost as if I'd dreamed the whole thing. I decided I was ridiculous, hormone addled and delusional. And I carried on to the narrow side street that would take me to the language school. I gave one last look towards *Stephansplatz* as I opened the door and climbed the stairs to class.

I never saw him again, but I've thought about him often over the years. In many ways that encounter freed me from the residual trauma of the encounter with the man who laid his hands on me. I went out more and I didn't think about making sure I had my city face on, like an accessory: hat, gloves, city face. I didn't try to adopt the look of the locals; I wore my own face as I traversed the city both above and below ground. It felt like enough.

28

ACCEPTANCE

RUTH LEYSE WALLACE

I find, as philosophers remind us, that I do traverse life alone. With aging came the question "How am I doing?" Perhaps others may ask the same questions of themselves . . . at a different rate, in a different order, with or without support from others through personal contact, writing or teachings.

The physical part of life is impossible to ignore at any stage of life, from health during youth, to compromised health at any age, to the acceptance of our own or another's death. Acceptance of decreased physical ability during aging seems especially difficult to accept.

As we grow mentally through innocence, to knowing/accepting/judging, we learn how the world works. Through formal and informal education we learn the laws and beauty of nature (what goes up must come down) . We learn and benefit by accepting the laws of nature (fire is hot; cooking improves some foods).

In various stages we progress socially. Idealism, practicality and compromise find their inner place as we learn how the world works socially, culturally and politically. We may (or may not) accept that others are different than us. Each individual's place in the world may hinge on where, when and how acceptance develops.

Growing emotionally potentially deepens one's links with others. Knowing other's feelings and thoughts often leads to understanding, and acceptance, even in disagreement.

This fosters the ability to support friends, a spouse, and the growing of the next generation.

Named, or just sensed, spiritual growth (one's deepest, basic beliefs and principles) can grow within or be inspired from outside one's self. From the depths can come acceptance of one's own life and prospective (or imminent) death.

One common denominator through all aspects of life is acceptance: acceptance of who you are, what you can / can't do (influence), re: self, others, nature, lack of control, your own strength, knowledge, ability, privilege/rights, power.

Acceptance of the realities of life can lead to realistic and satisfying answers to the question of to what /where will you apply your unique ability and interests as well as your energy, a limited resource. In a free country answering this question is each person's ultimate choice.

A reflective question for one's Self for each Life Front:
Where am I in the process? How am I doing Traversing Life?
Starting out   Accepting!
Physically ————————————————————————
Mentally ————————————————————————
Socially ————————————————————————
Emotionally_____
Spiritually _____

SECTION THREE - MEMOIRS

29

PSALM 139

KARIN F. DONALDSON

I had been through a harrowing experience. One that shredded my insides like cabbage for slaw. The soreness lingered as I glanced out of my bedroom window, the Bible open in my lap. Our garden, radiant with blooms, hummingbirds, and mourning doves, announced that spring had suddenly arrived.

I was memorizing Psalm 139 when out of the corner of my eye a flurry of motion beyond the pane of glass drew my attention. Turning my head slightly, I witnessed a young rabbit nibbling some tender shoots. His long ears rotated slowly left, then right, then left again. His fuzzy nose twitched but otherwise, he sat quite still on the lawn, dipping only his head slightly to grab little blades of grass.

This is magical, I thought. Living on the edge of a canyon was an invitation to skunks, raccoons, possums, and squirrels. Even a silver-coated coyote occasionally paid a visit. Yet at this moment, the innocent little bunny, nibbling peacefully in the safety of my garden, soothed the deep ache in my soul.

I envied the bunny his innocence, his calm, and his lack of anxiety. As long as I can remember, fear and apprehension have been constant companions of mine. In my family, expectations were always high. *Don't embarrass yourself. Don't disgrace the family name. Do this, don't do that. Careful! Careful! Careful!*

And yet, here nibbled a peaceful little rabbit, whose life was always fraught with danger. At any moment, that silver-coated coyote could leap out of the bushes and nab the rabbit for breakfast. How can he be so calm?

My eyes returned to Psalm 139.

O Lord, you have searched me and

you know me.

You know when I sit and when I rise;

you perceive my thoughts from afar.

You discern my going out and my lying down;

you are familiar with all my ways.

Here was the question. Do I really believe this or are these just lovely words that have nothing to do with real life? Is there a Lord that knows me inside out? Who is familiar with all my ways?

Well, just for argument's sake, let's say that there is.

So, where was He when the Nazis took over Germany and held my physicist father hostage? No! Not as a Jew. As a rocket scientist who was conscripted to help develop the V2 missiles that bombed London. Where was He, when my mother outran the allied bombers with two babies—a newborn and a three-year-old in tow?

Alright, I'll give Him a reprieve. Our family made it to the United States, and my father's intellect and abilities contributed to the creation of NASA.

Before a word is on my tongue

you know it completely, O Lord.

You hem me in—behind and before;

you have laid your hand upon me.

Such knowledge is too wonderful for me,

too lofty for me to attain.

. . .

I HAVE TO ADMIT—EVER since I decided to become a writer of children's books, I've relied heavily upon You. I feel Your guidance as I write. Sometimes I almost believe that You have laid Your hand upon me. Am I being hypocritical here?

Where can I go from your Spirit?

Where can I flee from your presence?

If I go up to the heavens, you are there;

If I make my bed in the depths, you are there.

If I rise on the wings of the dawn,

if I settle on the far side of the sea,

even there your hand will guide me,

Your right hand will hold me fast.

If You are who people say You are, God—Who even *You* say you are, then the above stanza from Psalm 139 must be true. But do I believe it, at the marrow of my bones, in my heart of hearts?

If I say, "Surely the darkness will hide me

and the light become night around me,"

even the darkness will not be dark to you;

the night will shine like the day,

for darkness is as light to you.

I have to be honest. My darkness was pitch black. And my night had no light in it. Where were You? Why do You hide yourself? Mankind cries out to You, and You don't respond. We're supposed to have faith in You, but it's hard to trust in a hidden God.

For you created my inmost being;

you knit me together in my mother's womb.

I praise you because I am fearfully and wonderfully made;

your works are wonderful, I know that full well.

My frame was not hidden from you

when I was made in the secret place.

When I was woven together in the depths of the earth,

your eyes saw my unformed body.

All the days ordained for me were written in your book

before one of them came to be.

I can't deny that You must have been present at my birth, on that horrific night. When a heartless doctor chided my mother during the delivery while bombs exploded all around the building, eclipsing my mother's screams. Only a miracle could have protected the two of us at that moment.

How precious to me are your thoughts, O God!
How vast is the sum of them!
Were I to count them,
they would outnumber the grains of sand.
When I awake, I am still with you.

Search me, O God, and know my heart;
test me and know my anxious thoughts.
See if there is any offensive way in me,
and lead me in the way everlasting.

Lord, I would be dishonest if I didn't admit that You have put thoughts into my mind that I've expressed in my writings. You have put people into my life through amazing, incomprehensible circumstances——my husband, my son, and my daughter, their wonderful spouses, and my beautiful grandchildren. I am thankful.

MANY YEARS AGO, when I read Mark 1:35, it was like a prophetic word, from God, directed to me.

Very early in the morning, while it was still dark,
Jesus got up, left the house, and went off to a solitary place,
where he prayed.

I believed it to be a call for me to put God first before everything else in my day. In the beginning, this was tough. I enjoy sleeping in. So, I prayed for God to wake me if He wanted to communicate with me. Suddenly, my eyes popped open at 2:00 a.m., sometimes at

5:00 a.m. Surely, He doesn't mean THIS early. That thought was quickly replaced by another. *This is My time! I have a whole universe to run!* I sat up straight. Did I just think that, or was God speaking? It certainly didn't sound like something I would have said.

I took it to be God's voice and couldn't wait to hear from Him again. I became obedient when He woke me—regardless of the time. Over the years, the Lord and I have settled to between 7:00-7:30 every morning.

As a result, I have become less anxious. A sense of peace and acceptance has replaced my obsession with performance and perfection. The more I hand over control of my will to Him, the more productive my days become. The Lord has called me to be His purpose in the world, without explaining what that means. But it doesn't matter. In submission, I meet with Him every morning, and He runs my life.

I scan the yard for the bunny but he has eaten his fill and has moved on— replaced by black-winged, yellow-breasted orioles fluttering to and from the birdfeeder while tiny hummingbirds await their turn. A lacy spiderweb, bejeweled with glittering drops of dew, hangs suspended between a magnolia and an ornamental pear tree.

I marvel at God's creative genius. How does He come up with such extraordinary creatures? But then, He designed the most incredible creature of all. A creature with the ability to choose, judge, procreate, love, hate, and accept or reject its creator. Humanity is the pinnacle of God's creation. I often think that He's made a big mistake by giving mankind free will. What a risk!

Each of us aches to be known and loved. Psalm 139 acknowledges that God knows and loves us—way beyond our understanding. What we may *not* know, or frequently forget, is that God too, yearns to be known and loved that same way —by us!

Jeremiah 9:23-24

This is what the LORD says: "Let not the wise man boast of his wisdom
or the strong man boast of his strength
or the rich man boast of his riches,
but let him who boasts boast about this:
that he understands and knows me,
that I am the LORD, who exercises kindness,
justice and righteousness on earth,
for in these I delight,"
declares the LORD.

Are you anxious, confused, or overwhelmed? Do you feel invisible, misunderstood, and unloved? Then I suggest you give this little prayer a try and see what happens.

Dear God,

I'm not sure if You exist. But if You do, and You are who people say You are, I need help. I don't know how to get to You, so please make yourself known to me. If You exist, I want to believe in You. Amen.

30

A HOARDER OF MEMORIES

JANICE COY

I don't know I'm a hoarder until I walk to the neighborhood park with my grandson and a pink soccer ball, I've discovered deep in a garage cupboard where it was lodged for years. We hold hands as we cross the street at the familiar corner. We watch for cars, his warm fingers curled in my palm. Safe on the other side, he reaches – fingers spread - for the ball tucked under my arm. The same pink ball my daughter kicked around more than twenty-five years ago.

I hand him the ball. He hugs it to his stomach and runs to the wet grass: his feet tangling and stumbling in this almost mastered skill. He flings the ball. *Shoes Off!* He shouts. A crow flies from a nearby tree squawking. I remember when the tree was little more than a stick. Now, a mature grove of trees shades the cement picnic tables and benches. We toss our sandals beneath a bench. And then, we play on the spongy grass, nudging the ball with naked toes and bare soles.

My daughter wore baggy soccer shorts that hung past her knees, long socks, shin guards and cleats; her over-sized team shirt – blue - billowed on her skinny frame when she ran; her blond ponytail streaming behind. The team's name: blue what?

The memory is faint. I tease it out. *Blue Devils*. I smile and run with my grandson. Our foldable chairs edged the same field back then; the players kicked up the same smell of freshly mown lawn. Now, memories of joyful shouts at blocked goals, tears and slumped shoulders at missed kicks, and daydreaming amongst the dandelions flood me.

I lift my grandson and spin him around, his dimples –my daughter's - his mother's- blur against the June sky. He giggles. I set him down and we run some more, our shadows merging and separating until we stop in a low spot. Our toes squish in the mix of mud and grass.

Done! My grandson shouts. I check my watch. Ten minutes are gone. But time means nothing to him. He's not a memory hoarder - yet – not like his grandmother.

We sit on the bench where I hold him on my lap. He doesn't sit still for long. He's already squirming, churning his legs in the air. I brush off his feet. Scattered blades of grass drift to the lawn. I help him slide on his sandals. He's ready to go. Bits of mud are stuck between my toes, but I'll wash them later.

Pink ball tucked under my arm, holding hands we walk home.

31

MIRACLES
CHLOE EDGE

My life is a miracle. I have seen so many miracles I can't remember them all. I didn't see miracles in the first part of my life because I didn't have my miracle eyes yet, but it was a total miracle that I didn't get busted for stealing cars when I was a teenager.

It didn't seem like a miracle at the time; it looked like a hopeless mess, a chaotic drama full of drunken despair, but it was a miracle that I was tricked into a treatment center, stayed there, and haven't had a drink or a drug since—forty-two years and five months clean! I was a street addict and I had nothing. I started at the very bottom in 1981. March 28, to be exact.

I also didn't believe in God. Little by little, because I had no choice if I wanted to live, I have practiced faith, acted as if there were a Higher Power, and come to really believe in an energy that some people call God. During my prayer experiments, a period of critical skepticism between 1981 and 1985, I learned to pray. I could write many pages about my prayer experiments. I had to find out for sure if there really is a God, so I continued until I knew, but right now, I just want to write about this one part, right after I married my friend, Don, and we were in San

Blas on our honeymoon. I was four months pregnant, and I had married my surfer. It was okay with me that we were actually there so Don could surf Matanchén Bay. The surf was flat. We stayed in a little place right on the beach; we walked around holding hands, being in love and eating well. By the second day, however, Don's shoulders started to slump in disappointment. This was his first trip out of the country, and there was barely a ripple in the water. Nevertheless, he'd paddle out and wait.

Finally, I could take it no more, and I left the beach to go back to our room to pray. I got on my knees by the bed and waited until I got a little sensation in my third eye area, and then I began, "Dear God, You know why we're here, and You know what I'm doing. I know I'm not supposed to be praying for specific things for myself, but this is important. Will You please make some surf? Like today or tomorrow because we have to leave pretty soon. Big surf, okay? I'll tighten you up later. I love you. Amen."

That evening we walked around in the little town, ate at a nice restaurant, and went to bed. Don wakes up very early, often thinking about surf. Sometimes, real early, the water is glassy, and that is an optimum surf condition, *the morning glass*. After he prayed, he opened the door to check the surf. We could hear the thundering of crashing waves. It was double overhead, which means twice his height on the face of the wave. He was so excited! He rushed around the room—trunks, flip-flops, board, and he was gone.

I got right on my knees, shaking, praying, "Are You sure You want me to know about this kind of stuff? You know I'm a trouble causer, and I'm not sure I should know about this kind of Power. Please let me know. Send me a sign I can't miss. Amen." The waves all that day were definitely a miracle.

Earlier, in my first year clean, I had written a letter to UCSD asking if I could go to their school. I had no ninth-grade graduation papers, no high school diploma, but I sent along a transcript from Palomar College, which had about ninety units of sketchy credits, times when I had conned my dad into giving me money for school. I dropped out often, but not always. And, I had that one piece of paper. I had no idea that it was unwise to apply to UCSD with under a 3.5 grade point average. In fact, I didn't know what a grade point average was. They accepted me. A lady called me just before Christmas in 1981, and said I could go to UCSD in the spring. Now I think that the admissions lady was also a person in recovery because everyone I have ever asked didn't get a phone call from the Admissions Office. Not one person did. Only me.

This was a miracle, but I missed it. I said, "Oh, cool," and went on thinking they called everyone.

There's another miracle in here: When I was in the treatment center, they said that there was something wrong with my brain because of so many drugs. It was a condition with a long name for which I received disability checks, but it meant that my neuro-transmitters weren't connecting. The doctors said they didn't know if my brain would ever function properly. They set up the disability case for me, and the checks started coming. The miracle is that in 1985 I graduated from UCSD, magna cum laude.

I was forty-two with a baby in my belly. The miracle baby who got through a Today Sponge, the contraceptive of the day in 1984, was born weighing nine pounds, seven ounces, and was delivered with no drugs. Another miracle.

When I had been clean for nine years, I felt I needed to find the son who had been taken from me when I was sixteen. I wanted to tell him that I love him and that I had not agreed to the adoption. I wanted him to know that I had been looking for him all his life. I found him when he was twenty-nine. He had just gotten sober. He was sober and in my life for 25 years. Sadly, he is drunk now, and we are out of touch again. The miracle was that I found him.

I was talking to Don the other night about miracles. He said, "The real miracle of your life is the amount of people you've reached and touched during your recovery." I hadn't even thought about that. For thirty-nine years, I have been going regularly into the jails and prisons and taking meetings to the inmates. I have many friends whom I met while they were doing time, who are now clean and carrying the message of recovery to others. I have been working nonstop with addicts, on a personal level, mostly by phone calls to Florida, Massachusetts, Texas, Iowa, Arizona, Northern California, and Hawaii, as well as right here in San Diego County. These addicts, after they recover somewhat, begin helping other addicts.

Long ago, I made a deal with God, and I prayed, "If You just let me live long enough to recover, I'll give You the whole rest of my life in service." So far, I've kept up my end of the bargain. Nikki Giovanni has a line in one of her poems, "One ounce of truth benefits like ripples in a pond," and that's how I think of my service—that I'm alive because of it, that I'm keeping myself clean one more day because of it, and that my service is going on and on, through others.

Female dope fiends do not live to be eighty. It is a miracle that I am alive, that I am not living in an institution. The daughter who hated me, whom I carried while I was doing time for sales of narcotics in 1965, has given us two grandchildren, one of whom graduated from Southern Utah University, where he went on a football scholarship. The younger one just started college at Arizona State University. My daughter is my friend— sometimes. That is a miracle.

We haven't seen the end of it. Our son graduated from Stanford, Phi Beta Kappa, and received two Masters degrees at Berkeley, one in psychology and one in statistics. He went back to Stanford on a fellowship and received his Ph.D. in biology. He's a genomic statistician. Oxford University Press published his book, *Statistical Thinking from Scratch: A primer for scientists by M.D. Edge.* Right this minute, he is working as a professor at USC. He married his undergraduate lab partner, who is doctor, and they have a son, seven years old, and a daughter, almost four.

I have watched myself recover, miraculously, from delusional paranoia, dissociative disorder, manic depression, speed sores, migraine headaches, sciatica, degenerative disc disease, and arthritis. I still have Meniere's Disease, and I am deaf in the left ear because of the beatings I took as a kid. I'm in better physical shape than I was when I was thirty. Don and I have been married for 38 years. All this is a miracle to me, and I am not finished yet. There are more miracles to come.

32

OMEN IN THE SKY
AL CONVERSE

The headlights appeared first, a glow over the rise about a mile away, then stronger, and finally, the truck, cruising along the lonely Route 66. As I approached and the glow grew larger, I eased my car more to the right on the two-lane highway. The nearly obliterated dashed white lines marking the center of the road gave me little leeway. My left foot reached for the dim switch on the floor and click, I dimmed my lights. After it passed I moved my right foot off the accelerator and my left foot onto it. I eased my numb right leg over on the passenger side to rest.

The talk radio host droned on. Some night owl caller had speculated that humans would eventually wipe out the earth in a nuclear war. After he hung up, the host had to fill the air time with chat. Fortunately, he was good at mindless blather.

Another truck appeared ahead, driving in my direction. I approached and blinked my headlights. He wagged his lights on the trailer and I moved out to pass. I zipped into the clear westbound lane, moved past him, and when he blinked his headlights I pulled back into the eastbound lane.

As I worked my way east on US 66 late one August night,

my mind wandered to the girl I left in San Diego. I had just mustered out of the Navy after a couple of deployments to Vietnam and a year of dating her. Off to graduate school with my military obligation behind me, I expected to be happy but I was blue. My ruminating on this subject had caused me to bypass several motels until the "vacancy" signs turned into "no vacancy" signs resulting in my present commitment to driving all night.

As the talk show host blabber continued I rolled down the window seeking some fresh air to keep me awake. A green light caught the edge of my left eye. In a microsecond, it appeared as a molten object streaming across the desert sky. An instant later it disappeared over the horizon. My first thought was "Christ" just "Christ" and nothing else . . . then, "what the hell was that?" Within minutes the talk show host was babbling on about phone calls reporting a meteor over the desert.

I crested a hill and another truck appeared, a big oil tanker moving slowly on an uphill grade ahead. The truck's sudden appearance flustered me. My position complicated my move to hit the brake pedal. I managed to get my right foot back in position as I moved my left foot out of the way. I pressed my right foot on the brake pedal. The car slowed—a close call. I forgot about the meteor.

I drove behind the tanker for a few miles to recover my composure before I blinked my headlights to pass. He wagged his lights and I passed.

Around four a.m. I spotted a rest stop and pulled off the highway. I turned off the talk show blather and slept. At eight a.m. the sun glare from the east woke me and I drove on. The unusual night prayed on my mind. The once-in-a-lifetime encounter with a meteor and the close call while driving reminded me of the awesome, tenuous, and short lives we all live.

Two days later I was in Syracuse at my parent's home, a planned respite before I was to drive to Storrs, Connecticut to register at the UCONN graduate school of business. I spent two days at home pacing and pacing, my thoughts unsettled. On the third day, I got in my car and drove back to San Diego.

I asked Melinda to marry me, made the long drive back to Syracuse, and then to Storrs. I registered, found an apartment in East Hartford, bought some cheap furniture, and started classes.

I flew back to San Diego to marry her on a weekend in October. We have been married for 55 years.

33

WHILE DANGLING FROM A TRAIN

REINA MENASCHE

What kid doesn't love trains? And what adult scribbler doesn't dream of a train story to tell?

My story is not the haunting whistle heard from a lonely motel room. Nor is it the lush blur of landscape glimpsed through overlarge train windows. This story isn't even a wistful wave goodbye and joyful lurch forward with baggage at the other end. Apart from including the usual clattering, sweat, and nostalgia, this train tale is different.

It is both metaphor and reality, protagonist and villain. My train from Montpellier to Paris—boarded so long ago now—enabled me to leave my adopted country of France, an ex-fiance named Antonio, and my best friend Brigitte. It is the train from which I ended up dangling, hands glued to handrails, feet flailing in the wind, voices screaming behind me.

The train in this story almost killed me. Yet that one crazy episode holds within its desperate grasp every longing of youth and regret and fear of maturity. These moments are blasted on my mind as I speedily traverse life.

Imagine a warm dry summer: Mediterranean heat and sun on stone. Imagine that summer winding down from heady outdoor festivals and dining, long bittersweet drives to vineyards and cubbyhole villages. Imagine a relationship decision that makes no sense due to its finality ... yet seems inevitable. If I can't be Forever French, and he is too French to be American, then what other choice is there? Maybe he'll change his mind. Maybe I'll find a way to change mine. Our situation might right itself, by itself, for there is no lack of love.

On that day, love comes in the shape of this man. He is torn by dual cultures—French and Spanish—as well as dual desires and loyalties. Love appears as romance, since embracing goodbye at train stations is as romantic as a medieval ballad. And love comes in the shape of a best friend, the kind who will hold your hand when you cry and take you in with almost no questions.

I didn't want to leave Montpellier. But I missed my family so much. I had no real job or job skills in French, no legal right to live there, and my engagement had broken under the stress. Or maybe, I hoped, our engagement was only postponed. If not, would I be able to live through the heartbreak?

You see, Antonio had a provincial lifestyle—long lunches with extended family, the women always cooking—and a reliance on guaranteed medical care. He was afraid of life in America. I, on the other hand, was American to the core. I had two close sisters and two aging parents and a career in English journalism. I didn't drive a car in France, I didn't cook hot lunches every day, and my family was waiting for me in California.

Only time will tell, I thought. What's meant to be will be.

Even now, I remember the warmth of his arms, the foreign words between us so comfortable that I hardly recognized myself. I remember the sticky sadness, too, with its choked-back tears and confusion. I pulled away from him to give another quick hug to Brigitte and then faced Antonio for what I prayed would not be the last time.

"*Au revoir, pas adieu,*" he whispered. *Goodbye for now, not forever.*

I remember managing to yank myself away from him and getting on that train and sitting down to gaze through the window—and then getting up and climbing down to the platform again, for one more last time, one last embrace.

My luggage and backpack were still on the train, mind you. I would only be a minute. The station always announced departures with a three-bell chime, and everyone knew that chime meant business. You hear, you board.

"Don't worry," I told Antonio. "They haven't rung the bell yet."

Ears keenly listening, I gave myself over to the other sensations. Love in the scent of hair and a sweater ... and reflecting in large hazel eyes ... love conquering all. Love can slay dragons.

But can it slay trains?

My first glimpse of what was to come was that steel beast slowly beginning to glide. But wait—where was the bell? The train was *moving.*

"*Merde,* the train," cried Antonio. "It's leaving!"

"Oh no," said Brigitte. "My God, it's going without you!"

And with my stuff, I thought in horror. My suitcase. My tickets. *My passport.*

In one frozen heartbeat, I eyed the train doorway. I took long measure of the distance to the doorway from where we stood ... and the accelerating pace of the train. With less than the time it would take to form a decision, I began to run. And I heard Antonio read my mind: "No—don't do it, Reina. *Don't!*"

But my feet were already moving. Too late to stop now. Slowing down would be even more dangerous; I had cranked into gear and could not, would not, shift. There was nothing to spare: no time to vacillate, no changing directions. My body had a will of its own. I watched in dumb fascination as my legs pumped—and then leaped. I'm not going to fall, began the mantra somewhere inside that vacuum of space. My vision had narrowed to the doorway, to those shiny railings, and me. In a duel. The rest of the station receded. Antonio and Brigitte vanished on the head of a pin. Drips of time slowed so sickeningly, I could hear the tick underneath as I made the calculation—*NOW*—and hurled myself into the air, over the crevasse—

I saw the gap between platform and train: saw the great clanking wheels in their monstrous spin and felt them reverberate in my solar plexus. And I thought, *I'm not going to fall.*

In midair, I reached for the silver railings. Poised over the canyon, I grabbed at them—and my hands gripped steel. Cold steel. A thundering noise rushed in … and screams. "Get her!" "Oh my God!" "Stop the train!"

With no emotion, I noted that my feet had missed their purchase. I was not on the train or standing inside the train.

I was dangling.

Interesting. Time slowed so much I could muse at my musings. Hey, look at that, I thought. My fingers are white where they grip the railing. Where they hold my weight. I can hear screaming. That's Antonio, poor Antonio. And Brigitte. But why are they screaming? I wondered, still laser-focused on the whites of my fingers. *I'm not going to die.*

And it went on like that. Forever. The sounds of the station from a great hollow distance. Emotions flat and brain alert. Wondering at the lack of fatigue. *I'm not going to die. Not. Going. To. Die.* Then I heard, or felt, or sensed, a change. Footsteps running—someone chasing the train. A man ran alongside, trying to catch up, shouting words that did not take shape. I was too consumed, now, to understand French. It had gone from me, like everything else, meaningless at ground zero.

Then a hand—that racing, pounding someone—came out of nowhere and shoved at my back. I felt the hand slam the breath from me. I went hurtling with incomprehensible speed and flew into the train like a crashed bird, tumbling along the floor where a crowd had gathered.

Time shifted again. Reality slapped me cold. Legs and feet moved at my eye level, and when I looked up, strange faces stared down. The screaming from the station had receded, *chug-chug-chug*, as I began to shake. My whole body was convulsing, teeth chattering, the fear and terror and adrenalin and fatigue throbbing through my body like heaving tides. I couldn't talk, couldn't ask for help, couldn't imagine how to stand, or walk.

I was convulsing alone, on a train.

Then a woman appeared. A woman with solid body and strong arms squatted down to my level, on the floor, and she took me into those arms as if it were the most natural thing in the world. She held me tight for seconds. And, eons. She held me until her humanity vanquished death, her warm assurances penetrated the dark. This stranger—I never saw her face. I don't know if I thanked her or how much time passed. Eventually, I *was* upright, clawing my way down a bouncing hallway by touching walls, here and here. I was crammed into a seat, reunited with my suitcase and my tickets and my goddamn passport.

My body still trembled, especially my hands. My teeth chattered. But I did not bite my tongue. I managed to sit there like a normal person and look out the overlarge windows at the fleeing landscape of my adopted city, my adopted country. I thought, *I could have died. Antonio. Brigitte.* And I shuddered in the way a soul shudders.

I didn't cry. In a blinking stupor, I drank water and nibbled bread while riding the train to Paris. I caught a shuttle to the airport. I boarded my plane, watching raindrops cleanse the small window I would be glued to for the next million hours until I arrived in California. Where I would exit the plane drunk with fatigue, but looking so stylish and slim that my own mother barely recognized me. Her face lit up with joy as she welcomed me to my new home. Yes, she knew I was heart-broken, but she didn't ask for the details. "I hope everything works out for you; you deserve it," she said. "How was your trip?"

I didn't mention the train. I never told my mother what had happened, not even in that last year before she died. I never shared the story in writing, until now.

Sure, it was stupid to jump the train. Passports aren't worth your life. It was foolish to get off the train in the first place, for a second goodbye. Love isn't worth your life, either. So, what was I taking away from all this? Certainly not Antonio. Yet that train ride was more than near-tragedy, more than fodder for a writer's usually ordinary life.

That second goodbye on the platform contained all of life's longing for what's whole and feels right—and then hurts and can't be changed. That split-second decision to jump, based on a passport, turned out to be survival poking through turmoil, though I wouldn't do it again. Dangling from a train made me a better teacher and a therapist decades later. When I talked to clients about the fight-and-flight response and the exhaustion that follows, I understood.

The kindness of the woman on the train will always remain with me as the Kindness of Strangers.

Even the secret I kept from my mother seems symbolic. I trusted her with almost everything in this life, yet here was my small effort to protect her from fear.

Truth, like love, is not the whole story.

So, My Train is an excellent lesson. It showed me how much I value love but that I can—and *will,* when life demands it—be able to continue alone. My Train taught me to recognize my own strengths. As a kid, I couldn't even climb the ropes in gym class. Yet I held onto those train railings with superhuman strength because I *am* human, and I want to live. Even while trembling. This, I believe, is resilience.

And, by the way, to this day I still love to travel.

I'm afraid of planes but feel mesmerized boarding a high-speed train.

34

INNKEEPER
CHLOE EDGE

I was widowed at thirty—suddenly. Unable to get a grip, floundering in grief, mother of a nine-year-old daughter, I agreed, reluctantly, to manage one of my father's motels. Motel San Diego was located below the level of the street. There was a driveway going down into the property across the parking lot and back up to the street, then an asphalt oblong. After my daughter's inspection on our first day at the motel, she bounced into the office declaring, "You're not just a single parent, you're a single parent with twenty-six bedrooms and five kitchens."

It was a lot of work. I felt like I had put myself on a Ferris wheel that never stopped. Travelers rang the bell at all hours of the night. The two maids began working at nine a.m. There were deliveries, the pool guy, the laundry man with the sheets. We washed our own towels and there were always towels to fold. There were bills to pay and paperwork, rude customers and weeds to pull, but the worst task was the trash.

On Tuesday evenings I had to drag all the trash cans up the long driveway to the street. Then on Wednesdays at about ten, they all had to come back down. I hated it.

I was tapped out in more ways than one. I had been eating more than usual, trying to stuff my grief, and I was spreading out of my size nine jeans. I was studying astrology; I'd learned everything in the books I owned, and the books I needed in order to continue learning were going to be expensive. I had no money, and my dad wasn't paying much. I would never be able to afford a fifty-dollar book. I had moved from a small one-bedroom in Mission Beach to a large two-bedroom manager's quarters, and I needed plants and baskets to make the place feel cozy. I felt so poor.

Plus, I was agonizing over my loneliness. Although Richard had been my husband for only five months, he'd been my friend for twelve years. I didn't understand my emotions and they were strong. I was wondering about spiritual stuff: when someone close died, it was like a giant floodlight was flipped on and everything showed, like my psyche was on review.

Anyway, I was thinking about people's reactions to spiritual awakening, and I was wondering if, when someone was awakened on a spiritual level, if maybe they sometimes nut up and act like they're crazy for a while, because I thought I was acting that way, and I was hoping it was going to be for a good reason.

So, there I was, one Wednesday morning, working alongside the maids, Hideko and Jill, who knew how I felt about the trash. The cans were up and emptied, but no one had dragged them back down yet. There were about twenty empty cans sitting up there. I had gone into the office.

Hideko discovered it first and came running, yelling, "I solly, Chloe, somebody fill you cans."

I looked up and the cans were full again. I couldn't believe it. Tromping up the driveway, cussing, I thought maybe I'd imagined having seen the trash truck earlier. When I got up there, I was dumbfounded. Someone had dumped what looked like a whole life into the cans.

I dragged them down to their place, next to the office and took a look. There were four pairs of perfectly good size eleven jeans, blouses, baskets, plants, and books. Not just any books, but the very expensive astrology books I needed! There were jewelry and sandals, records, and pottery, and at the bottom of one of the cans, a book, *Psychosynthesis*, by Roberto Assagioli, M.D., and there was a piece of broomstick marking a page in chapter 3, "Self-Realization and Psychological Disturbances." The heavy print in the middle of the page said, "3. Reactions to the Spiritual Awakening."

Since then, I have wondered many times who delivered everything I needed at the exact moment I needed it most.

35

BLOOD SISTER – MEMOIR

GERED BEEBY

What's it all about? Somewhere, and at some point in time, many of us ask: What have we done that is important?

Everyone has accomplishments. Early on many have hopes and aspirations that seemed unlimited. Coming of age can fill one's thoughts with such promising deeds and hoped-for experiences. Some even trend into romantic idealism. As time goes on, not all these lofty ideals may arrive as expected, but at least you should try.

My own contributions exhibited some range. I helped defeat Ronald Reagan's Evil Empire during the so-called Cold War. Later after leaving Navy active duty, I was part of a notable environmental improvement program in the San Diego region. Along with my first wife we did many things to raise a decent family. As an engineering professional my California State licenses were earned with appropriate effort on my part. The most notable benefit from these was rebuilding our single story tract house into a two-story home for a growing family. Later and sadly, I tried to get her the professional help she most desperately needed. On that note, things do not always work out, and our marriage did not survive. However, this enlarged house served well during my single parent years in the last decade of the 20th century.

But things change, and early in the new millennium I remarried. Happily, this union works to this day. Also, as a drilling Naval Reservist for most of these years I served parallel careers in both civilian and military. In the words of Winston Churchill I was "Twice a Citizen."

Still, these kinds of developments occurred for many other people. And retirement eventually comes for most people. Combining reserve affiliation with my engineer work, retirement evolved as a series of milestones. But with a broad sense of irony the best reward for me did in fact come last—early in 2007.

I grew up as the eldest kid in a large family. We moved around a lot since our Dad was a career Navy pilot. We were close knit and helped each other out. I had two younger sisters and two younger brothers. We had our joys over the years. But the lowest point for us all came when we lost our eighteen-year-old brother David to Hodgkin's disease in 1970.

Still, life went on and we experienced many satisfactions as a supportive family. Then, decades later the cancer crisis struck again. Our youngest sister Debbie was afflicted with a form of leukemia that resulted in esophageal cancer. She underwent an arduous surgery that addressed the immediate cure for her throat. However, even with the devoted help of our sister Barbara, a registered nurse and retiree from the Navy Nurse Corps, the looming specter would not go away. Follow-up tests showed that Debbie's blood forming system had become compromised. Debbie would need a bone marrow transplant; a whole new blood forming system—a risky but necessary procedure if she was to have a chance at life.

The first step was finding a suitable bone marrow stem cell donor. The best candidates are close relatives, such as siblings or children. Debbie, though once married, had never had children. So, each of us, Barbara, our brother Phil, and I, had our bloodwork drawn for analysis.

Well, lo and behold, the only suitable match was me. *Suitable* means the one with the most gene-based, antigen matchups that would allow the donor bone marrow cells to go to work and not be attacked by the host (i.e. Debbie's) own defense mechanisms. Such an attack could potentially lead to a tissue (i.e. donor stem cell) rejection and failure. Of the more than 100 possible matchup factors for bone marrow stem cell success, twelve are the most important. Turns out Debbie and I had not only all twelve but many more. This is what researchers call a Twelve Point match or a 12/12 match. An analyst observed it was almost as if we were identical twins, although we were nearly twelve years apart in age and with opposite genders. The old Genetic Lottery works in mysterious ways.

Immune systems are extraordinarily complex with many antigen factors involved. Debbie lives in Beaverton, Oregon, just west of Portland, which has one of the best medical facilities around for treating these cases. In that sense she was lucky. We set about planning for my bone marrow stem cell extraction and subsequent delivery into Debbie.

You may have heard, as I had, the old gothic horror tales of the pain of bone marrow extraction on the part of the donor. During those times such extractions involved large triangular needles jammed deep into large bones, such as the pelvis and femurs. Recovery from this was a trauma all its own for the donor.

For me, however, a newer and better process got used.

This is called apheresis. Basically, it is a centrifugal separation process wherein the donor's blood supply is slowly withdrawn, gets sent through a slick separator, then returns to the donor's other arm, minus billions of bone marrow stem cells. Density differences between the stem cell liquid versus other blood components allows the whole thing to work. The machine used was portable, about the size of a small refrigerator. In some respects this worked like a super blood transfusion. The whole process would take three or four hours.

In early February 2007, Barbara and I visited the hospital in Oregon and received preliminary indoctrination. Barbara would be Debbie's recovery care giver. She received detailed information on the numerous antibiotics and medications Debbie would need. Despite the close genetic match there were still concerns about possible reactions or other unforeseen circumstances. I learned that just prior to Debbie's Delivery Day (DD-Day!) I would receive a series of daily hormone injections over a five-day period to maximize my stem cell production.

Meanwhile, my engineering career was coming to an end. My final A&E (Architect and Engineering) company was well respected and had even asked that I stay an additional six months past my previous planned retirement date.

It's nice to be wanted, but leave I did.

The last week in February 2007 Barbara and I returned to Oregon for our meet with destiny.

By this time the rest of our story was well on track. My stem cell booster shots were underway. Debbie was admitted to the hospital and her own preparations began. One of these steps was the insertion of a catheter in a vein below her collarbone, which would facilitate not only medications, but the eventual injection of my stem cells. Another part of her regimen was her own hormone workup. This included the necessity to destroy any remaining blood forming tissue so her tissue(s) would not conflict with mine. There are a great number of other clinical details that I am leaving out and indeed do not even know.

For my part, after a day or so of injections, I could literally feel the results. The accelerated cell growth caused my bones to ache. Although not really painful, this was surprising. Strangely, I felt the stress in my breastbone. And then another side effect came about. Imagine having a cold or the flu, but without the usual symptoms of coughing, nausea or headaches. One did show up however. My nose ran as it had never done before or since!

As the big day approached, one final concern occurred within me. Debbie had said at the beginning that this train of events, once started, could not be stopped. I was her only link to her future. I had to stay alive. Any terrible fate that might hypothetically take me out would lead to the inevitable demise of my sister. I have never shared this thought until now. I took pains not to mention it. This contingency was never discussed by the medical staff, at least not with me. But I knew enough of probability risk to realize that healthy people simply do not get killed. The odds are millions-to-one against that for any given day. So I put that to the back of my mind and ignored it. Things would be fine.

Morning of the big day dawned and revealed there had been a light snow overnight. Barbara and I would take it easy driving the relatively few miles to the hospital on surface streets.

In the procedure room, staff suggested a last minute head call since I would be partially immobilized on the bed until past midday. Then I was hooked up. The extraction process began and I felt fine. We immortalized the event with photographic evidence—smiles all around. Part way through Barbara displayed her well practiced nursing skills and she gave me the best foot massage I can ever remember. She knew patients can get leg cramps from prolonged inertia. That would not be a problem today.

When the apheresis process was done, a quick test for stem cell inventory showed the amount harvested was prodigious. In less than an hour the full load was injected into Debbie. By this point for the most part my contribution had ended.

Barbara's work on the other hand was just beginning. Both sisters knew that months lay ahead for rest, medication, and recovery. Medically speaking, my undifferentiated stem cells set about invading Debbie's bone marrow to grow, morph, and replace her now missing blood forming cells. Much of the overall monitoring and recovery stage was to allow Debbie's body to assimilate this tissue donation with minimal adverse reaction and to prevent infection. To make this very long story short—it all worked.

We all stayed connected as progress went on. Brother Phil would visit from his place in southwestern Washington State, an easy drive to Debbie's home. In time, she no longer needed constant care. During one of our phone calls she even mentioned a surprising fact. Before all of this developed, she had Type O Blood. Now she had Type A blood; the same as me. We smiled about this new twist on the Frankenstein effect. Debbie even joked about whether she would inherit some of my technological interests.

All these events occurred sixteen years ago. Debbie continues to be fine and when we talk we recall those days. The experience had a profound effect on me. I realized this one-of-a-kind action on my part is the single most important thing I have ever done.

I was able to give the gift of life. On that day and forever more Debbie had become my blood sister.

36

TO JOSH—WELCOME TO DADDY-HOOD

TY DAVID PIZ

Be open to learn from the child within

This is the most amazing and timeless journey we can ever travel with another person.

Love 'em with all you have. Love 'em morning noon and night.

There are times to step aside and let them grow. Other moments to wrap snuggly in one another's soul and carry each other through this thick forest of the great unknown.

Occasionally tread softly, be in support mode of this wonderful little being, then no matter what happens, whatever they just did, whatever became of their decision—really, just be there for them. Then side by side, you can assist one another with putting the pieces together as you move forward ... and yes, kind sir, it's easier said than done. This journey takes a lot of practice and patience, so be kind to yourself in these travels!

As the world crowds in, smile wholeheartedly and again when this fragile little one tests your sincerity—in the end, you will love everything about this wonderful small human because they are a special part of you! And be open-minded with yourself as you grow, as you change and as you trek through your own steep learning curve of daddy-hood. You are the role model that kids watch, that they listen to, and they model their parents' behaviors like a tiny tape recorder. Another important detail is be loving, nurturing, and always express outwardly the unlimited love you have toward your spouse! Additionally, my dad had a major positive impact on my childhood, throughout my youth and into adulthood. My dad, alongside my mom, is my greatest role model. Next to them are my five great siblings without whom, for certain, I would not be the respected man that I have become.

Be willing to show your child the real you, because then, when they are grown and gone, they will know you, not the person you thought you should be for them, or the person that society tries to tell us we have to be. This bond is pure, and it is an essential part of true development, for your child and for you!

Show compassion. Listen—and truly hear when they speak to you. Let this child be who they are. Lift them and you will raise each other like beautiful flowers in an open field.

Best wishes from Ty and daughters, Jessica, Cireen and Alicia Piz, and their significant others, along with the amazing grandchildren they have brought into this world. As well as from my amazing wife. We selected three areas in life that we thought were important and really wanted to share with them. We selected these to give our children a base to learn to make choices for themselves, later in life. The opportunity to play an instrument or sing in the choir. Go to Sunday school and learn about prayer. Play a sport, play two or three or five if you want. Find one element that you really like, and make friends with a common passion.

~

IN MY EXPERIENCE as daughter and mom, people who haven't done the day after day after day with a child in a long time can tend to have selective memory for only the wonderful loving side of being a parent. So for someone who's in the thick of it every day, my input would be there will surely be the highest of highs and the lowest of lows on this roller-coaster adventure, but try to trust that these extremes in the ride won't last long (even if those times feel like they'll never end). If you embrace each moment of the experience for what it truly is—beautiful, scary, joyful, painful, gentle, disgusting—and you put all distractions aside, then you'll realize that your child has taught you one of the most valuable life lessons ... how to exist fully in the present. And while this gift of being a parent will be a part of you for the rest of life, know that daddy-hood is only temporary as you prepare your young child to one day handle, in their own independent way, all that the world has to throw at them!

Wow! Stunning input and quite enlightening additions from these three ladies. While being independent, they are deep in the trenches of living mommy-hood right now! Love each of you. Thank you for sharing your insight, and for caring and for growing with your wonderful hubby. And all of your pets too.

Renew your commitment to love and start fresh every day.

37

NINETY DEGREES TO THE LEFT, A MEMOIR

ROBYN LITT

I found the forgotten box today.

I run my fingers along the tarnished-brass kaleidoscope. The metal smells of neglect. I push aside dusty tissue paper. A lost memory triggers a smile.

"Are you interested in a trade?" the woman once asked me. She was dressed in a long floral skirt and t-shirt typical of a vendor at the Harvest Festival.

"A trade? I guess, uh, sure," my twenty-something entrepreneurial self, answered back. I'm not certain that's exactly what I said, but that's close. Bottom line? I ended up with one of her kaleidoscopes and she got one of my watercolor paintings.

Now I hold the scope up to the early morning light. With each twist of my wrist to the left, shards of fiery red, sky blue, and earthy amber shove against a deep violet ocean Fire. Air. Earth. Water. All jumble together, out of order, at times visible, other times hidden.

Past memories entice me today, pieces shift in place. What do I know about living life now? About the important things? I'm thinking efficiency wasn't my strong suit. But quality?

I smile. Quality. I think I've captured some of that.

I set the heavy scope back down and pick up my coffee for a sip. The image of the red, blue, yellow, and violet gem sticks with me, not in any specific order—more like a scramble. Just like my life, a meandering path filled with surprise and wonder. Come to think of it, I emerged into this world bottom first, breech. Why should I travel in a direct line now?

RED TRIANGLES—Fire's Burning

The fiery heat from the oven adds a sense of urgency to the summer air. Hurry, the tiny kitchen is warming up. It's time. I position the stool next to Grandma and lean into the tiny Formica countertop to see the best show ever. She picks up eggs, puts one in each hand. With a swift crack against the bowl lip she opens the shells. Yolks and whites pour out. She gives each egg one last shake and drops the shells in the bin.

"We'll need ..." Grandma recites, as she watches Granddad through the organza-covered kitchen window. He's mowing the lush lawn in neat rows.

"Sugar?" I ask.

"Yes, and ..."

"Eggs," I add.

"Yes, and ..."

We play our game of fewest words and efficient movements like a keyboard. Our notes rise and fall with our breath and concentration. Birdsong floats through the open windows to join us. I watch her hands slide along the ingredients. She whisks the eggs with one hand and measures the sugar with the other. Her perfectly applied nail polish flashes by my curious eyes as she adds ingredients to the big ceramic bowl. She stirs. I step down from the stool.

I look up at the open shelves near the stove. Grandma has a collection of colored glass and ceramic miniatures. One is Cinderella's coach, complete with four perfect prancing horses. I move close. I bet I could climb even closer. My arm pushes against the top of the stove for a split second before the searing heat of the hot burner will mark it forever.

"No!" Grandma's voice calls out as the burning burrows deep into my skin.

Tears flow as I open my mouth in a silent cry that finds volume as my skin reddens.

Grandma rushes to grab a stick of butter from the refrigerator to put on my arm. "Hold this here." Her glistening eyes match mine as she scoops me in her embrace.

THE SUN-WARMED KITCHEN counters are full of mixing bowls, measuring spoons, and cookie sheets. At one end, far from the separate oven and stove tops, perches my daughter. Her short legs dangle over the counter to reach down just past the pull-out drawers.

"Sugar?" she asks.

"Yes and ..." I say and smile.

"Eggs?" she asks.

"Yes and ..."

"What else, Mommy?" Wide eyes stare up at me. A bird chirps outside the garden window as the porch wind chimes join in.

"Hugs, tickles, and kisses," I say.

Her giggles bounce through the air, off the buttercream walls, and into my heart.

I touch my inner arm and look down. A faint outline of concentric circles barely peeks through my summer tan. The pain long forgotten. The warm cookie memories still fresh.

"Cookies! I'm ready to bake cookies," she demands and raises her arms to me. I swing her down to the tiled floor like an airplane coming in for a safe landing.

"Cookies it is. You know, this is your Great-grandma's recipe. She could crack two eggs at a time."

BLUE CIRCLES—Air Currents

The harness tightens. "Run toward the water," he says for the fourth time.

I nod. What am I doing? My two-piece swimsuit starts to ride up in the back as I run across the sand. The adrenaline shoots through me and before I know it, a strong tug lifts me into the air and up. The water below me distances itself and the shore cliffs slide into position as I find myself flying close to them.

Parasailing? Crazy! Fabulous!

My stomach drops as my heart soars. So, this is how the birds feel. It must be. The draft moves past me and the gorgeous blur of turquoise water, green and brown cliffs, with the pale sand below take me to a place of dreams. But this is real. The boat has turned. It's time to pull on the cords, ease into the landing. What if I started too late? Too late to worry. I feel the wet sand tap dance against my feet and I know that gravity has claimed me. The guides release the harness. I'm earth-bound again. I'm alive. I flew and I'm alive. What kind of crazy person tries this? Deep inside, I know, I will never try this again. But today I flew.

AMBER SQUARES—Earthly Treasures

I turn the agate heart over and over in my palm. The smoothed shape warms in my clenched fist.

"We need to put a fastener on it." Granddad looks at me for a moment. "Bring it over here," he murmurs as he carefully places several loose stones out of our way and clears a small space on his scratched counter for us to glue the metal in place.

I reluctantly hand over my prize. We've worked on cutting,

shaping, and smoothing the caramel and mocha stone over several visits. Today is the day we make it into a necklace. I place the heart upright in a small stand that winches together to hold it tight and safe. Granddad hands me the glue to dab onto the stone. As he leans close, I can smell the spiced tobacco he loves that is stealing his breath. The oxygen tank and tubing have sat in the corner the last few visits. His unshaved beard looks scruffy and forgotten. His piercing eyes laser-focus on the rock in front of us as he pulls a magnifying glass stand close and picks up a set of tweezers lying next to his favorite rock hammer.

"What kind of glue should we use?" I ask. I don't want to talk. I think, just like his rocks, he likes silence.

"Cement," he grunts. He has completed a project with each grandchild before me and he will probably do one with each grandchild after me. It is his legacy.

I look around his basement workroom. Every space seems occupied by rocks, saws, hammers, drills, piled up books, papers, and unfinished projects. At the far end, he has a glass cabinet filled with crystal, amethyst, agate, tourmaline, turquoise, opal, and the random arrowhead he's found on his travels.

How much of his life has he spent looking down? Digging in the hard earth, pulling up its treasures. Gazing at the stones and seeing magic within each one. Granddad lives in the basement, underground with his stones, emerging into the sunlight only on special occasions, cemented in his passion.

VIOLET RHOMBI—Underwater

I'll just say it.

I'm feeling snarky at age sixty-two. Old enough to know better, but senior water aerobics class has amped it up.

The Octopus is treading water right in front of me, the Synchronized Smoochies are to my right, and Hairy Beast is to my left. I glance at the clock. Class will start any minute now. Maybe I could move to the back row. I glance behind me. Nope. The three Besties are back there chatting away.

I close my eyes and focus on the silky water moving around me as I tread in the deep end. Appreciate your surroundings. Be grateful you're not working anymore. Enjoy the moment. Thoughts flood through my mind. Find your Zen spot.

The last one floats and lingers. Don't be a judgmental jerk.

I'm not sure why I've been so cranky lately. Usually, I'm pretty positive and downright perky. But ever since the COVID shutdowns and reopening of society as we know it, my disposition resembles some of the strip malls around town: lights turned off, worn paint, and signs with missing letters.

Ah, here we go.

"Let's get started!" The water aerobics instructor flashes us a toothy grin as she poses in front of us on the rubber-mat covered tile. She starts an exaggerated walk-jog step with wide swinging arms.

We do the same in the pool.

As the routine begins, my mind wanders. It might as well. The routine is exactly the same every time with this instructor. My limbs do their thing as my brain travels through this week's shopping list unchecked. Sweet potatoes, kale, eggs, Greek yogurt, and some of those ... "Oof!"

Hairy Beast bumps into me. "Sorry," he laughs.

I try not to shudder.

"I wish there was music," says one of the Besties behind me. Her words bounce around the walls like a loose racquetball.

"Right? We've asked her so many times," another responds.

"She's a little weird," the third one tries to whisper but isn't successful.

"I heard she's against all music. Some religious thing or the other."

"I heard she just doesn't—" The sound stops.

Someone next to the trio must have let them know their voices are carrying.

Right about now I'm feeling guilty for my earlier snarky thoughts.

I grab a pair of water paddles to increase the drag. My arms mysteriously expanded in circumference these past two years. It may have had something to do with the Banana Bread Trials. You know, several versions of recipes tried out over COVID-time with quarantined family members. Now, we are all visiting the gym on the regular.

We turn to the right for four counts, then turn to the right again, four counts.

Oh. The Smoochies are practically swallowing each other's tonsils. Ew.

Alrighty then.

My mind travels deeper in the waves.

I'm glad I retired. Really! I am. I push out with my hands and jump up in a move that reminds me of high school cheer-leading days. Isn't water wonderful? It holds an amazing amount of bouncing indulgence.

Now, I get to pursue what I want to do with my time. That's what everyone keeps telling me. I love painting and writing ... but now ... is it too late for me? Is it important that I'm taken seriously? Was I before, back when I was working? People listened to me. They respected me. They followed my lead and raved about my contributions. Where are they now? They're working, I remind myself. No time to placate grouchy retirees.

Octopus reaches out and shifts into my personal bubble to exercise. I try to move to my right, but the Smoochies are mirroring arm movements. I think an Olympic judge would give them at least a three on synchronization techniques.

That doesn't solve my problem though.

Do I get closer to Octopus so she slithers back to her area? How is it possible to feel claustrophobic in a pool, for God's sake. I move in her direction, but her compass is off as usual.

We move into high intensity jogging and jumping jacks. I put the paddles away. My arms are getting a little tired.

Why do I have to feel validated by others? Or am I just so used to next steps? My whole life is made up of tiny steps forward, first word, first hug, first school, first race, first tornado drill, first move, first best friend, first kiss, first college degree, first award, first raise, first promotion, first mentee, first, first, first. Do others see the end of steps before we do ourselves? I don't feel like the stairway is going down exactly, but with every ma'am and offered seat or opened door am I getting closer to the downstairs journey?

Cool down exercises start.

The waves stop pitching against the sides of the pool and over each of us. Concentric ripples move out and away as I glide one arm and then the next in slow movements.

I find myself calming with the water.

Life is good. New opportunities exist. Breathe in, breathe out.

Maybe I should introduce myself to Octopus this time.

I GET HOME, change and make tea. Then, I pick up and turn the kaleidoscope another ninety degrees to the left. New pieces fall into place. The temptation to keep sifting through old memories is enticing.

I glance at the clock. Today is moving forward.

I put the kaleidoscope down and run to catch it.

38

A HARROWING EXPERIENCE

GWENDALLE COOPER

I n 1947, two years after the end of World War II, I was a student at the University of Miami in Coral Gables, Florida. While the airport was not as huge then as it is now, it still took two hours and four buses to reach the south campus of the university, resulting in a four-hour roundtrip, Mondays through Fridays.

So, I invested in a 1939 Ford Coupe two-seater with a rumble seat. Essentially, a rumble seat is a reverse trunk lid that opens to reveal a hidden bench seat, converting a car made to transport two people into one which can carry four. Now I could reach my destination in twenty to twenty-five minutes by driving around the west side of the airport.

I liked being a student at the university, and I joined Kappa Kappa Gamma, a national sorority. In my second year of being a sorority member, I became the *big sister* of a pledge named Judy. My new pledge's family lived in Havana, Cuba, where her father managed the USA-based Armour Meat Packing Company.

I had another friend, my best friend Peggy, a Chinese resident of Canada, who lived on campus like my pledge Judy. The Thanksgiving break at the university was approaching, and most of the students, myself included, made plans to go home for the holiday. This is the season where compassion, caring, and love become more evident around the globe—usually.

Unfortunately, college students living away from home sometimes allow isolation, loneliness, and despair to bully their way in and allow depression to put a damper on the annual days of joyful celebration.

A few days before the holiday started, Judy and her family invited me, and Peggy, to spend Thanksgiving with them in Cuba. General Batista was no longer in power, so we gleefully accepted the invitation.

My dad offered to drive us to the airport. The plan was for Judy, who had already joined her family, to meet us at the Havana Airport upon landing.

At the airport, I asked my dad, "Can I bring you anything from Cuba?"

"Yes," he replied, "a bottle of rot-gut rum because Cuba is known for producing high-quality run. I want some for the eggnog I always make at Christmas."

I waved to my dad as Peggy and I boarded the plane. This was my first trip by airplane. I looked forward to visiting Cuba, but I was not excited at all about flying. Held captive in a twin-engine metal tube moving rapidly above the earth was not my idea of an adventure.

The plane took off for the slightly more than an hour-long trip to Havana. A lovely flight attendant served everyone beverages and snacks. I chose coffee. *This isn't so bad after all,* I thought.

Suddenly, the flight from Hell ensued. The airplane bounced around the sky like a celestial toy. I grabbed the arms of my seat, holding on for dear life. I don't remember breathing.

Once, the plane dropped so suddenly that the coffee in my

cup sitting in the cup holder in the tray in front of me sloshed out to eye level. Just as swiftly, the plane rose and my coffee miraculously fell back into the cup.

Then as now, I believe there is a Creator in charge of everything. So far, however, the Creator has not resigned and put me in charge, and I understand that will not happen. So, what could I do? I closed my eyes and gripped the armrest. And I prayed.

Bobbing around in the heavens for what seemed like a long time, I decided to apply for citizenship in Cuba, if I lived to get there. No way did I intend to subject myself to another experience like this.

My prayers were answered as the weather subsided just before reaching Havana. Our plane descended and landed safely. Judy and her father met us at the airport. Peggy and I took turns telling them about our distressing flight. We inspected the outside of the plane, and to my surprise, it looked fine.

I shook off the bad experience and began a wonderful four-day adventure in Cuba. During our visit, Judy's father treated us to sightseeing tours around various locations in Cuba, including the lush countryside where some sugar cane cutters lived in poverty-stricken villages. The most beautiful place we visited was the world famous Veradero Beach, known for its fine sands and warm crystal clear water.

As our holiday drew to a close, I realized the only way to return to Miami was on our scheduled return trip. Thinking about it frightened me. I reminded myself that the last four days had been filled with beautiful, uneventful weather, and I didn't see a cloud in the sky.

I decided to hazard another flight.

When I landed in Miami and stepped safely on solid ground again, I had cause to celebrate. I took a moment to thank my Creator for an excellent flight home.

Since that first airplane flight, I've learned many more times that moving through life can be harrowing, but it is always exciting.

SECTION FOUR - POETRY

39

NEXT ONE

ANDREA SUSAN GLASS

H ave you ever had a funky sales job
     Where the phone hang ups have caused you
     to sob?
So, you cried to super salesman, Joe
Hey all I get is "NO, NO, NO!"
"Don't take it personal, it's not you,
Sales is a numbers game, do what I do.
Here's what I say to get through the day,
Repeat this mantra, say what I say,"

REJECTION, rejection
     It's not a projection
     "N-O" means next one.

I'VE BEEN SHOPPING my book, the next bestseller
     'bout a struggling writer and her wayward fella.
     It's been making the rounds to agents and eds
     Coming back so fast, wonder if it's been read.

So, I called my bud who's been having more luck
And said, "Hey, girlfriend I seem to be stuck."
She said, "Hang in there, have patience and tenacity,
'Cause we've all got so much capacity."

REJECTION, rejection
It's not a projection
"N-O" means next one.

MY HUSBAND LEFT, my guy flew the coop
I didn't know how low they could stoop.
Wasn't having much luck asking guys out
They wouldn't call back, leaving me in doubt.
Did anyone read my personal ads?
It was getting badder than bad.
When I looked in the mirror and liked what I saw
I thought, "Well okay, I'll go back for more.

REJECTION, rejection
It's not a projection
"N-O" means next one.

WHAT ALL THIS means is keep on, I guess
'cause the very next one could be the one to say, "Yes."

REJECTION, rejection
It's not a projection
"N-O" means next one.

40

DEMENTIA

KAREN FOGELBERG-HILL

The changes came and took the truth of you.
Gone without goodbyes, without amends,
Old Woman, how I hated you whom I could not
comfort.
How I hated those who loved, but never came.
How I needed you then—MOTHER!

41

NOW

ROBERT JORDAN

My memory of my nanny stopping the bleeding
with a thin layer of onions before binding
the wound tight with her bandana is fading,
like an old sepia-toned photograph; so, too,
the white lights at the hospital, the doctor
telling my mother how lucky I was to be alive
(while pricking my wrist with a long, thin,
steel needle—anesthetizing the wound—before
stitching it shut, making me cry yet again).

NOW THAT I'M closer to this end of life,
I don't remember the shame I carried all
those years at punching the plate glass window
because my temper got the better of me—again.
Now that I'm closer to this end of life, when
I look at the scar, I see my brother standing
on the other side of that window, thumbs planted
on both temples, wagging his fingers, sticking
his tongue out, smiling, rocking side-to-side.

. . .

NOW THAT I'M closer to this end of life,
I see how easy I was to be set in motion
—so sensitive; just sport for him. I see
how much of that I endured all of my life;
and I feel sad for all of us.

42

ANNOYING PEOPLE
ANDREA SUSAN GLASS

The sign at the zoo reads: *"Please do not annoy, torment, pester, plague, molest, worry, badger, harry, harass, heckle, persecute, irk, bullyrag, vex, disquiet, grate, beset, bother, tease, nettle, tantalize, or ruffle the animals."*

While traversing life, I've found that...

People who annoy come in many shapes and sizes,

Doomsayers and pessimists and haughty criticizers.

Self-centered and arrogant, they're often smug and lewd,

Abusing self and others, they're forgetful, late, and rude.

When you see something white, they see it in black,

They act like they're your best friend, then stab you in the back.

Not returning emails, or doing what they say,

Cancelling appointments, here tomorrow gone today.

Talking endless chatter, they don't listen to you,

Loud and lying, cheat at cards, these people are taboo.

Phones are always at their ear, they take and never give,

Quick at finding fault with you, they're often combative.

They keep repeating angry words, they're always losing keys,

Incompetent, perfectionist, don't say thank you and please.

They're cheap, closed-minded, unaware, limited, and boring,

They smell, they smoke, they drink too much,

At night they're always snoring.

They cut you off in traffic, they take your parking place,

They hog lane #1 or drive at a snail's pace.

They try to sell you anything, they call at dinner time,

They really are the pushy types, it ought to be a crime.

They drop in unannounced and don't return your books,

Because you eat tofu and sprouts, they give you funny looks.

They wear too much perfume, they pull too many pranks,

They tell the end of movies, well hey, thanks, but no thanks.

I plan to post a sign because these folks have left me fumin'

"Please do not annoy, torment, pester, plague, molest, worry, badger, harry, harass, heckle, persecute, irk, bullyrag, vex, disquiet, grate, beset, bother, tease, nettle, tantalize, or ruffle the human."

43

PERSPECTIVES IN TIME
LISA GIRDLESTONE

Morning alarm interrupts much-needed sleep.
Far away explosions roll and thunder.
Birds chirp beyond the window, in a tree.
Not rude or obnoxious in their persistency,
But halt the descent into dreaming's wonder.
Blissful shower to awaken the senses
Water flows like old dreams, reflective and pensive.
Hot wind, with its stinging grit in my face
Assails the soul to know its place.
Cool water splashed from a porcelain carafe
A relic from the bygone past.
Day set in motion, the morning rushing
Amid slamming doors and children laughing.
Jets scream overhead and tanks roll by
Eyes keenly watch for enemy fire.
Newspaper, coffee cup, and silent plea
Eager for his walk, my dog gazes at me.
Endless freeways, cars slowly marching
The clock keeps time in ticking anxiety.
Gun checks, equipment checks, and orders to follow

Tasteless rations feed a gut so hollow.
Dog panting, we climb that trail's woody slope
Fishing pole carries a silent hope.
A sea of work, with ebb and flow, demanding functionality
A flexible, malleable, and ever-ready battery.
Reams of paper and groaning machines.
Bursts of bullets and wounded screams.
The gentle sound of bait plopping in water
Spreading ripples of hope farther and farther.
Pause to be thankful, ever mindful
Survival in these hard times, so hurtful
A job to be had and a job to be done
Peacefulness of a job well done.
Bid my labors goodnight, at last
Homeward, oh horizon, my eyes do cast.
Count myself lucky, count the dead
Count the stars, now peaceful and exhausted.
Count another day, the bells intone
Dog at my side, the rest is hard won.
The paradox of time that marches steadily by
Ever glad for its passage, and yet I
Mourn its passing, its memory faint
All blurry pictures and fading paint.
Who I was, became, or yet shall I be
Tears mingle with relief as time flows free
No past, nor future, even present undone
For on this day, three become one.

44

LAND LORD

KAREN FOGELBERG-HILL

H ectic Poet, bird in flight,

SEEKING LANDFALL, garden bright,
Eden's waiting, take a stand,
Make your marriage with the land.

HEW YOUR VISION from the hill,
Bend the branches to your will.
Stretch your arms, your mind, your hands,
Master all within your span.

SNAKE AND VINE and blood intwine,
Staff and trunk and arm divine.
Ancient priesthood trials passed,

Sacred vows and bonds hold fast.

EARTH'S the bride that you must groom,
Life's the threshold of the room.
Love's the only thing you own,
Come to her and you are home.

45

KINGFISHER

CAROL HEASLEY

I want to bite into the Anna apple
golden red on the tree. Bitten, the meat is white
and moist. I bring it inside where from your bed
you salivate, motion with your hand, say plaintively,
"Give me some." Beyond the frantic look of dying,
you grasp for what you leave behind. Straight down,
blazing blue, brash kingfisher, soft orange underbelly,
into the waters you always plunged. Hardwired to love
an apple, you sink your teeth in its flesh.
But the act of eating escapes you, so you gesture
for me to lie down. Lying there I stroke your
face and arms; while you turn inward, I wonder what
you see think feel
Inexplicable even to you this space between dark
and light like Caravaggio's bold chiaroscuro,
John the Baptist in the Wilderness.

"CAROL, WHAT IS HAPPENING TO ME?"

Too painful to answer you are dying,
I say, "I love you."

ABOUT THE AUTHORS

ShuJen Walker Askew – Short Story (pg. 185)

ShuJen Walker Askew has been a member of SDWEG for three years and is currently a Board member. She has published her work in the Guild anthology two times. She served as a content editor for the 2023 anthology.

ShuJen writes short stories, poems, scripts, and plays in various genres. Her works are published in local anthologies at San Diego Mesa College, Grossmont College, San Diego Writers and Editors Guild, and San Diego Writers, Ink. Her short stories have made top 10 in the San Diego Decameron Project and the San Diego Public Library Local Author Contest. ShuJen is working on her first novel, *Across All Skies*. She loves learning and is taking acting and creative writing classes with San Diego Continuing Education and the San Diego Public Library. In addition to serving on the SDWEG board, she is a member of Word Weavers, the Society of Children's Book Writers and Illustrators, and other various writing organizations. ShuJen is working toward her creative writing certificate and does some freelance editing. She is an Electrical Engineer by trade, a mother of two, and enjoys writing. Telling stories about the world around her helps ShuJen capture life. She hopes that someday her kids can read her works.

She grew up as a military brat—in the Philippines and Taiwan—and speaks fluent Mandarin Chinese. ShuJen resides in San Diego, CA, with her family.

Gered Beeby – Memoir (pg. 257)

Gered Beeby has been a Guild member for twenty-four years during which time he served on the Board of Directors for twenty years: Secretary (2001-2003), President (2003-2004), and as a Director-at-Large (2004-2020).

Gered was appointed to the United States Naval Academy by President John F. Kennedy in 1962. After attending, he served as a Navy nuclear submarine officer for twenty years, and afterwards as a licensed civilian engineer, holding many technological positions. His last assignment was as a subject matter expert for the California Engineer Licensing Board, where he reviewed various technical issues brought before the Board. His novel, *Dark Option* about industrial espionage was published in 2002 and was nominated for a Benjamin Franklin Award in the category: Best New Voice—Fiction. His screenplays include *The Bottle Imp*, which is a deal-with-the-devil story based on Robert Louis Stephenson's 1892 classic tale, and *Dark Option*. Gered has contributed to most of the editions of *The Guilded Pen*.

He currently resides in Encinitas, California, and believes that writing is a vehicle for ideas that are not typically available in the course of everyday life.

You may contact Gered Beeby at: geredbeeby06@gmail.com.

Bob Boze – Short Story (pg. 35)

Bob has been a member of the San Diego Writers and Editors Guild for over ten years and has published short stories in the anthology several times.

In addition to the Guild, Bob is an active member of the San Diego Professional Editors Network (SD/PEN), Southern California Romance Writers (SoCalRW) and Publishers and Writers San Diego (PWSD), as well as blogging for Books Go Social in Dublin, Ireland. He has served as a content editor for the 2023 anthology.

Bob and his writing partner and wife, Robyn Bennett, live in the South Bay area of San Diego. They are both internationally published romance and nonfiction authors, editors, teachers, workshop presenters, speakers, and bloggers. Combined, they have over seventeen books and five short stories published, with several novels and short stories currently in the works.

Originally from New York, Bob's travels have covered most of the world and he has lived in London, England; Istanbul, Turkey; Houston and San Antonio, Texas; Los Angeles and Paso Robles, California; before finally calling San Diego home.

Bob's education includes: Studies in Creative Writing, Literature, English Literature and English at NYU, William and Mary, University of Maryland, and the University of Delaware. He holds a dual BS degree in Electronic Engineering in Systems Design and Development and Project Management from Northrop University.

He has been an Information Volunteer, Interpretative Volunteer (Docent), and Volunteer Mentor at the San Diego Zoo for over 30 years.

Bob and Robyn also belong to a number of writer's groups in New Zealand, Ireland, and England, and have attended and presented workshops at writing conferences and festivals in San Diego and New Zealand. They were selected to present their workshops at Dublin's International Writers Festival, The San Diego School of the Arts, and writer's groups across the United States.

You may contact Bob Boze through email at: bobboze70@gmail.com or their web site: writingallsorts.com.

Lawrence Carleton – Short Story (pg. 13)

Lawrence Carleton is a long-time member of SDWEG and has published in multiple Guild anthologies.

Larry took up writing when Parkinson's Disease ended his hobby as a jazz trumpeter. He has published or otherwise presented scholarly work in philosophy, cognitive science, and software development. He holds advanced degrees in computer science and philosophy and a post doctorate in cognitive science.

He currently amuses himself, and he hopes others, by writing short stories with interesting characters in unusual situations. He is particularly proud of his published short story collection, *I'm Not Roger Blaine* and *Other Curious Phenomena*.

Contact Lawrence Carleton by email: lrcarleton@gmail.com.

Susan Gere Carter – Short Story (pg. 191)

Susan Carter has been a Guild member for one year and is included for the first time in the *Guilded Pen*.

Susan's debut novel, *The Trolley to Renwick Park*, a historical coming-of-age novel, set in the early 1900s, is currently in rewrite, soon to be shopped for publication. Susan retired from a fulfilling career as an instructional designer/technical writer, contracting to a variety of Fortune 300 companies. Susan has multiple film credits and an IMDB profile. A lover of the theater, she is a longtime volunteer with the San Diego Old Globe Theater and the La Jolla Playhouse. Susan is past presi-dent of the San Diego Bonsai Club and a volunteer at the San Diego Zoo Safari Park Bonsai Pavilion. Susan and husband, Keith, who reside in Santee, California, enjoy travel and have completed over seventeen home-swap vacations throughout Europe and the United States. When not at her computer, pounding out potentially award-winning stories, she can be seen riding an e-bike with her husband over hill and dale in Southern California.

You may contact Susan Carter at: susangerecarter@ gmail.com.

Al Converse – Memoir (pg. 243)

Al Converse has been an active member of the Guild for eleven years and is proud to have contributed to every issue of the San Diego Writers and Editors Guild anthology. He served as a content editor for the 2023 anthology.

Al is the proud great-great-grandson of Justin C. Converse who served as a private with the Union Army at the Battle of Gettysburg. This ancestor is the subject of his current project, a historical novel called *Vermonter* which was released in 2023. Al earned a BS in Business Administration from Boston University in 1965, attended Naval Officer Candidate School, and served on the USS Eldorado AGC-11 during two deployments to Vietnam. Following his active service, he attended the University of Connecticut where he obtained an MBA. He then spent several years in banking before joining the US Small Business Administration in San Diego, where he retired in 2004 as Chief of the Finance Division. Al began writing after his retirement and has published nine books: *Bitch'n, Die Again, Boston Boogie, Baja Moon, News from the East, Hornwinkle Hustle, Flagship, and Jack Blue.*

Al and his wife, Melinda, currently reside at an independent living community in Colorado Springs.

Gwendalle Cooper – Memoir (pg. 275)

Gwendalle Cooper joined the San Diego Writers and Editors Guild one year ago at age ninety-four and will celebrate her ninety-fifth birthday shortly after the publication of her contribution to the 2023 anthology.

Gwendalle, an Emerita Professor at San Diego State University, has traveled four directions of the world from the Arctic above Norway to Columbia and South America, much of Europe, and the Far East to give lectures and workshops on self-help practices. She was the first Psychologist for the women's prison in Colorado and spent a month with the Sami in the Artic Circle above Norway. Gwendalle has taken several creative writing workshops and classes at Oasis Learning Center and joined a San Diego writers' group where she produced several short stories and poems.

She currently resides in La Mesa, California, and is delighted to have the opportunity to write and publish with San Diego Writers and Editors Guild.

You may contact Gwendalle Cooper at: gwendalle@ juno.com.

Steve Corkery – Short Story (pg. 89)

Steve Corkery joined the San Diego Writers and Editors Guild approximately two years ago and looks forward to becoming more active with the organization. An email from the San Diego Writers Guild requesting submissions for the 2023 Anthology motivated him to attempt writing. He took the Short Story Guild Workshop, and the story he developed there resulted in his first inclusion in the Guild anthology. Steve served as a content editor for the 2023 anthology.

When Steve announced his retirement date, friends and family asked, "So what are you going to do when you retire?" as if the absence of working for a company paycheck would somehow isolate him from society and prompt him to withdraw from meaningful activities. Notwithstanding making and executing his daily to-do lists, he narrowed his options to four pursuits, pleasure being the common denominator: golf, fishing, reading, writing. Four years have slid by since day one of Steve's retirement. He has discovered infinite pleasure in reading and writing, as much as he ever did during his muse-struck, English-major college days. Golf and fishing are still there, waiting off-stage.

Steve gets lost, found, and completely absorbed when reading: Fiction, nonfiction, history, editorials, poetry, and biographies. He currently resides in Vista, CA.

Janice Coy – Memoir (pg. 233), Short Story (pg. 101)

Janice Coy has been an active member of SDWEG for about six years and has had work published in four *Guilded Pen* Anthologies. She served as a content editor for the 2023 anthology.

Janice is the author of seven fiction books. She is a contributor to numerous anthologies including SDWEG *Guilded Pen*, San Diego Writer's, Ink: *A Year in Ink*, and The San Diego Decameron Project Anthology. She is published in *3 Elements Review*: A Literary Journal and is a suspense finalist at the San Diego Book Awards Association Annual Awards. An award-winning journalist, she has worked as a beat reporter for a daily newspaper and as a feature writer for a weekly newspaper. She is a committed journal writer and hopes to keep writing in some fashion for the rest of her life.

As a second-generation native Southern Californian, she enjoys spending time outdoors: hiking, biking, or swimming in the ocean. Janice currently resides in San Diego, CA.

C. H. Currier – Short Story (pg. 161)

C. H. (Scott) Currier has been a member of SDWEG since 2018 and has had two pieces included in the *Guilded Pen*, in 2018 and 2019.

Retired from the horticultural industry, Scott was originally from Pasadena, CA. He earned a BS from Cal Poly San Luis Obispo. His original goal was to complete writings from his grandfather, who was born in 1858. He passed in 1933 but left his family handwritten and typed stories that began in the 1930s. Scott has used these stories, and the portrait of his grandfather that hangs over his desk, as prompts for his many short stories and his poetry.

Scott, a cancer survivor, is currently writing his first novel and resides in Poway, CA, where he enjoys playing softball and driving his 1967 Alfa Romeo Boattail Spider.

You may contact Scott through email at: chcurrier@cox.net.

Patricia Daly-Lipe – Essay (pg. 209)

Patricia Daly-Lipe has been a member of SDWEG since 2020, and is contributing for the first time to the *Guilded Pen* anthology.

Patricia was born in San Diego, California, and grew up in La Jolla graduating from The Bishop's School. She spent time living on the east coast in Washington, DC, the home of several generations of her mother's family. She earned a BA degree in Philosophy from Vassar College (with a year at the Catholic University of Louvain, Belgium) and completed her Masters Degree, followed by a Doctorate of Philosophy in Humanities, specializing in Creative Arts and Communication.

As a single parent of three children, Patricia raised and raced thoroughbred horses (winning at Santa Anita, Hollywood Park, Golden Gate Fields, and Del Mar racetracks) and showed in the hunter and jumper divisions at horse shows on both sides of the country. She taught English and writing at universities, wrote for the *Evening Star Newspaper* in Washington, DC, had stories published in several magazines, and had a weekly column with the *Beach and Bay Press* Newspaper Group in San Diego.

Patricia is a well-published author with eleven books, each in a different genre, was past President of the National League of American Pen Women, La Jolla Branch, and later President of the DC Branch. She has won multiple awards and honors including: 2002 State of California Book Award winner by Governor Cruz M. Bustamante Commendation to Patricia Daly-Lipe for *La Jolla, A Celebration Of Its Past.* La Jolla Pen Women; NLAPW Woman of Achievement 2004. 2009 "Golden Nib" Contest, Special Achievement Award, Second

Place in Poetry for *A Poetic Meditation*. Royal Dragonfly Book Awards for Historical Fiction, First Place for *A Cruel Calm, Paris Between The Wars,* 2013. IAOTP: Top Author of the Year, 2016-2017. Global Book Award and New York Book Award for *Patriot Priest.* Kops-Fetherling Book Award, Silver Award for *Miami's Yester'years, Its Forgotten Founder Lo c k e Tiffin Highleyman 2020.* IAOTP: top author of the decade, 2021. Preferred Profes-sionals: Top Author, 2022, Top Shelf First Place Winner 2022 Book Awards, for *Miami's Yester'Years.*

Currently Patricia resides in Ponte Vedra, Florida, where she rescues thoroughbred horses and loves to paint and draw. She is often contracted to give presentations about creativity.

You can contact Patricia Daly-Lipe through her website: www.literarylady.com.

Karin F. Donaldson – Memoir (pg. 227)
Karin Friedrich Donaldson joined SDWEG in the spring of 2023. Her work is published in the 2023 anthology for the first time.

Karin founded "Power Reading" in 1974 and taught over three thousand San Diegans the art of speed reading. She was honored as a Women of Dedication by The Salvation Army's Women's Auxiliary in 2016.

At the end of World War II, Karin immigrated to the United States from Germany with her family. She'll never forget the day American Army trucks rolled into her village and GIs tossed Hershey bars to the children running after the Jeeps. She can taste that Hershey bar to this day.

For twelve years, she served on the pastoral staff of La Jolla Presbyterian Church. Upon retirement, Karin joined The Salva-tion Army as a volunteer, serving as President of the Women's Auxiliary and Chairman of the Metropolitan Advisory Board. She currently sits on the Advisory Boards of The Salvation Army and Big Table in San Diego.

Her careers include stockbroker, speed reading instructor, pastor, grief counselor, wife, mother, and grandmother. Karin has been published in *Chicken Soup for the Soul* and *OASIS Journal*. She also writes contemporary middle-grade fiction with faith-based themes.

Karin and her husband, John, currently reside in La Jolla, CA, where they enjoy sailing and are benefactors to numerous nonprofit organizations.

You may contact Karin at: <u>kfdonaldson@san. rr.com</u>.

Chloe Kerns Edge – Memoirs (pg. 237 & pg. 253)
Chloe Kerns Edge joined SDWEG in 2010. She has been published in the anthology each year since 2012.

Chloe sold her first poem when she was nine, and she's been a journalist ever since. She graduated from UCSD, Magna Cum Laude, with a degree in Literature and Writing. Her published work includes; *Tattoo*, a book for women in prison, published 1988 to celebrate seven years free from drugs, alcohol, and incarceration. She is also published in Maize, Volume 6 in 1983 and Birdcage Review, 1982.

Chloe has three children, is happily married, and is a young grandmother and great-grandmother. She and her husband reside in Escondido, CA, where Chloe teaches Yoga and Creative Writing. She has plans for another book, *Rule Number One: Don't Get Caught!*

Contact Chloe Edge through email at: <u>AuntieWild@ aol.com</u>.

Karen Fogelberg-Hill – Poems (pg. 283 & pg. 291)
Karen Fogelberg-Hill is a new member of the San Diego Writers and Editors Guild and is contributing to the anthology for the first time.

Karen graduated high school in the 1960s, married, had children and got her RN. She worked, then retired. She was blessed with parents who revered books and an older sister who loved reading to her and became a voracious reader. At eight, she created her only published work: an anatomically complete, red ribbon bound pictorial about her family. Her parents were delighted, her sister, mortified.

Over the years, writing poems became her sustenance and sanctuary. Now, late in life, Karen belongs to a writing group-- still writing poetry--but also exploring fiction and non-fiction storytelling. She finds joy in sharing her work and listening to what others have written; she feels emboldened to present her work on a larger stage.

Karen currently resides in Escondido, CA
Contact Karen- Fogelberg-Hill through email at: kfogel berg@hotmail.com.

Tiffany Noel Froese – Essay (pg. 213)
Tiffany Noel Froese joined SDWEG in 2022 and is published in the Guild anthology for the first time.

Tiffany is a native Californian and near-native San Diegan. She has over fifteen years of experience working in the story- telling industries. Her career began in Hollywood as an assistant at one of the biggest talent agencies in the world. She then went on to work at Disney TV Animation, Original Series Development.

Currently, she's a freelance writer and editor and resides in Encinitas, CA.

You can learn more about and contact Tiffany Noel Froese on her website: www.TiffanyNoelFroese.com.

Michael O. Gibbs – Short Story (pg. 73)
Michael O. Gibbs has been a member of SDWEG for two years and is publishing in the anthology for the first time.

Mike was in the military for nine years, serving as a green beret. Following military service, Mike joined the San Diego Police Department, from which he retired after thirty-six years.

He has studied Native American cultures for about four decades, is an animal behaviorist, man tracker, animal tracker, and enjoys writing fiction about prehistoric native cultures.

He will soon publish the third book of his High Plains Warrior series: *Crow Boy.* Mike's next project will cause him to spread his writing wings with a move to a covert military thriller, tentatively entitled, *Primitive: Black Wolf.*

Mike and his wife of thirty years reside in San Diego, CA.

Contact Michael O. Gibbs through email at: <u>highplainswar riornovel@gmail.com</u>.

Lisa Girdlestone – Poem (pg. 289)

Lisa Girdlestone is a new member of SDWEG and is published in the anthology for the first time.

Lisa was born in Tennessee, the youngest of seven children in a military family. They relocated to north Texas where she enjoyed small town life and spent summers at Lake Texoma, waterskiing and sunbathing. She then moved to Oklahoma where she ultimately began a career in the legal industry and started a family. In the midst of a divorce, Lisa relocated to San Diego in 1998, where she continued her career working as a legal assistant while raising her two daughters.

Inspired by her mother, who was an accomplished poet, Lisa has written several poems and has two novels in progress. Entirely self-taught, with no formal higher education, Lisa's writing is influenced by her keen interest in Egyptology, science, and spirituality. Lisa is hearing impaired and plans to learn American Sign Language.

Lisa is a self-taught knitter and she loves to solve cryptograms. She resides in San Diego, CA.

Andrea Susan Glass – Poems (pg. 281 & pg. 287)

Andrea Susan Glass is a ten-year member of San Diego Writers and Editors Guild.

She is also a board member of San Diego Professional

Editors Network and is active in Publishers and Writers of San Diego, and San Diego Writers, Ink.

Andrea Susan Glass, CEO of WritersWay since 2000, is a leader in personal and professional development book coaching, ghostwriting, and copyediting. She assists both emerging and seasoned authors in developing their nonfiction books from idea to publication.

She is the bestselling author of *Your Fabulous FIRST BOOK: How to Write with Clarity, Confidence & Connection* and *My Fabulous FIRST BOOK: A Companion Workbook to Your Fabulous FIRST BOOK*. She's also a winner of the San Diego Book Awards for ghostwriting. As a ghostwriter Andrea has written and/or copyedited several hundred books. Additionally, Andrea teaches "Marketing for Copyeditors" and "Building a Business Around Writing" for UCSD (University of California San Diego) Extended Studies.

Writing is an outlet for her voice, her creative expression, and her dreams of having a successful career as an author. As a multimedia artist, she is involved in the art forms of jewelry/wire wrapping, mosaics, and fused glass.

Andrea makes her home in Oceanside, CA.

She can be contacted through her website: Andrea@WritersWay.com.

Anna Hallett – Short Story (pg. 1)

Anna Hallett joined SDWEG early in 2023 and is published in the anthology for the first time.

Anna lives in the Anza Borrego Desert writing under the blazing sun and shining stars. Her works appeared in 101 Words and Five Minute Lit, online blogs; Five Minute Lit: Wicked Shadow Press Anthology *Murder on Her Mind*; *Literature Today*; *Bright Flash Literary Review* and *10 By 10 Flash*, online ezines. She is cofounder and director of The Writing Party, an entertainment company offering a fun environment to explore creativity through writing. She wrote and published *Waiting*

Games and Amusements for Families and *The Writing Party Inspirations.*

Anna is a freelance writer, editor, and proposal manager with Hallett Associates with more than twenty years of experience in proposal writing, RFP Response, research, analysis, and white papers. She finds writing to be the fun part of traversing life.

She has recently fulfilled a childhood dream to take an acting class and perform on stage. And she may try it again!

Anna resides in Borrego Springs, CA.

Contact Anna Hallett on Instagram: @the_writing_party.

Margaret Harmon – Short Story (pg. 109)

Margaret Harmon is a prolific author who has been an active member of San Diego Writers and Editors Guild since 1989. She served as a content editor for the 2023 anthology.

Just before Margaret's fifth birthday, she decided to become an author—and was permanently expelled from kindergarten for reading during nap time, an act that did not cause her to waiver in her decision.

She is the author-illustrator of *The Man Who Learned to Walk in Shoes That Pinch: Contemporary Fables, A Field Guide to North American Birders: A Parody, The Genie Who Had Wishes of His Own: 21st-Century Fables,* and *Mr. Helpless Gets Organized.* Awards earned by Margaret include the San Diego Book Awards Association Best Anthology and Best Humor.

Margaret loves exploring how life really works—and then trying to live the discoveries. She believes that fables work to help us stop self-sabotaging and become who we mean to be. Her fables (like Aesop's originally) do not end with pithy little morals because, though we all read the same words, we each read our own fable. Our favorite characters become our private troupe of empowering allies. Margaret's fables air on National Public Radio, are taught in college literature and oral interpretation classes, and are analyzed in a French doctoral dissertation. Her fables are currently being told, via European podcasts, to Ukrainian IT workers practicing their English.

Margaret resides in Pacific Beach, CA.

She can be contacted through her website: www.Margaret-Harmon.com.

Carol Ann Heasley – Poem (pg. 293), Short Story (pg. 143)

Carol Ann Heasley joined SDWEG in 2022. She is publishing in the anthology for the first time.

Carol's work has been published in the *OASIS Journal*, the San Diego Anthology 2023 – Honorable Mention, and the Grossmont College Journal.

In the act of writing, Carole illuminates her creative being, giving her an irrefutable state of self. She has taught college-level writing and has been active as a poet for 30 years.

Carol resides in San Diego, CA with her four-year-old Schipperke named BlackBerry. She enjoys the company of fellow poets in several writing groups and is an avid lover of plants and gardens with great joy.

R. J. Jordan – Poem (pg. 284)

R.J. (Robert) Jordan has been an active member of the Guild for twelve plus years and has contributed to four anthologies.

He was born in Mexico City in the 1960s and by all accounts had a happy childhood. That state of mind extended through his high school and college education in Massachusetts and California. He worked on both sides of the US–Mexico border as a business manager for thirty years before retiring in San Diego to dedicate more time to writing.

Recently he traveled to Spain to walk El Camino de San Francisco, a little-known pilgrimage alongside the more famous Way of St. James.

He holds advanced degrees in History and Creative Writing

and is a proud father and happily married. He currently resides with his wife in Coronado, CA.

Robyn Litt – Memoir (pg. 267)

Robyn Litt has been a member of SDWEG for one year and is looking forward to becoming more involved in the future. She is published in the anthology for the first time.

Robyn is an author/illustrator active in the Society of Children's Book Writers and Illustrators, San Diego Chapter. She is enrolled in UCSD's Children's Writing and Illustration Certificate programs. Current projects include a humorous middle grade coming of age adventure and several picture books. Robyn writes like she paints, with whimsy, curiosity, ethereal threads of social justice, and characters with heart. Her family moved six times by the time she graduated high school, so often her writing reflects the foibles of being the new kid in town. She thinks kindergartners could probably rule the world.

Robyn has lived in San Diego, CA, for over thirty years, teaching, raising a family, exploring nature, and promoting civic awareness.

Contact Robyn Litt through email at: robynlitt101@gmail.com.

Jeff Mason – Short Story (pg. 45)

Jeff Mason is publishing in the Guild anthology for the first time. He has been a member of SDWEG for approximately three years.

Jeff Mason, MD, FACP, MSHA has more than forty years of experience as a practicing physician, with physician organizations, and California Health Plans. He most recently served as Senior Medical Director for UnitedHealthcare where he had overall responsibility for medical care of members in California. Jeff is a graduate of New York Medical College, a fellow of the American Academy of Physicians, and he earned his master's in healthcare administration from the University of Colorado.

In 2017 Jeff retired and moved to San Diego where he has started a second career as writer, bicyclist, and attentive grandparent. He is polishing his first novel, a story about a young doctor in training, and is working on a second novel featuring a nurse.

Jeff has backpacked in the Sierras every year for 30 years and is relearning Spanish using Duolingo. He resides in Del Cerro, San Diego, CA.

You can contact Jeff Mason through email at: jeffma sonmd@gmail.com.

Wendy Matthews – Short Story (pg. 175)

Wendy Matthews, a new member of SDWEG, is published in the anthology for the first time. She is looking forward to serving on the Board of Directors in 2024.

Wendy grew up reading every Nancy Drew book published and always knew she would be a writer. Over the course of a 25-year corporate career, she wrote many things: annual reports, presentations, speeches for executives and herself.

After interviewing more than fifty people, she wrote and self-published a book about people who had been laid off from their job, then found a new purpose in life. The book is called Tweeners: True stories of people who have successfully made mid-life career changes.

In 2018, Wendy attended a writer's retreat in Tuscany, which was the jump start to her current writing effort: an adult fiction novel called Choices. She is currently hoping to find an agent to represent her work.

On her fiftieth birthday, Wendy went skydiving and found it be almost as thrilling as she finds feeling the words flow when she is in the "writing zone."

She resides in San Marcos, California.

Contact Wendy Matthews through email at: <u>wendyi sawriter2@gmail.com</u>.

Caroline McCullagh – Short Stories (pg. 21 & pg. 31)

Caroline McCullagh joined SDWEG in 2008 and is published in three prior anthologies.

Caroline McCullagh, award winning author, editor, and writing teacher, earned a master's degree in cultural anthropology at UC San Diego. Her life-long interest in the Inuit (Eskimos) has led her to write a series of six novels—two published so far—*Quest for the Ivory Caribou* and *Twenty-Six Eskimo Words*. The third, *Let Me Count the Ways*, will be published in 2023. She has also authored *American Trivia and American Trivia Quiz Book* with her writing partner, Richard Lederer, and *Sing for Your Supper: Opera Memories & Recipes*, a project for San Diego Opera. In addition, she was a book reviewer for fifteen years for the San Diego Horticultural Society and for the past eight years has written book reviews for the Mensa Bulletin. She has published extensively in newspapers and magazines.

Caroline resides in San Diego, CA, where, when not writing, she spends time with her daughter and granddaughters, playing with her dogs, gardening, and listening to classical music and jazz. She also edits for friends.

Contact Caroline McCullagh through her website: <u>www. CarolineMcCullaghAuthor.com</u>.

Reina Menasche – Memoir (pg. 246)

Reina Lisa Menasche has been a member of the SDWEG for over two years and is looking forward to becoming more active in the guild.

Reina's fiction has been honored by organizations such as the San Diego Book and Writing Awards, and the Southern California Writers Conference. Her first two novels, *Twice Begun* and *Silent Bird* were finalists in the San Diego

Book Awards. Her third novel, a paranormal suspense titled *The Spirit Of Shy Moon Lake*, was released in 2021. She is currently working on her first children's book as well as on a sequel (and prequel) to *Twice Begun* In addition to her time spent writing, Reina works as a licensed clinical social worker for a non-profit. She has been strongly involved in the writing community and spent years as host of Bookshelf for *East County Magazine*, interviewing local authors about their creative process.

Her website includes blogs on psychology and wellness, writing, and other social commentary.

She resides in Spring Valley, CA.

Contact Reina Lisa Menasche through her website at: www.reinamenasche.com

Pennell Paugh – Essay (pg. 199)

Pennell (Penny) Paugh joined SDWEG two years ago. She was a member of the marketing group for one year and has served several roles in 2023 including Vice President, President, and Events Coordinator on the Board. The 12th edition is the third time she has published in the anthology.

Penny has published extensively in nonfiction newsletters and magazines in the fields of mental health, corrections, speech, and hearing. In 2021, her debut fiction story, "Thrift-Store Luck", was published in San Diego Writers and Editors Guild Anthology. "Changing the World", her second story, appeared in 2022. Additionally, she has written two fantasy novels for nine-to-twelve-year-olds, and another fantasy for young adults.

Penny resides in La Mesa, CA, where she spoils her cat and reviews novels written by San Diego writers for East County Magazine.

You may contact Penny Paugh by email at: curiositypen@gmail.com

Richard Peterson – Short Story (pg. 110)

Richard (Rick) Peterson is a long-time member of SDWEG, 15 years, and served as Membership Chairmen for seven years. He has been published in *The Guilded Pen* since 2012, every edition to date. He has served as a content editor for several anthology editions including the 2023 anthology.

Rick has written magazine articles and was a former staff writer for "Wholistic Living News." He authored the article "Stained Glass Television" in the *Journal of Popular Culture* (Vol. 19, No. 4); and a chapter called "Electric Sisters" in *The God Pumpers: Religion in the Electronic Age* (Bowling Green State University Popular Press). He functioned as a judge for the San Diego Book Awards for nine years.

Retired from federal civil service in Human Resources in January 2023, Rick has continued to enjoy ballroom dancing and collecting art. He resides in Mission Valley, San Diego, CA.

Contact Richard Peterson through email at: quiller6354@gmail.com.

Ty David Piz – Memoir (pg. 263)

Ty David Piz, has been a member of SDWEG for twelve years. His work has been included in all editions of the *Guilded Pen* Anthology.

Before retiring, Ty spent fifteen years working with special needs students in the public school system and has a deep commitment for special needs students and education in general. He wrote several documents for motorcycle safety programs in California and Colorado that have been used to improve an instructor's commitment to mechanical reliability of motorcycles, as well as improving tire safety standards. In his work with SPED students, he documented the activities they participate in throughout the day. These notes are then used by teachers, administrators, parents, and physiologists in determining what needs the students have in their day-to-day interactions with peers and staff, which assists young people in being successful in school and beyond.

He is the father to three amazing daughters and grandfather to three sensational grandkids. They have spent happy summer vacations making an annual four-thousand-mile road trip together in order to experience new events in a wide variety of places.

Ty resides in Lakewood, CO.

Contact Ty David Piz through email at: typiz54@gmail.com.

Frank Primiano – Short Story (pg. 165)

Frank Primiano joined SDWG in 2015. His work has been included in *The Guilded Pen* Anthology every year since 2015.

Frank, a biomedical engineer by training, has published in engineering, scientific, and medical literature, both during his careers in industry, academia, and as an entrepreneur. He writes primarily fiction and creative nonfiction in retirement. In addition to the Guild anthology, his short stories have appeared in three editions of the San Diego Writers, Ink's *A Year in Ink*, and in the last three San Diego Community College Continuing Education Program's Writers Workshops' anthologies, for which he also served as an editor. He has been a finalist in the San Diego Book Awards' Unpublished Novel and Unpublished Short Story categories. He enjoys creating characters and making up stories, listening to recorded fiction while driving, and reading biographies. Writing keeps his mind active and exercises his memory. At one time, Frank, a native of Philadelphia, PA, was a professional cartoonist and, up until a decade ago, he'd mention, in casual conversation, that he went to high school with Bill Cosby.

After living in Cleveland, OH, for over 30 years, he and his wife, Elaine, moved to San Diego at the turn of the century and now reside in Carmel Mountain Ranch, San Diego, CA.

Contact Frank Primiano by email at: fppjrster@gmail.com.

R. H. Riffenburgh – Short Story (pg. 5)

R. H. (Bob) Riffenburgh joined SDWEG five years ago and has served as Vice President and Board Member for two plus years. This is the second *Guilded Pen* Anthology that includes Bob's work.

Bob Riffenburgh, Ph.D., retired in 2021 at the age of ninety, after working as a university professor, consulting firm CEO, government scientist, Navy operations research modeler, NATO officer in Europe, and designer/analyst of medical research studies. Along the way, he has been an ocean sailor and a Navy undersea diver. He has published one hundred and sixty-four scientific papers, four editions of a leading medical textbook, and poetry and short stories in literary journals. Currently, he is launching a final career as a novelist. He has written a YA book, *Thank Ye, Mr. Sun*, that is half story and half portrait of depression-era Appalachia, and the first two volumes of a techno-thriller series: *A Theft of Sanity*, telling of an undersea search for a weapon of mass destruction—and a kidnapped scientist. Also, *A Theft of Joy*, about a naïve artist being falsely accused and blackmailed for faking a painting by a master.

Married sixty-three years, until cancer took his wife, Bob resides in San Diego, CA. He enjoys his five children and seven grandchildren.

Contact   R.H.   Riffenburgh   through   email   at: riffenbu@sdsu.edu.

Mardie Schroeder – Short Story (pg. 69)

Mardie Schroeder joined SDWEG in 2014 and has been a very active member. She served as Board President in 2017, 2018, 2019, 2020 and 2023. and as past president in 2021. In 2019, she was awarded the Rhoda Riddell award for her contributions to the Guild. Her work has been included in the anthology every year since 2014.

Not only is Mardie active in the writing community, for many years, twice each year, she went on week-long horse adventures (drives and roundups) including a pack trip over the Continental Divide. She played tennis three times a week until age eighty-five, and pickleball until eighty-six.

Mardie published *Go West for Luck, Go West for Love* in 2015. She currently resides in North Park, San Diego, CA.

You may contact Mardie through email at: <u>mardiewho@</u> <u>yahoo.com.</u>

Chavah Siegel – Short Story (pg. 79)

Chavah Siegel's short story submission to this anthology is her first piece of fiction submitted for publication.

In 2019, Chavah won second place in a national essay contest sponsored by San Diego Oasis Learning Center. She is currently working on two novels—a medical mystery about a patient with a rare illness searching for a diagnosis and a second mystery centered around an infamous art heist. Despite the serious themes used in her fiction writing, she infuses humor into her characters and plots, because humor has been her companion throughout life and has saved her, even in the most difficult of times.

Chavah holds a Bachelor of Arts degree in creative writing, but she worked for many years in an unrelated field and returned to writing only ten years ago. She attends three professional read and critique groups a week and finds these groups to be essential for improving her writing and editing skills.

She truly believes that it's never too late to become a published author. Writing is the same as breathing for her—necessary for living.

JR Strayve JR – Short Story (pg. 125)

JR (Jerry) Strayve JR has been a member of the Guild since 2018, served as the Treasurer for a brief time in 2023, and is contributing to the anthology for the first time. Jerry served as a content editor for the 2023 anthology.

Strayve was born to a nomadic military family, attending nine schools before entering college. Following service in the United States Marine Corps, he raised a family while working as a financial representative and serial entrepreneur. Raising his young children, he discovered his talent for "spinning tales," regaling them with spontaneous bedtime stories. Soon his passion for history spoke to him and he jumped into writing.

His published fiction works include the first two books in a four-book series, *Braxton's Century, Volumes One and Two, First Spouse of the UNITED States*, and its sequel, *POTUS Down*. Strayve has also written a novella and multiple short stories. He contributed to the anonymously authored memoir of fellow Marines, *Another Marine Reporting, Sir!*

The third book in Braxton Century Series will be published early in 2024. Writing is the very essence of Strayve's life—a profound passion that defines his existence. Whenever he's not immersed in this creative pursuit, a sense of incompleteness overwhelms him, occasionally leading to moments of grumpiness. His literary endeavors revolve around weaving captivating novels that delve into pressing societal issues, captivating readers with the journeys of individuals confronting and, more often than not, triumphing over adversity—but not without the occasional twist of fate.

Strayve has many outside interests. They serve as sort of a tonic. He enjoys spending time with other authors and readers. He enjoys reading books on varied topics. Sitting down with a big bowl of popcorn and a diet Coke while watching various series and movies is nirvana!

Currently residing in the Hillcrest Area of San Diego, California, he enjoys biking, hiking, swimming, walking on the beach, and hitting the gym.

You may contact JR Strayve JR through his email: info@ jrstrayvejr.com.

Janet Travers – Short Story (pg. 153)

Janet Travers joined SDWEG in 2023 and is looking forward to serving on the Board of Directors in 2024. Her submission to the 2023 Anthology is Janet's first published story.

Janet Travers has written many short stories over the past fifteen years. This year (2023), she started to submit them to literary magazines. She has written and performed original songs and has written a stage play. For Janet, writing is not an escape from reality, but rather a way to understand and figure out people and life experiences. She is a singer who started performing professionally at age sixteen. She graduated from SDSU with a degree in theater and has enjoyed performing on stage and in film and TV in New York and California.

Janet enjoys cooking recipes from many cultures and is usually proud of how well they turn out. In elementary school she was voted most accident prone and best dressed even though everyone wore uniforms.

She currently resides in Normal Heights, San Diego, CA.

You may contact Janet Travers through email at: janettraver s92@gmail.com.

Ruth Leyse Wallace – Essay (pg. 223)

Ruth Leyse Wallace is proud of her more than fifteen years of active service to SDWEG. She served as the Newsletter Editor, Board Secretary and as the Board President. During her tenure as the Board President the Guild anthology was initiated. Ruth has contributed to the anthology every year since the Guild initiated it. In several years, Ruth also served as coeditor.

Ruth enjoyed a 35-year career as a clinical dietitian in the field of mental health, including serving as adjunct faculty in community colleges. She has published two books about nutrition and mental health—one self-published, one published by Taylor and Francis. In addition, Ruth contributed chapters to three textbooks in her field of expertise.

On her flip side, Ruth co-owned and flew a hot air balloon named The Green Apple while living in Topeka, Kansas!

She currently resides in Chandler, AZ.

You may contact Ruth through email at: ruthwallace78@gmail.com.

Ken Yaros DDS – Short Story (pg. 137)

Ken Yaros has belonged to SDWEG for more than twelve years. During that time he was a Board member for two years and has contributed to the anthology every year since 2013. Ken served as a content editor for the 2023 anthology.

Ken is an Alumnus of Albright College, Temple Dental School. He served thirteen years in the Airforce and Air National Guard and practiced general dentistry for forty-five years.

For some, retirement means more golf and travel, but for Ken it means more time for family and new pursuits. Writing has opened up a new world of possibilities and challenges. Along the way he has had support and encouragement and access to some of the most interesting and talented people dedicated to excellence in thought and writing. His short story was selected for national recognition in the Oasis Journal.

He resides in San Diego County and is about to dip his toe into commercial publishing. In the fall of 2023, he plans to introduce his first two e-books, entitled *The Dental Story* and *The Dental Bible*. Both are geared for dental consumers who have largely been left on their own to fend for themselves. He is originating a website to foster conversations geared to improving reading for our kids as well as a forum for discussing problems facing our younger generations at a critical time in our history.

Contact Ken Yaros through email at: kyaros@yahoo.com.

Sandra Yeaman – Short Story (pg. 57)

Sandra has been an active member of the Guild since 2013.

During that time she held multiple positions including webmaster (2014-2020), member-at-large (2020), treasurer (2022), and is currently the financial administrator (2023). Sandra has also volunteered her time for three years as the copyeditor for the anthology and is a contributing writer in the Twelfth Edition, 2023, for the tenth time, having skipped submitting something in 2022. In 2018, SDWEG presented her with a Rhoda Riddell Builder's Award for her contributions to the growth of the Guild. She is proud to say that she was born in Fargo, ND, and is not the only SDWEG member to have that honor (but she's not telling who).

Sandra Yeaman considers herself fortunate to have lived more than one life during her seven plus decades. She started out as an English teacher, but to students whose first language was something other than English, in both the US and overseas. Her first overseas work experience was in Tehran, Iran, in the days before the revolution. Following Iran, she taught on a Fulbright lectureship in Iasi, Romania for a year. When she found herself living back in her home state of Minnesota, where teaching English as a second language wasn't recognized as requiring any special skills, she became a software engineer for a word processer manufacturer. Sixteen years after her high school declaration that her career goal was to join the US Foreign Service, she succeeded. She worked as a United States diplomat for 23 years, adding to the list of foreign countries she had lived in, bringing the total to 11, most of them so small you may not recognize their names.

Since moving to San Diego from the Washington, DC, area in 2012, she has been writing about her foreign experiences, hoping others will enjoy, and perhaps even learn a bit, about those countries that she knew nothing about growing up.

Sandra currently resides with her husband in El Cajon, California.

You may contact Sandra Yeaman through her website at: www.SandraYeaman.com.

www.ingramcontent.com/pod-product-compliance
Lightning Source LLC
Chambersburg PA
CBHW060420030726
47495CB00003B/669